BEHIND THE LINES

CONTEMPORARY NORTH AMERICAN POETRY SERIES

Series Editors Alan Golding, Lynn Keller, and Adalaide Morris

BEHIND THE LINES

WAR RESISTANCE POETRY ON THE AMERICAN HOMEFRONT SINCE 1941

PHILIP METRES

UNIVERSITY OF IOWA PRESS, IOWA CITY

University of Iowa Press, Iowa City 52242
Copyright © 2007 by the University of Iowa Press
www.uiowapress.org
All rights reserved
Printed in the United States of America

Design by Teresa W. Wingfield

The University of Iowa Press is a member of Green Press Initiative and is committed to preserving natural resources.

Printed on acid-free paper

ISBN-10: 0-87745-998-3
ISBN-13: 978-0-87745-998-9
LCCN: 2006935965

07 08 09 10 11 C 5 4 3 2 1

To my parents, Phil and Kay Metres, who taught me the discipline and honor of serving one's country, outrage against social injustice, and an abiding thirst for peace — at least three kinds of love.

Contents

Preface

"Where is their home?" This was my question as a four-year-old, when my mother and father explained that we were sponsoring a Vietnamese family, refugees from the war, and bringing them home. My father, who served in Vietnam as a U.S. naval advisor on a South Vietnamese patrol gunboat, and my mother, a lifelong pacifist, navigated the maze of tents stretching into the distance at Camp Pendleton. The fourteen members of the N—— family huddled in a dusty tent, one family among hundreds, and we greeted each other without words. For a short time, I would share my room with Lam and Dũng—boys a few years older than me—while my parents tried to find the family an apartment, battling racist landlords reluctant to rent to foreigners. Thirty years later, when my wife and I visit the N——s' beautiful home in suburban San Diego, they throw open the door and welcome us with open arms. When we sit down, Ba, the patriarch, tells the story of how we became one family in 1975, and he does not hold back his tears—tears of gratitude, tears of sorrow—as memories of that war and its aftermath flood back.

Despite our geographical distance from battlefields in the past century, war has always come home. Soldiers who don't make it back alive, and the soldiers who do—war returns in the bodies and minds of veterans who return but are altered by its fire. Veterans who weep behind dark sunglasses as my father pins medals onto their worn fatigues during the 1986 Vietnam veteran parade in Chicago. The vets who dive into the closet when thunder strikes. Uncle D—— who never talked about his Purple Hearts from the Second World War. Great-uncle C—— who spent his entire adult life in an asylum after he returned from the First World War. The loved ones, the communities, the workplaces, churches, and other groups who await and absorb their return— each of us is only one or two degrees of separation from our country's mostly distant battlefields.

Indeed, as the peace movement has shown, war is never just *over there*; in a democratic republic, our daily lives as citizens, taxpayers, voters, and consumers, connect us inextricably to the decisions and structures that aid and abet warfare. Further, the peace movement's radical wing has shown the ways in which structural injustices at home—racism, sexism, class inequity—manifest violence that is almost inseparable from the violence that soldiers experience in the confusion that is war. (War is, after all, derived from the Indo-European root word meaning *to confuse*.) This book shows how civilian poets have played a crucial role both in the peace movement and in war resistance more generally; these poets on the homefront—through their poetry and their involvement in resistance—have made visible the moral confusion of war and its ultimate damage to societies (including to the ones who win). Alongside antiwar veterans, these poets articulate more than a vision of war— they summon a portrait of resistance that both mirrors and exhorts the peace movement itself. While it may be true that some wars are inevitable, and some may even be necessary, this book argues that a vital peace movement, aided and prodded by poets, is also necessary to ensure our common futures. Living in a society where the military-industrial complex exerts a dangerous influence over our politics, in the center of empire, we need voices that counter the insistent drumbeats of war, to remind us that we live in an increasingly interdependent world.

I am grateful to those who aided in the writing of this book, especially Tom Foster, as well as Eva Cherniavsky, Jeanne Colleran, Michael Davidson, Chris Green, and Susan Gubar—all of whom contributed extensive advice. Thanks as well to Steven Gould Axelrod, Dick Bennett (COPRED/Omni), Michael Bibby, Purnima Bose, Robert Cording, Alan Golding, Tom Gottschang, Peter Kvidera, Jon LaGuardia (for help with the index), E. J. McAdams, Aldon Nielson, Helen Sword, and Michael True for their encouragement and advice on aspects of the project. Thanks to John Carroll University and Indiana University for providing research funding during various phases of the project. Thanks to the Swarthmore College Peace Collection librarians for their help in locating some lost links between the peace movement and poetry. Thanks to the Houghton Library for permission to visit Robert Lowell's archive. Thanks to the FBI for not destroying all of their files for Levertov and Lowell and to the Freedom of Information Act for letting me see them. Thanks to all the poets, critics, and activists who participated in interviews, including John Balaban, Jan Barry, Robert Bly, Ralph Di Gia, W. D. Ehrhart, Jim Haber, Sam Hamill, Kent Johnson, Jackson Mac Low, Jay Meek, Lowell Naeve, Mark Pawlak, David Ray, Jerome and Diane Rothenberg, Leslie Scalapino, Todd Swift, and Barrett Watten. And thanks, finally, to Amy Breau, for her support throughout, and to my two daughters, Adele and Leila—may this book make other futures possible.

Acknowledgments

Portions of this book have appeared—in different versions—in the following journals and anthologies: *Big Bridge* (2007), *Contemporary Literature* (2000), *Indiana Review* (2000), *Peace and Change* (2004), *Peace Review* (2003), *Pleiades* (2006), *Postmodern Culture* (2003), *Prison Etiquette: A Convict's Compendium of Useful Information* (2001), and *Still Seeking an Attitude: Critical Reflections on the Work of June Jordan* (2004).

Grateful acknowledgment is due to the following for permission to reprint from these works:

John Balaban, "The Gardenia in the Moon," "Along the Mekong," and "Mau Than" from *After Our War* (University of Pittsburgh Press, 1974, copyright ©1975 Cooper Canyon Press). Reprinted by permission of John Balaban and Copper Canyon Press.

William Everson, "War Elegy I," "War Elegy II," and "War Elegy X" from X *War Elegies* (Untide Press, copyright ©1944) and *Chronicle of Division* (Black Sparrow Press, copyright ©1997). Reprinted by permission of Jude Everson.

John Fogerty, "Fortunate Son," courtesy of Jondora Music. Used by permission of Concord Music Group, Inc.

William Heyen, "1. (Vegas)," "2. (The Reich)," and "38. (The Truth)" from *Ribbons: The Gulf War: A Poem* (Time Being Books, 1991). Reprinted by permission of William Heyen and Time Being Books.

Kent Johnson, "The New York School (or: I Grew Ever More Intense)" and "Lyric Poetry after Auschwitz, or: 'Get the Hood Back On'" from *Lyric Poetry after Auschwitz* (effing press, 2005, copyright ©2005). Reprinted by permission of Kent Johnson and effing press.

June Jordan, "Apologies to All the People in Lebanon," "The Bombing of Baghdad," and "War and Memory" (copyright ©2005 June Jordan). Reprinted with permission of the June M. Jordan Literary Estate Trust, www.junejordan.com.

Denise Levertov, "Airshow Practice," "News Report, September 1991: U.S. Buried Iraqi Soldiers Alive in Gulf War," and "In California During the Gulf War" from *Evening Train* (copyright ©1992 Denise Levertov). "Life at War" (copyright ©1966 Denise Levertov) and "Enquiry" (copyright ©1971 Denise Levertov) from *Poems 1960–1967*. "In Thai Binh (Peace) Province" and "The Pilots" (copyright ©1975 Denise Levertov). Reprinted by permission of New Directions Publishing and of Pollinger Limited and its proprietor.

Robert Lowell, excerpts from "The March II," "Memories of West Street and Lepke," and "Waking Early Sunday Morning" from *Collected Poems* (copyright ©2003 Harriet Lowell and Sheridan Lowell). Reprinted by permission of Farrar, Straus and Giroux, LLC. Draft of "Memories of West Street and Lepke" in the Robert Lowell papers, call number bMS Am 1905 (2203), reprinted by permission of Houghton Library, Harvard University.

Michael Magee, "Political Song (Confused Voicing)" from *MS* (copyright ©2003). Reprinted by permission of Michael Magee.

Clarence Major, "Vietnam #4" (copyright ©1970 Clarence Major). Reprinted by permission of Clarence Major.

Ben Reyes, "Juan Carlos Gonzáles" from *Aztlán and Viet Nam: Chicano and Chicana Experiences of the War* (copyright ©1999). Reprinted by permission of George Mariscal.

Adrienne Rich, "Newsreel" (copyright ©1971 by W. W. Norton & Company) from "Shooting Script" (copyright ©2002 Adrienne Rich). Lines from Part V of "An Atlas of the Difficult World" (copyright ©2002, 1999 Adrienne Rich). Used by permission of the author and W. W. Norton & Company.

Karl Shapiro, "The Conscientious Objector" from *Trial of a Poet and Other Poems* (Raynal & Hitchcock, 1947). Reprinted by permission of Robert Phillips, Literary Executor, Estate of Karl Shapiro.

William Stafford, excerpts from "Watching the Jet Planes Dive," "Peace Walk," "Something to Declare," and "Entering History" from *The Way It Is: New and Selected Poems* (copyright ©1960, 1977, 1991, 1998 the Estate of William Stafford). Reprinted by permission of Graywolf Press.

Edwin Starr, "War," as sung by Edwin Starr. Reprinted by permission of Linsey Tower.

Barrett Watten, excerpts from *Bad History* (copyright ©1998). Reprinted by permission of Barrett Watten and Atelos Publishing.

Introduction

The armies took their seats, marshaled into ranks.
But one man, Thersites, still railed on, nonstop.

—HOMER, *The Iliad*, TRANS. ROBERT FAGLES

Is it time to bring the troops home? The first war protestor in literature, Thersites, proposes precisely this solution to the king's abuse of power in the *The Iliad*, that classic of war literature and cornerstone of Great Books curricula. The singularly exceptional Thersites, who pokes his shaggy head into the epic poem to become its only voice of dissent, is dispensed with quickly. Still, his irruption into the paradigmatic war story demonstrates the high stakes of dissent in a time of war and anticipates the desire of those authoring the dominant narrative (both politicians and poets) to stifle such testimony:

> The armies took their seats, marshaled into ranks.
> But one man, Thersites, still railed on, nonstop.
> His head was full of obscenities, teeming with rant,
> all for no good reason, insubordinate, baiting the kings—
> anything to provoke some laughter from the troops.
> Here was the ugliest man who ever came to Troy.
> Bandy-legged he was, with one foot clubbed,
> both shoulders humped together, curving over
> his caved-in chest, and bobbing above them
> his skull warped to a point,
> sprouting clumps of scraggly, woolly hair.
> Achilles despised him most, Odysseus too—
> he was always abusing both chiefs, but now
> he went for majestic Agamemnon, hollering out,
> taunting the king with strings of cutting insults.
> The Achaeans were furious with him, deeply offended. (106)

The only voice in *The Iliad* to rail against the abuses of the war is a soldier. But to our post-Vietnam eyes, Homer's Thersites would have fit right in among the sundry but deceptively stereotypical media images of protestors (civilians and veterans alike): he is *unruly* in all senses of the word—uncouth, foul-mouthed, clownish, physically deformed, unkempt, scraggly-haired, and antiauthoritarian.

And he will not shut his mouth:

But he kept shouting at Agamemnon, spewing his abuse:
"Still moaning and groaning, mighty Atrides—why now?
What are you panting after now? Your shelters packed
with the lion's share of bronze, plenty of women too,
crowding your lodges. Best of the lot, the beauties
we hand you first, whenever we take some stronghold.
Or still more gold you're wanting? More ransom a son
of the stallion-breaking Trojans might just fetch from Troy?—
though I or another hero drags him back in chains . . .
Or a young woman, is it?—to spread and couple,
to bed down for yourself apart from all the troops?
How shameful for you, the high and mighty commander,
to lead the sons of Achaea into bloody slaughter!
Sons? No, my soft friends, wretched excuses—
women, not men of Achaea! Home we go in our ships!
Abandon him here in Troy to wallow in all his prizes—
He'll see if the likes of us have propped him up or not." (106–108)

For Homer, Thersites's argument is as deformed as his physical form. Yet Thersites is also an "emerging democratic voice among Greeks . . . [who] represents the rank and file," "a war-weary soldier who has at last realized that his sacrifice means nothing and only serves to enrich his lord" (Tritle 12). Thersites levels a class-based critique of war, accusing his leader of endangering his soldiers' lives for his own greedy whims.[1] In response, Odysseus attacks Thersites verbally for his "taunts," "wrangles," "babbles," "rants," and "slanders," accusing him of being a coward and to blame for the problems of the war—"*you're* the outrage" (108). Finally, Odysseus invents the canard still circulated today: that to stop the war would be a "humiliation" (109) and desecrate the memory of those who died in battle. After this tongue-lashing, Odysseus beats Thersites "like a cur" (107–108), much to the delight of the other soldiers—thus eliminating Thersites and the dissent he represents.[2]

The Iliad—for all its insight into the psychology of warfare—also manifests disturbing elements that haunt so many depictions of war: (1) the narrow focus on the (male) soldier on the battlefront—one which naturalizes war, distracts from its causes, and turns away before its final devastation; (2) the fascinated gaze upon violence, rendered in stimulating visual imagery; (3) the perpetuation of gender stereotypes; and (4) the absence or ridicule of dissenting voices.[3] In this way, The Iliad is the prototype for war literature—the Ur–war story, in Miriam Cooke's definition—a *bildungsroman* which typically begins at the front, tracks a soldier's initiation into the intensities and terrors of war, dramatizes the existential break from the homefront[4] (often figured as female), and leaves us with the soldier's eventual transformation into manhood. The epic poem's narrative frame, in particular, permits the fantasy that war is always with us by eliding the conditions that led to the war, and cuts away at the precise moment when the war ceases to be a contest among great men—when it involves the raping and pillaging of the civilians of Troy.[5] The Iliad ends the way the Gulf War ended for American television viewers; while for Iraqis, the Gulf War entailed economic blockade, civil strife, and near total social collapse.

Despite its blind spots, The Iliad is still held out as a universal representation of war. For Bernard Knox, who wrote the introduction to Robert Fagles's 1990 translation, The Iliad is both truthful and pleasing, and speaks to our essentially warlike nature.[6] War might be "a terrible beauty," he poses, echoing Yeats, but it makes for good literature. Simone Weil argued, on the eve of the Second World War, that "the true hero, the real subject of The Iliad, is might" (153), and of this force she described how the "power to transform man into a thing is double and it cuts both ways; it petrifies differently but equally the souls of those who suffer it, and those who wield it" (173). Yet the heroes' deaths come with exquisite visual detail; the images of spears and weapons penetrating flesh have an unmistakably erotic texture. If these depictions are pleasing, for whom are they pleasing? Whose interests do they serve? What future warriors will they inspire? The Iliad is an eminently masculinist and aristocratic perspective of war, where homosocial relations dominate and where women are the cause of and obstacle to (alpha) male bonding; no wonder Alexander the Great kept his copy "in a jeweled casket" (Hadas 23). While the lives and deaths of the great warriors hold our gaze, the masses of soldiers have all the personality of a bee swarm.

We have listened to Thersites, if only for his moment. If we could hear them, what would the people of Troy say, as they suffer the siege behind the city's walls? And what would the Greek women at home say, worrying over their absent husbands? We can only imagine. The exclusion of dissenting voices—either by disappearing or by demonizing the bodies from which they come—has continued throughout our history, even in our literature, though the soldier poets of the First World War have put to rest, at least for our historical moment, the uncomplicated glorification of warfare. Yet, despite the fact that nearly every English-language anthology of war poetry from the last fifty years articulates the importance of antiwar sentiment, the soldier-poet alone is still held up as the principal proprietor of viable antiwar poetry: e.g., Wilfred Owen, Siegfried Sassoon, Randall Jarrell, Louis Simpson, Karl Shapiro, Michael Casey, Bruce Weigl, Yusef Komunyakaa, Brian Turner, and others.[7] These poets certainly deserve our attention; but in an age when total war affects nearly every citizen—whether man, woman, or child—do *only* soldiers have the right, or the ability, to speak about war? According to Sayre P. Sheldon, "during World War I, 5 percent of the casualties were civilian. The figure rose to 75 percent during World II. In the 1990s, 90 percent of the millions of casualties in wars around the world were civilians, most of them women and children" (x). In her critique of Paul Fussell's *The Great War and Modern Memory* (1975), Lynne Hanley confronts his myth "of soldiers as the [only] tragic victims of war" (31); privileging only English male soldier-poets on the European front not only excludes perspectives about war from women, noncombatants, pacifists, and people in the colonial world, but also limits a broader analysis of the culture and economics of warfare. Should we even seek out war poems, when, as in the case of Wilfred Owen, "the individual's protest is overwhelmed by the institutions of the military and the nation, and contained within the value system of heroism, stoicism, and self-sacrifice on which the war machine runs" (Van Wienen 28)? War poetry anthologies since the First World War witnessing the "terrible beauty" of war inevitably have relied upon the soldier poetry of first person autobiographical lyric. But given W. D. Ehrhart's experience of reading Owen and immediately enlisting with the Marines during the Vietnam War, does such poetry actually promote and idealize warfare *even as it protests* against its brutalities? Why study war poetry at all, when, to quote Seamus Heaney, "no lyric has ever stopped a tank" (7)? Is it time to abandon the lines?

A Poetics of War Resistance

The loss of the great range of dissenting voices damages cultures and peoples—not only the cultures from which they come but also those that live at the end of the missile trajectory. Though the role of soldier poetry occupies a critical place in the war resistance literary tradition, this project retreats from the scene of battle, "behind the lines," back to what has been termed the "homefront," precisely because of the unique role that civilian poets have played in shaping and representing war resistance and the contemporary American peace movement. The tradition of American war resistance poetry, with its beginnings in the First World War, crystallized in the mid-twentieth century, with the rise of conscientious objector poets such as Robert Lowell, William Stafford, and William Everson, and persists to the present.[8] Yet poetry that resists war has largely been dismissed by critics as unlyrical (cf. Robert Bly's "Leaping Up into Political Poetry"), too easily categorized (cf. Robert B. Shaw's "The Poetry of Protest"), dangerously ahistorical and self-righteous (cf. Cary Nelson's *Our Last First Poets*), politically unviable (cf. Paul Breslin's *The Psycho-Political Muse*), or not self-critical enough (cf. Robert von Hallberg's *American Poetry and Culture, 1945–1980*). Undoubtedly, some Vietnam-era antiwar poetry was self-righteous, rhetorically clumsy, and tonally arrogant.

But these critiques miss the intricate dance that war resistance poets have executed, negotiating between the claims of their art and the claims of their conscience, and between the two communities they court: the nation and the peace movement. Despite the poetic excesses of the time, the Vietnam War era proved a critical moment for the articulation of war resistance poetry as a tradition. Such anthologies as A *Poetry Reading against the Vietnam War* (1966), *Out of the War Shadow* (1968), and *Winning Hearts and Minds* (1972) offer an extension to and a critique of the war literature canon. More than just a gathering of voices, these anthologies announce the poetics of war resistance, confronting the limits of lyric poetry in representing a distant war, employing identificatory rhetoric and documentary evidence, mediating between poetic disinterestedness and partisan ideology, and addressing both the nation and the peace movement.

Bly and Ray's A *Poetry Reading Against the Vietnam War* provides an exemplary (and in some sense still unsurpassed) war resistance poetry anthology. First, it bypasses the conventions of war poetry anthologies by including not only first person witness poems but also explicitly pacifist and anti-imperialist poems from William Stafford, Robinson Jeffers, and ee cummings. Further, these poems appear alongside nonpoetic texts from government dissenters, such as Senator William Fulbright; official U.S. news sources (the *New York Times*; the *New York Herald Tribune*); military information sources (the *Reserve Marine*); French journalism (*Paris-Match* and *Le Monde*); leftist and pacifist alternative publications (*I. F. Stone's Weekly*, among others); quotes from pacifist thinkers

(Dr. Spock, A. J. Muste) as well as an array of military and political leaders from the Second World War; activist sources (a "Women for Peace" bulletin); and literature from past wars. The mélange of sources in A *Poetry Reading against the War* demonstrates the creativity with which poets and activists deconstructed the official narrative presented by the administration, showing how civilians attempted to know what they often could not personally witness; even if independent journalists, dissident intellectuals, antiwar soldiers, and government officials (former CIA employee Daniel Ellsberg) would later become crucial resources for the movement, in its historical moment, this anthology suggests that the truth was not just out there on the battlefront but also in the mainstream papers of the day.

Second, the anthology presents itself as poetry for use, conceived as a kind of script or score generated from readings given by American Writers against the War to enable other communities to create their own war resistance events. Thus, the anthology's utility and ephemerality as a text of the moment, rather than delimiting its cultural value, actually renders it more valuable. Providing a window into the production of a counternarrative of the war and enabling further acts of dissent and war resistance, A *Poetry Reading* exemplifies the dialectic between visionary language and pragmatic didacticism that marks war resistance poetry.

Another anthology, *Campfires of the Resistance*, reflecting the era's zeitgeist, bypasses the constraints of a national address by speaking to and about the activist community and the counterculture. A collective subjectivity other than the nation-state emerges from these poems: "there is a different We behind this anthology—a political movement. . . . We have not only common enemies, but a sense of ourselves as united by bonds stronger than those of nation, class origin, and organization" (Gitlin xv). The "movements'" poets, who worked for the progressive causes of the time—civil rights, peace, women's liberation—write with a sense of a larger *we* that belies the potential isolationism of the lyric. Todd Gitlin's anthology demonstrates how war resistance poetry necessarily foregrounds the problematics of poetic address. War resistance poetry discloses the open secret of modern American poetry, revealed most plainly in times of war: the presumption that poetry should be bounded by, limited to, or produced for the nation. War resistance poetry thus requires us to pay attention to the ways in which poetry constructs, addresses, and negotiates its nation(s). The dangers of employing that *we* are obvious: it can produce a lyric subjectivity that refuses to acknowledge its own epistemological limits while speaking to the already converted in a language that fails to challenge the writer or the audience.

Undoubtedly, embattled resistance communities occasionally require such encouragement, in the face of societal apathy or governmental harassment. Still, the most memorable war resistance poetry rarely spurns the chance to speak to the wider nation, even when it represents the longings of war resistance communities. This study thus extends and applies Emile Benveniste's analysis of the subject's appeal to "the other" and Phillip Brian Harper's analysis of Black Arts rhetorical address—which argued that Black Nationalist poetry relied upon a split not only between black and white nations but also within the black nation itself—to the peace movement. "The other within" for Black Nationalism was the Negro who wanted assimilation with whites, who "sold out" his race. Relatedly, war resistance poets can at the same time represent the longings of the peace movement, extol its virtues, exhort its members to action, *and* occasionally argue with those in the movement whose absolutist positions threaten to defeat the fragile coalitions and social networks that knit it together. The tenuousness of a peace movement, and the unwillingness to let go of imagined communities beyond the peace movement, has often compelled war resister poets to acknowledge both the daring *and* the dangers of absolutist resistance.

Peace Movement and War Resistance in the Age of Pure War and Empire

But just what is this imagined community, this phenomenon called the peace movement? The term "peace movement" has no single meaning, because as a movement, it is always coalitional by nature, sustained by a patchwork of groups with radically different political agendas, analyses, and histories: the historic peace churches—Quakers, Mennonites, Brethren, and others; longstanding internationalist and nonviolent groups—Women's International League for Peace and Freedom (founded in 1915), Fellowship of Reconciliation (1915), War Resisters League (1923), and Peace Action, formerly SANE (1957) and FREEZE (founded in 1981); socialist, communist, and anarchist groups—Communist Party, Workers World Party, Green Party, and Black Bloc anarchists; war veterans—Veterans for Peace and Vietnam Veterans Against the War; mainstream churches and religious organizations; feminist antiwar groups such as CODEPINK; specific ethnic groups, for whom each U.S. war is a kind of civil war; and even, though rarely, our mainstream political parties. And each new war gives birth to new generations of peace groups. In "The History of the American Peace Movement," Howlett and Zeitzer refer to Lawrence Wittner's useful analogy of the peace movement as an "onion, with the absolutists at the center and the less committed forming the outside layers. At times of popular enthusiasm for war the less committed outside layers peel off, leaving the pacifist core; in times of strong aversion to militarism new layers appear, and the onion grows in size. This structural fluidity accounts both for the peace movement's repeated weakness in times of international tension and for its peculiar resiliency" (226).

That the peace movement has been marked by such fluidity—both in terms of its varied definitions of peace and its varied constituencies—raises the question as to whether "peace movement" is a movement at all. Noam Chomsky, in 1967, questioned the ways in which the phrase peace movement was acting as an impediment to war resistance: *"The 'peace movement' exists only in the fantasies of the paranoid right.* Those who find some of the means or ends pursued objectionable can oppose the war in other ways. They will not be read out of a movement that does not exist" (italics mine, 680). The peace movement as a concept occasionally has homogenized the diversity of war resisters and war resistance. Chomsky's argument, however, seems dangerously indistinguishable from official narrations of war. In the words of Hakim Bey, "The Media however produced (i.e., simulated) the impression that virtually no opposition to Bush's [1991 Persian Gulf War] existed or could exist; that (to quote Bush) 'there is no Peace Movement'" (25).

Yet the peace movement—even if the term may reduce the heterogeneity of war resistance—is an important, even essential aspect of a healthy democratic society. The peace movement acts as a necessary brake to the enthusiastic acceleration toward the next "necessary war," though it seems destined for permanent oppositional status. Gwyn Prins has likened the peace movement to "a leaping, diving whale . . . When the 'whale' disappears in a dive, those on the right believe the movement no longer exists. Supporters of the movement, on the other hand, see the leaping whale and claim it can fly" (qtd. in Everts 27). Whether critics might wish that it were dead or supporters might wish that it could fly, the success of the peace movement ought not be measured by whether or not it stopped a war; rather, its impact, however decentralized or marginal, must be registered in the constancy of its witness to the evils of warfare and its resistance to the smooth functioning of an imperial, militaristic culture of war. That constancy requires not only institutional support (both academic and activist) but also the existence of what Evert calls "prophetic minorities" (27–28)—those who are totally committed to bringing about peace and nonviolent social change.[9]

Though my title foregrounds war resistance over peace movement—an allusion both to the venerable War Resisters League (and its program of Gandhian nonviolence and social radicalism) and Barbara Harlow's theorization of resistance literature from the postcolonial world—I believe that the peace movement is an enabling fiction, not a disabling one, because it proposes that local and seemingly isolated acts are part of a larger imagined community of resistance. However, I employ "war resistance" also because it includes the peace movement and those other antiwar, anti-imperial, and antiracist efforts that do not always fit easily under its umbrella, that bristle against being defined as peace movement. Because the peace movement emerges from multiple ideological bases, it is often in conflict about the best ways to resist war. Kenyon Farrow notes how African American resistance to the recent Iraq War, while not always represented visibly in public marches (where African American protest is routinely criminalized), can be registered in the dropping rates of military enlistment—a large employer of African American youth. Farrow's example shows one of many legitimate ways that people have resisted war. Resistance actions range from (1) counternarration (educating, lectures, readings, flyering, petitions, letters, protests); to (2) physical and financial support for resisting war, boycotts, strikes, claiming CO status, or supporting COs; and even to (3) extreme or illegal acts of resistance, from sit-ins to tax resistance to other more violent acts of resistance. Gene Sharp's crucial *The Politics of Nonviolent Action* lists 198 nonviolent tactics that resisters have employed to counter illegitimate power and effect social change, many of which have been used by war resister poets in the twentieth century.[10]

The modern peace movement was born of the devastations of the First World War; however, the American peace movement owes its particular identity to the cultural transformation during and after the Second World War. This book thus tracks the historical trajectory of war resistance in American poetry from 1941 to 2006 through the flash points of the Second World War, Vietnam, the Persian Gulf War, and the recent wars post–September 11, a period in which the U.S. has achieved a military superiority perhaps unparalleled in world history. Simultaneously, war resistance in the United States has confronted imperialism and the militaristic cultural values that have been described by Paul Virilio as "Pure War." Virilio argues that we live in a state of Pure War, in which the real war is not the battle itself, echoing William James, but the endless preparation for war.[11] Virilio dates the military-industrial complex from the 1870s—around the time that U.S. political and economic power had solidified and begun imperial expansion—yet he argues that our era is actually an extension of the Second World War, in which "all of us are already civilian soldiers, without knowing it. . . . The great stroke of luck for the military's class terrorism is that no one recognizes it. People don't recognize the militarized part of their identity, of their consciousness" (26). Pure War thus pervades all aspects of culture, from the increasingly violent and technophilic video games like "Duke Nukem," "Quake," "Doom," or "Grand Theft Auto" that invite people to view the world through the target eye, to less violent but no less virulent displays of nationalism such as television coverage of the Super Bowl. Such "illusionary identifications," in the words of Jochen and Linda Schulte-Sasse, create an "illusion of mastery" that effaces our declining democratic power as citizens (70). ("Pure War" is, by the way, now also the name of an online video game, thus completing the circle.) Pure War manifests itself economically in what Eisenhower famously called the military-industrial complex—impacting the globe not simply through U.S. military engagements but also through counterinsurgency and covert operations; military training of Latin American officers in Fort Benning's School of the Americas; maintaining hundreds of military bases in other nations (from Cuba to Okinawa); and in skyrocketing sales of weapons, at times to opposing sides in conflicts. Pure War amounts to "endocolonization" (95)—a situation in which one's own population is colonized by state power. While Virilio's formulation elides key differences between colonization and the general situation of Americans in the United States, Pure War provides a fruitful cultural analysis that echoes anarchist and Marxist critiques of the coerciveness of state power.[12]

Virilio's focus on the militarization of U.S. culture provides a necessary supplement to Hardt and Negri's recent theorization of Empire, their term for the "political subject that effectively regulates . . . global exchanges, the sovereign power that governs the world" (xii). For Hardt and Negri, even though nation-states have declined in power, "sovereignty as such" (xii) has not; though they reject the notion that we live in an age of American imperialism, they acknowledge that the U.S. "does occupy a privileged position in Empire" (xii) and thus a central site where Empire as such requires constant ideological justification and cultural support. Characteristic of Empire is that war making is always framed as a project for peace and in defense of rights; in Hardt and Negri's formulation, "although the practice of Empire is continually bathed in blood, the concept of Empire is always dedicated to peace—a perpetual and universal peace outside history" (xv).

Precisely because the homefront—a space ineluctably connected to the more visibly militarized and beset battle zones throughout the world—is a contested site in the legitimation of Empire and its self-justifying military adventures, Virilio argues that American war resisters are in a unique situation to effect change: "there's no doubt that the American 'pacifist' militants are at the center of the machine. . . . They occupy the best position insofar as they have an extraordinary amount of information on the war-machine at their disposal, which doesn't exist elsewhere" (132). War resistance in the United States, then, plays a crucial role in how wars are conducted from the centers of Empire; but access to information, *pace* Virilio, is not the only requisite to war resistance. For Hardt and Negri, "our deconstruction of this [ruling spectacle of Empire] cannot be textual alone" (48); they look to the "militant" to model resistance in ways that reverberate beyond individual acts of insurrection. Whatever we call the new resisters of global Empire, they will not come *ex nihilo*; rather, a *culture* of war resistance, and a textual apparatus that articulates what such a culture might look like, is crucial to sustain a critique of militarism in America and the Empire it necessarily protects. If this textual foundation derives not only from political analyses but also from the repository of literary texts and art already centrally preoccupied with the questions of resistance, it will guarantee war resistance a greater imaginative lability and pragmatic fluidity than if it relied only on the occasionally ossifying ideological architectures of Marx or Mao, of Gandhi or Galtung.[13]

War Resistance Poetry and the Political Lyric

Though it would be difficult to argue, as Jan Clausen has regarding feminist poetry, that "there is some sense in which it can be said that poetry made possible the movement" (5), American poets and poetry—in its multiple modes and forms—have played a crucial and even defining role in articulating, representing, and sustaining war resistance. American poets have contributed uniquely to war resistance and to the peace movement, both in their physical involvement in activism and in their poetry. No other literary genre has been as conducive to the performative, immediate, and often homespun symbolic actions of the peace movement. In addition, war resistance activists have long relied on poetry, and its popular counterpart, song, to build a shared culture—relaying the narratives that name the movement and its longings.

However, given that the predominant mode of modern poetry has been the lyric, how do war resister poets attempting to make visible Empire and its culture of Pure War, negotiate the lyric's tendency to privilege the transcendental moment over narrative, the effusions of subjective experience over cold knowledge, the immediate and the momentary over the distant and narrative, the individual voice over the din of the crowd? It is not difficult to understand why few poems directly address such abstract phenomena as weapons sales, nuclear stockpiles, or U.S.–funded military regimes. Richard Wilbur's "Advice to a Prophet" warned prophets and poets alike:

> Spare us all word of the weapons, their force and range,
> The long numbers that rocket the mind;
> Our slow, unreckoning hearts will be left behind,
> Unable to fear what is too strange. (336)

Though there have been some striking exceptions to the quietism of American poetry during the American Century, including Carolyn Forché's *The Country between Us*, Adrienne Rich's *An Atlas of the Difficult World*, and Peter Dale Scott's *Coming to Jakarta*—all of which represent the unseen connections between American privilege and economic/military domination— the larger picture of American poetry displays a quiescence when it comes to the militarism of American culture. The rationale for organizing my discussion of war resistance poetry around three symbolically central wars—a structure that participates in the problem of viewing war as a discrete event rather than a pervasive cultural symptom of expansionist capitalism—speaks to the limits of the modern American lyric. Because of the predominance of the lyric in American poetry for the past fifty years, we must face it, take it apart, and see how it works as a mode of war resistance.[14]

Theodor Adorno's argument for the utopian potentiality of the lyric as oppositional to societal values in "On Lyric Poetry and Society" provides a theoretical basis for the lyric as a mode of resistance to state coercion, militarism, and war. War resistance poetry that relies upon a lyric subjectivity at odds with its society authorizes dissenting subjectivity and complicates the nationalist discourse of war. Further, Denise Levertov's theorization of political poems adds specificity to Adorno's argument by foregrounding the dovetailing of lyric and war resistance in "short, or fairly short [lyric] poems written without personae: nakedly, candidly, speaking in the poet's unmediated character" ("OED" 166), often "written by people who are active participants in the causes they write about, and not simply observers" (167). Levertov's activist-focused definition theorizes a poetry that aims either to convince the unconverted by interpellating them into an imagined subjectivity or to energize the morale of war resisters. Her definition exposes what is unsaid about the traditional Wordsworthian lyric—that, in speaking representatively (i.e., to the nation), one must avoid divisive topics—but proposes a new form of lyric that would embrace its subjective position.[15]

There are good reasons to be wary of oversimplified celebrations of oppositional poetry; Robert von Hallberg's call for an accommodational poetry that "speaks to the center" comes out of a democratic longing for poetry to return to the mainstream, to end poetry's affair with aesthetic and political elitism. But von Hallberg also veers into an apologia for empire; he notes that "empires are not made and broken by poems, but through poetry they are remembered and somehow even justified" (28). War resistance poetry worries over the problem of address for precisely the same reasons that von Hallberg does. Insofar as war resistance poetry only speaks to the peace movement, it marginalizes itself, abnegates from the responsibility to address the unconverted; however, insofar as war resistance poetry speaks to the center of the nation, it risks the opportunity to enter into the peace movement's work of counternarration.

Yet there is a tradition of political lyric in Anglo-American modern poetry. William Butler Yeats's framing of the political lyric in his poems about the Irish rebellions (in particular, "Easter 1916") informs, inspires, and haunts poets W. H. Auden, Robert Bly, Robert Lowell, and Adrienne Rich—as well as critics James Mersmann, Robert von Hallberg, and Paul Breslin. Yeats's formulation, "We make out of the quarrel with others, rhetoric, but out of the quarrel with ourselves, poetry" ("Per Amica" 331), still frames many discussions of American political poetry and suggests that one way to complicate the lyric is through dialogic structure. Yeats is both exemplary of and deeply problematic for war resistance poetry, because his political poems ultimately promote a lyric subjectivity that upholds the dichotomy between poet and political movement; in the end, the poet can only elegize as he levels a half-fascinated, half-repulsed gaze on the Irish rebels, who, like stones, inhumanly trouble the living stream, in "Easter 1916." The "terrible beauty" at once proclaims the fated brilliant failure of the rebels and also the failure of poetry to move beyond the primacy of the aesthetic. Adrienne Rich, in particular, transforms her early debt to Yeats by inverting the dogma that political poetry is not aesthetic enough; she argues that an engaged art fails "not because it is engaged, but because it is not engaged enough: when it tries to express what has been logically understood but not yet organically assimilated" (WIFT 47). For Rich, a poem's lyric subjectivity must permeate its politics fully enough to emerge with a truly political vision, a truly visionary politics; if it fails to assimilate its politics in an organic way, it settles for an impoverished journalistic or propagandistic version of reality.

Because American war resister poets negotiate between the expectations of an antiwar audience and the demands of American poetry as "national" genre—that poetry must be a Yeatsian "argument with ourselves" that demonstrates loyalty to the nation—war resistance poems often expose, as an X-ray might, the ideological skeleton of the contemporary American lyric. War resistance poems that test the limits of lyric poetry—extending the lyric through the use of narrative sequencing, collage or other disjunctive techniques, dialogic structure, multiple voices, documentary sources, and discursive heterogeneity—offer a re-visioning of the possibilities for poetry engaged with the political realm.[16] Poets such as Robert Lowell, William Everson, Denise Levertov, Adrienne Rich, John Balaban, Daniel Berrigan, and June Jordan express "dissatisfaction with the lyric as it is codified in contemporary practice—with its representing a single epiphanic moment, its reliance on a unified speaker, its imagistic coherence and tendency toward closure, its restricted intellectual or cultural range" (Keller 22). Relatedly, some war resistance poetry situates itself on the trajectory of postmodern poetries—experimenting with seriality, polyvocal collage, and fragmentation—that harnesses the centripetal forces of language, in contrast to lyric's centrifugality; Jackson Mac Low, Bruce Andrews, Leslie Scalapino, Barrett Watten, and Michael Magee abandon the lyric in favor of what Marjorie Perloff heralds as a postmodern poetry that will "accommodate narrative and didacticism, the serious and the comic, verse *and* prose" ("PIL" 49). Such poems offer a heightened attention to how language can frame and complicate ongoing conversations within and outside movements for social change.

War resistance poetry, therefore, spans various camps of recent American poetry and renders visible the epistemological and ideological blindnesses that inhere in the traditional lyric and the war story—that prototypical story we tell about our wars. Yet what unites lyric and experimental war resistance poetry is what I would call "political desire." In contrast to what Roger Gilbert describes as the polarities of pleasure and politics—"the rival claims of pleasure and politics, the aesthetic and the social, private experience and public responsibility" (243)—war resistance poetry often emerges from the subjective longing, even pleasure, produced by reaching beyond the bounds of the privatized and commodified self into a negotiation with the political realm in general and with the peace movement in particular.

A crucial nexus in which to examine war resistance poetry, therefore, is between the poet as maker of poems and the poet as citizen-activist. In other words, in order to account for war resistance poetry, we must go behind the lines of individual poems and situate the poems in the wider biographical and social contexts that inform their multivalent meanings. Going behind the lines also means drawing out emerging patterns within war resistance poetry;

three theoretical problematics recur throughout this book: lyric subjectivity, representation, and poetic form. First, the problematic of lyric subjectivity and its relationship to the psychoanalytic discussions of subjective identification and address; in other words, how does a war resistance poet project herself as a lyric subject when she is speaking from a position of dissent? How does the poet invite the reader into a position that the reader might not initially want to inhabit? In particular, how does the poet deconstruct the illusionary identification with the State but still offer the reader an emulable subjectivity? Is the poet able to avoid making the poem about "the poet's own tender sensibilities" (Scully 5)? Second, the problematic of representation — of war, of what constitutes the scene of battle, of resistance, and of "the other"; in other words, does the poet approach the problem of describing or representing an event not witnessed with his own eyes, and if so, how? How does the poet deal with not only the unrepresentability of war but also the politics of representing other cultures, in light of Orientalism? And third, the problematic of poetic form. In other words, how does the poet engage the poetic tradition's forms and modes to articulate, question, and sustain war resistance culture?

But the examination of war resistance poetry cannot take place only through a discussion of individual poems or poets; it must go behind the lines in another sense: beyond the page and into the public square. The wider poetry archive during the Second World War, the Vietnam War, and the Persian Gulf War demonstrates how war resistance poetry can be found not only in books or anthologies but also, to echo James Sullivan, on the walls and in the streets. The recovery of such occasional and ephemeral poetic acts as poetry readings, demonstration placards, leaflets, and even symbolic actions expands our definition of poetry and the cultural work that it can do. In the hands of war resistance poets, language is a symbolic action, and symbolic action becomes a language with poetic implications. In recovering these poems, we can pose further questions not only about the limits of the individualized poem but also about the individualized poet, and propose ways that poets and activists might work to find ways of making poetry *active* again and of making activism a labor of making as much as a labor of protest and unmasking. Thus, the survival of war resistance poetry depends not just on the aesthetic value of the poems but also on what these poems offer as cultural productions.

This study, therefore, oscillates between chapters that contextualize the war resistance work of individual poets and chapters that draw from the broader archive of American war resistance poetry and considers those in the contexts of their production, circulation, and exchange. The debate between a poetry that favors the aesthetic, the formal, and the individual, and a poetry that favors the political, the rhetorical, and the cultural-political movement suggests the ongoing and necessarily provisional rapprochement between artistic production and the peace movement. This debate manifests itself differently at different moments. During the Second World War, William Everson and the War Resisters League struggle between a poetry of pacifist ideology versus a propagandistic poetry against war. During the Vietnam War, Robert Duncan and Denise Levertov engage in a parallel negotiation between poetry and its relation to war resistance (also visible in the dichotomies between electric Dylan and acoustic Dylan, between New Left and Old Left). During the Persian Gulf War, Jean Baudrillard and Christopher Norris, Barrett Watten and June Jordan articulate different, even opposing critical and poetic strategies to resist war. During the Iraq War, Kent Johnson's upbraiding of the avant-garde position of the radicalism of form articulated by Charles Bernstein demonstrates the persistence of these debates. These disagreements represent not an unbridgeable impasse between politics and poetry but an ongoing negotiation over how poetry's particular power might best bear witness to and serve a culture of war resistance. The following précis of the book illuminates the ongoing struggle of poets to bring their craft into the fray of politics—mediating between the national political realm and the peace movement.

Despite the compelling motives for U.S. involvement in the Second World War, an estimated 50,000 Americans refused to fight, including about 12,000 who opted for conscientious objector status and worked in Civilian Public Service camps, performed noncombatant service in the armed forces, or went to prison. Many had religious or pacifist convictions, though some—Robert Lowell, for instance—argued that the Allied demand for unconditional surrender was tantamount to a betrayal of American principles. About 6,000 objectors went to prison (Zahn v–vi). After 1942, 90 percent of war resisters served multiyear sentences (Sibley and Jacob 353). Though the number of CO prisoners is relatively small, they vastly outnumbered their First World War counterparts and constituted a significant portion of the prison population as a whole; the objectors from the Second World War were, according to Howard Zinn, "four times the number of C.O.'s who went to prison during World War I. Of every six men in federal prison, one was there as a C.O." (Zinn 409).

Their experiments in nonviolent cooperation and resistance in both camp and prison inspired and battle tested future crucial participants in the Civil Rights and peace movements in the Cold War. David Dellinger, one of the

Union Theological Seminary objectors, would later become a leader in the peace movement during the Vietnam War; James Farmer, George Houser, Jim Peck, and Bayard Rustin would propel the Civil Rights movement. Houser helped form the Congress of Racial Equality with James Farmer in 1942 and confronted segregation in Chicago's White City Roller Rink (April 1942), the University of Chicago barbershop, and various restaurants (1943) (cf. Tracy 32–33). Houser and Rustin also helped plan the Journey of Reconciliation (1947), the precursor to the Freedom Rides in 1961; seven of its sixteen participants were COs, two black and five white. Rustin would later organize the 1963 March on Washington and was in Martin Luther King's inner circle, providing a "wealth of tactical experience . . . informing King's conclusion that there was a viable nonviolent path to a successful outcome in the boycott" (Tracy 96). Two other COs, Lew Hill and Roy Kepler, would found Pacifica Radio at KPFA in the Bay Area. Sun Ra (born Herman Poole Blunt) was first jailed for five months, then later served in Civilian Public Service and went on to become a legendary pioneer of free jazz. Gordon Zahn, Larry Gara, and others would become influential academics.

In *Direct Action: Radical Pacifism from the Union Eight to the Chicago Seven*, James Tracy notes how "for those who forged the radical pacifist movement, the inviolable constitutive unit of society was the individual . . . theirs was a thoroughly American radicalism" (40). The radical pacifists rejected Soviet communism as vociferously as they did American capitalism, and their distrust of authority—which they saw in the U.S. as leading to totalitarianism—led them to "a rather mystical commitment to total Democracy" (40), an orientation that A. J. Muste termed "holy disobedience." In this way, the radical pacifists embody Thoreauvian individualist resistance; they did not scorn all social organization, but they felt themselves in a battle against the state, its military-industrial complex, and a society of crushing conformity.

While resisting alongside radical pacifists, the CO poets uneasily dissented and didn't join the war against the State. Robert Lowell, William Stafford, and William Everson emerged from the proving grounds of internment to change the landscape of American poetry, in part because of their nuanced struggle against the claims of state and of absolute resistance.[17] Unlike the elder cynic Jeffers, who could trumpet against "the mould of [American] vulgarity, heavily thickening into empire" (168), and unlike the soldier-poet Karl Shapiro, who could depict the conscientious objector as a Noah in the ark of conscience, the CO poets struggled to articulate a resistance that neither protested from on-high nor retreated from addressing the nation. Perhaps because they were not granted the authority of the soldier to speak about their convictions and experience, the CO poets wrote a poetry marked by self-accusation and, at times, outright disavowal of their war resistance. The monikers I once ascribed to Lowell, Stafford, and Everson invoke the dominant culture's reified images of protestors—"fire breather," "yellow belly," and "beat," respectively—only to reject them as too extreme. They are a satire of pop culture journalism, what the dominant culture projects upon war resisters, but they also are doppelgangers, self-represented negations that haunt the poets.[18]

In chapter 1, I explore how Robert Lowell's conversion to Catholicism informs his singular and definitive act of conscience—a letter to President Roosevelt declaring his "personal responsibility" to refuse to participate in what he saw as an unjust war. Despite this dramatic violation of the status quo, his refusal to fight did not compel him, while in Danbury Prison, to participate in a radical pacifist action organized by Jim Peck, Lowell Naeve, and other radical pacifists to desegregate the prison. Years later, in his ironic disavowal of his war resister youth, "Memories of West Street and Lepke," Lowell reuses an image from his early antiwar poems from *Land of Unlikeness*—the "fire-breathing" dragon of martial America—to characterize his earlier, "naive" self who refuses to go to war. The poem itself makes no mention at all of the successful rebellion against the racial divisions of the penal system. Still, Lowell's characteristic self-revision and self-scrutiny, however, never release him from addressing—and occasionally, dressing down—the State's abuses of power, as he became a key figure in opposing the Vietnam War through poems, letters, and symbolic actions.

In chapter 2, I examine how William Stafford—whose poetic process and project crystallize in his internment experience—stages his haunting account of CO life in his memoir, *Down in My Heart* (1947), against an absolute pacifist named George. For Stafford, George becomes a kind of Zizekian saint to which he must explain why he did not choose final noncooperation against the State. Stafford painstakingly distinguishes his more accommodating mode of nonviolent resistance from George, perhaps a literary version of the legendary absolute pacifist Corbett Bishop, who while in prison refused to eat or even go to the bathroom for over a year, before the authorities finally released him. The memoir is a striking Ur-text to Stafford's own lyric poetry— which articulates a lifelong pacifism based on noncooperation but pointed toward community—a poetics of loyal dissent unwilling to conform either to the militarism of the state or the militancy of violence-minded Vietnam War protesters. Though Stafford's poems demonstrate the limits of the lyric in its monological thrust, they also demonstrate the lyric's ability to illuminate and embody the work of the peace movement.

In chapter 3, I consider how William Everson's crucial role in founding the Fine Arts Camp at Waldport, Oregon, distilled the artistic impulse within the Civilian Public Service experiment in pacifism during the Second World War. His work as printer and publisher of Untide Press offered a crucial means for disseminating war resistance poetry, while his poetry (particularly the X *War Elegies* and *Chronicle of Division*) both affirmed war resistance and bore witness to its personal and spiritual costs. Further, I argue that Everson's rejection of the War Resisters League's attempts to propagandize through publishing a poetry anthology demonstrates CO poets' characteristic resistance to issue-oriented poetry in favor of a peace culture. As a result of internment, Everson's pacifist poetry sets him on a track away from public political activism and instead further inward, to confront his own violence through spiritual life, as he enters a religious order for a period in the 1950s and adopts the name Brother Antoninus. Yet Everson's "minor civilization" at the Fine Arts Camp spurred on the San Francisco Renaissance and paved the road for the Beats; however, Everson's critique of the Beat's absolute refusal of the "square" world is clearly informed by his experience of internment during a popular war.

Why do these CO poets find themselves—war resisters, each in his own way—rhetorically opposing some *other*, even when that other is himself? First, emerging from the marginality of war resistance during the Second World War, the poets then had to confront the Cold War containment culture of the 1950s, compelling a poetry of accommodation—one which required a pledge of allegiance and a disavowal of the rebellious other. Second, the experience of resistance during the war yielded certain lessons about the dangers of *absolute resistance*, a notion that haunts Stafford's writing. Finally, these writers were particularly interested in probing the internal limits of their pacifism, what Paul Lacey has called "the inner war." These poets, more perhaps than any recent generation of poets, felt compelled to address "the center" of their culture. Lowell's self-criticism, Stafford's miniaturism, and Everson's refusals of orthodox politics or poetry complicate any simplistic or self-congratulatory reading of the attempt to marry poetry and war resistance. However, the daring act to refuse war and make poetry a principal mode of testifying to that dissent distinguishes the project of these poets. More effectively than other imaginative writers, these poets provided an accurate internal and external narrative of war resistance, articulating the vexing dilemmas of nonviolence and direct action. Their desire to *represent resistance itself*—even in the compromised, incomplete, or idiosyncratic ways of these poets—marks one of the essential characteristics of war resistance poetry: that need to create a document, a testimony, of refusal, where none was presumed to exist. In this way, they emerge from a long tradition of dissenting poetics and are by virtue of their extreme marginality, *sui generis*.[19]

In contrast to the Second World War's marginalized war resistance, the Vietnam War witnessed the burgeoning of a mass movement that altered the ways in which the U.S. could conduct its wars abroad. The war resistance movement was both a success (in braking U.S. imperial adventurism) and a failure (in its inability to end the war immediately), and it transformed into something more than a dissenting movement against war by becoming a counterculture in itself. Buoyed by New Left radicalism and the counterculture, and yet increasingly subject to the crackdowns of the State and ridicule by mass media, Vietnam War resistance poets such as Allen Ginsberg, Denise Levertov, and Robert Bly shifted from a rhetoric speaking to the center and addressed their work to the resistance community. These poets' new allegiances with war resisters challenged the most basic prohibitions of poetry that prevailed during that period, especially regarding lyric address. Poetry—in its many manifestations, from lyric poems to songs to symbolic actions—played a role in the movement's self-conception and its ongoing vitality, though it occasionally fell prey to the logic of a fantasized revolution.

In chapter 4, I examine the broader archive of Vietnam-era war resistance poetry, privileging and highlighting the strengths of antiwar anthology collections, poetry readings, and more ephemeral hybrid forms such as the poem-placard, the demonstration, and other modes of symbolic action. Extending Burke's notion of language as symbolic action, I read a number of kinds of texts—from a placard poem by Ginsberg, to poetry performances by Jackson Mac Low, to the Catonsville Nine burning of draft files using napalm—as poetic acts *exscribing* themselves into the public sphere and designed to be consumed by the public. The debate carried forth in letters between Denise Levertov and Robert Duncan about the kind of poetry needed during a time of war frames my reading of the possibilities and limits of activist poetry. While Denise Levertov saw as part of her poetic project imagining the war and sustaining the movement, Robert Duncan held fast to a poetry that would, in its very alterity, propose another way of living and, in its form, act as protest. In light of this debate, I argue for a keen attention to how these actions, a kind of poetry whose page may be public space itself and whose mode of re-publication may be televisual, allow us to extend our notion of poetry and its ability to reach outside of the audience of poetry readers.

Yet given that mass media distorted resistance, symbolic acts court dangerous misreadings and may lead to acts of greater extremism. Todd Gitlin's *The Whole World Is Watching: Mass Media in the Making and Unmaking of the New Left* (1980) details the deleterious relationship between mass media and the Students for a Democratic Society during the 1960s. Though SDS experienced initial gains as a result of media coverage, their new recruits—often "articulate, theatrical, bombastic, and knowing and inventive in the ways of packaging messages for their mediability" (154)—altered the fragile consensual community that brought SDS its political strength. Since, according to Gitlin, "the archetypal news story is a crime story . . . an opposition movement is ordinarily, routinely, and unthinkingly treated as a sort of crime" (28) and thus "a demonstration is treated as a potential or actual disruption of legitimate order, not as a statement about the world" (271). The media focus on events raised the stakes: "where a picket line might have been news in 1965, it took tear gas and bloodied heads to make headlines in 1968" (182). In the end, SDS became the distorted issue and image that they had struggled to contest.

Responding to the skewed mass media coverage of the war abroad and at home, war resistance poets during the Vietnam War sought to produce a counternarrative. They attempted to overcome their distance from the scene of battle by a variety of modes. Thus, in chapter 4, I also map out the modes that poets employed, from the visionary to the eyewitness, to render the war an inescapable fact for people on the homefront. From the visionary mode— as demonstrated by Robert Bly and Adrienne Rich—to the documentary mode—as demonstrated by Daniel Berrigan, Allen Ginsberg, and John Balaban; from the first person witness—as demonstrated by CO John Balaban— to translation and acts of cross-cultural collaboration; war resister poets adopt a host of poetic (and political) strategies to confront their own (and fellow civilians') geographical distance from the war.

In chapter 5, I consider how Denise Levertov, perhaps the exemplary war resister poet of the Vietnam War, came to represent both the promise and the perils of Vietnam War resistance. Though Adrienne Rich, W. S. Merwin, or Allen Ginsberg may have produced more defensible poetry about the war, Levertov's work—precisely because of its excesses as poetry and its uncanny parallelism to the antiwar movement—is a rich resource as a cultural text of the dominant narrative of the war resistance movement. In particular, I show how the shift in address in her lyric poetry from *The Sorrow Dance* to *The*

Freeing of the Dust parallels the shift in movement strategy from dissent to resistance. Levertov's poetry moves from a rhetorical courting of the national *we* to a more accusatory pose, speaking from the collective voice of the antiwar movement. This pose, while indicative of the antiwar movement's influence and the full flowering of the counterculture as a result of alienation with contemporary American life, also reflects the limits of New Left ideology's romantic identification with Vietnamese revolution. This limit manifests itself most explicitly in her poetry about the Vietnamese; these poems expose the perils of representing the other from the homefront. Gayatri Spivak's "Can the Subaltern Speak?" informs my analysis of Levertov's lyric dilemma. While Levertov's early poems fail to render Vietnamese experience in a meaningful way, her later poems—first when she visits North Vietnam, and later when she confronts the Persian Gulf War—consciously foreground the difficulties of representing the other.

Despite the rapid organizing efforts of the antiwar movement, which responded even before the war had been voted for, media framing of the Gulf War offered a fantasy regression to the Second World War—when dissent was marginalized and media coverage censored and cleaned of corpses—while at the same time it presented futuristic "missile-eye" views of Baghdad buildings being destroyed. Recast as the Second World War, the Gulf War thus invited a rewriting of the Vietnam War, in which mass media and protestors became the cause for U.S. failure in Vietnam. Due to the pressure on U.S. mass media to support the troops, war resistance coverage typically found itself balanced against tiny prowar demonstrations. U.S. media yielded to—and in some ways outdid—governmental desires for a patriotic war narrative without images of battle death or scenes of flag-draped coffins. The theoretical debate between Jean Baudrillard and Christopher Norris about dissent in postmodern conditions frames my discussion of Gulf War resistance poetry. Because the war itself was both virtual (Baudrillard)—particularly to those viewing it on television—and actual war, with demonstrable physical consequences to the Iraqis who bore its power (Norris), I stake a claim for a poetry flexible enough to acknowledge both war's virtuality (an extension of Virilio's Pure War) and war's physical and psychic unmaking.

In chapter 6, I demonstrate how the debate between Baudrillard and Norris parallels the impasse between Barrett Watten and Amiri Baraka over how one remembers 1960s resistance poetry; while Watten argues for a "turn to language" and the experimental poetries represented by the language poetry movement, Baraka holds fast to the Black Arts aesthetic of a rhetorical poetry working in concert with resistance. On the one hand, the language poets offer for war resistance is a politics of form, where language itself becomes the site of a postmodern resistance. On the other, the Black Arts and performance poetries offer a continuation of oppositional poetry. When examining the archive of Gulf War resistance poetry written during and just after the war, and the anthologies that collect them, however, one finds mostly a retreat to the lyric mode. Further, the editors replicate the journalistic desire to appear patriotic, thus echoing the rhetorical stance of Second World War CO poets. If the anthologies occasionally demonstrate how the individualized lyric can reflect the most embattled and self-absorbed aspects of war resistance movements, they reflect the lonely struggle for the peace movement to counternarrate in the face of the media's unanimity. Finally, I conclude with a brief examination of *Ribbons*, William Heyen's book-length real-time meditation on the war, as a successful experiment in extending the lyric into a narrative of resistance.

In chapter 7, I consider June Jordan's contribution to bridging African American struggle and war resistance, emerging out of the Black Arts and feminist movements of the 1970s. I analyze Jordan's stance of "righteous certainty"—a performative pose she adopts in order to claim her own authority to talk back to power. Righteous certainty emerges from Jordan's struggle against personal and social violence, and thus enables a revaluation of the Yeatsian lyric's self-oppositionality. In addition to focusing on her involvement in war resistance—through her column in the *Progressive*, her course "Poetry for the People," and her readings against the war—I read Jordan's "The Bombing of Baghdad" as a powerful chant poem that harnesses the lyric as an oppositional and documentary form and invites a transnational progressive audience to identify their own struggles with the struggles of Iraqis.

In chapter 8, I demonstrate how Barrett Watten, emerging from the avant-garde language poetry movement, addresses the conditions of postmodernity in his book-length prose poem *Bad History*. Watten's poetry realizes and extends Lindley's notion of "the openness of lyric to modulation by neighboring kinds [of literature]" (13), insofar as his poem modulates not only other literary genres, but also nonliterary writing (journalism, financial prospectuses, and the like) as well. His counter-epic—a self-conscious deconstruction of Homer's epic poem—also runs counter to the war resistance tradition's reliance on lyric voice, imagery, and subjective immediacy. Instead, it cannibalizes other discourses as it thematizes the problem of representing traumatic experiences to which we are not direct witnesses, yet which nonetheless implicate us. Finally, through its formal presentation—which resembles the margin of a news column—and its voluminous footnotes, *Bad History* dramatizes as it confronts the disappearance of History in a postmodern age.

Finally, in a coda, I address the conditions for war resistance and war resistance poetry after the terrorist attacks of September 11, 2001, and in light of the recent Iraq War. In particular, I argue how September 11 complicates the work of war resistance insofar as the War on Terror now flagrantly adopts and exploits the very terms of leftist critique—that of U.S. empire and of the conditions of Pure War. At the same time, I note how poetry has re-emerged as a popular cultural force, as thousands of Americans chose poetry as the most effective occasional mode to elegize. I analyze the most controversial poem to emerge from September 11, Amiri Baraka's "Somebody Blew Up America," as a text situated on the fault line between anti-imperialist critique and conspiracy theory and dramatizing the dangers of conspiracy thinking and of the use of Web evidence as documentary fact.

In light of the Iraq War and the renewal of poetry as a mode of cultural dissent, I examine the proliferation of traditional print poetry anthologies, such as *Poets against the War,* and on the Internet—drawing forth the implications of both "old" and "new" media for war resistance poetry. I also examine how Kent Johnson's *Lyric Poetry after Auschwitz* revived the ongoing debates about the role of poetry in war, and offer Michael Magee's "Political Song (Confused Voicing)" as a poem that unites political lyric, oppositional performance, and the experimental traditions into grief-stricken protest against the politics of retaliation. Finally, I highlight ways poets can play a role in the peace movement by articulating, complicating, and sustaining war resistance—not only through poems but also through daily involvement in the forms and genres of activism: media press releases, flyers, placards, and songs.

PART 1.

World War II

THE POETICS OF CONSCIENTIOUS OBJECTION

FIGURE 1: *William Anderson, CO and volunteer for the starvation experiment*

Like all men hunted from the world you made
A good community, voyaging the storm
To no safe Plymouth or green Ararat;
Troubled or calm, the men with Bibles prayed,
The gaunt politicals construed our hate.
The opposite of armies, you were best
Opposing uniformity and yourselves;
Prison and personalities were your fate.

You suffered not so physically but knew
Maltreatment, hunger, ennui of the mind.
Well might the soldier kissing the hot beach
Erupting in his face damn all your kind.
Yet you who saved neither yourselves nor us
Are equally with those who shed the blood
The heroes of our cause. Your conscience is
What we come back to in the armistice.

— KARL SHAPIRO, FROM "THE CONSCIENTIOUS OBJECTOR"

1. Robert Lowell's Refusals

MEMORIES OF WAR RESISTANCE IN PRISON

[H]istory as a palimpsest of two durations — then and now, the earlier period that is overtly "under consideration," and the current period, uneasy about its potentially apocalyptic destiny but so far uncertain about its concluding date.

— CARY NELSON, *Repression and Recovery: Modern American Poetry and the Politics of Cultural Memory, 1910–1945*

Poems move out into many futures, which are their own real futures as well, unknown to themselves.

— JEROME MCGANN, "The Third World of Criticism"

In his biography of Robert Lowell, Ian Hamilton tells an anecdote that still adorns discussions of Lowell's poem "Memories of West Street and Lepke." During his arraignment on the charge of refusing to register for the draft, Lowell spent a few days in West Street Jail, where the infamous Louis "Czar Lepke" Buchalter awaited execution on death row. Lepke, a notorious mafia gangster who led a gang of professional killers known as "Murder Incorporated," had been arrested on narcotics charges and convicted of ordering the 1941 killing of candy store owner Jacob Rosen. According to Hamilton's 1980 conversation with Jim Peck, a longtime antiwar activist, "Lowell was in a cell next to Lepke, you know, Murder Incorporated, and Lepke says to him: 'I'm in for killing. What are you in for?' 'Oh, I'm in for refusing to kill'" (91). It's easy to imagine Lowell saying such a thing, acutely aware of the ironies and contradictions of state power. Every indication is that Lowell did meet Lepke; certainly "Memories of West Street and Lepke" recounts the profound impression of the poet's encounter with the head of Murder Incorporated. *But this conversation probably never happened.* Peck likely assumed that Hamilton was asking about Lowell Naeve, thus confusing Lowell for Naeve, a fellow war resister who like Lowell and Peck passed through West Street Jail to Danbury Prison and whose prison memoir, *A Field of Broken Stones* (1951), is one of the important documents of war resistance:

Somewhere in the conversation we got around to the fact that I was in jail because I refused to kill people. The Murder, Inc., boss, who was headed for the electric chair, said: "It don't seem to me to make much sense that they put a man in jail for that." We looked at each other. There we were, both sitting in the same prison. The law covered both ends—one in for killing, the other in for refusing to kill. (29)[1]

In Hamilton's retelling, Lowell Naeve has been erased and replaced by Robert Lowell, whose memory of his "naïve" years in "Memories of West Street and Lepke" remains one of the few canonical poems to emerge from war resistance during the Second World War. The continued circulation of this story serves to illuminate some of the principal dynamics between war resistance and poetry.

First, the erasure of Naeve is symptomatic of the disappearance of the war resister from history. Despite the fact that Naeve himself was an artist and a writer, and the fact that some of his most courageous actions in prison involved continuing his art through subversive or underground means, he dropped out of literary-critical consciousness. Further, Naeve's replacement by Lowell suggests that literary celebrity and canonical status offer war resistance a way to achieve cultural legitimacy, wider publicity, and ultimately, a way to breach historical memory. Literature is produced and circulated both in the academy and in the marketplace at a scale exceeding the homespun social networks that support war resistance. Even if poetry remains one of the least popular of the literary arts, American poets still retain a symbolic significance—as laureates or as inaugural presenters, for example. In Robert Lowell's case, his poetry, family background, and cultural dissidence during a tumultuous period in the United States led to a unique celebrity that spanned a quarter century.

However, even though literary celebrity may lend cultural capital to war resistance, literary representations can also succumb to the distortions of dissent endemic to mass media and journalistic history. Lowell's most famous prison poem, "Memories of West Street and Lepke," offers an intriguing but problematic representation of war resistance during the Second World War. Written over ten years after his time in jail, Lowell's poem tells the story from the point of view of a presumably wiser, but more ineffectual, speaker. Lowell's poem has an almost photographic accuracy regarding the physical particulars of his early arraignment, yet his depiction of pacifists uses distortions typical of mainstream media to demean war resistance as ineffectual, immature, disloyal, or crazy. If literary representations invariably tend, over time, to reify the way those experiences get remembered, then paying attention to the particular circumstances that produce these representations might enable a more accurate—or at least, more rigorous—accounting of the economics of poetry and war resistance. However, a simplistic accounting of social conditions will not yield a satisfactory analysis of literary texts. As Mikhail Bakhtin and Pavel Medvedev warn, literary criticism often mistakenly limits literature to a mere reflection of ideology, takes literary representations as direct representations of life, or turns ideas reflected in the work into grand ideological theses (18–19). Since the contents of literature, to use Bakhtin and Medvedev's formulation, "signify, reflect, and refract reality" (10) and "the reflections and refractions of other ideological spheres (ethics, epistemology, political doctrines, etc.)" (16–17), literary criticism must balance between the generalizing claims of ideology and the particularizing insistences of the genres themselves. This critical balancing between history and literature becomes even more difficult when the literary work presents itself as a kind of documentary realism, as in Lowell's mature confessional poems.

Because critics have delegitimized Lowell's politics as mentally imbalanced ("manic"), I first reconstruct the original contexts of the poet's refusal to serve in the Second World War, outlined in his letter to President Roosevelt and reflected in his early apocalyptic verse. In the second section, reading of "Memories of West Street and Lepke," I argue that Lowell encouraged the critical commonplace that his refusal was manic because the poem itself revises his resistance to the war. Lowell's self-revision, while clearly a strategy of his mature poetics, also speaks to the larger cultural context of the 1950s, when the House Un-American Activities Committee bullied intellectuals and artists and demonized dissent. I read "Memories" therefore as a containment text, one that displaces the 1950s onto 1943, demonstrating broader connections between containment culture and confessional poetry. Finally, in the third section, using fellow war resisters Lowell Naeve's and Jim Peck's memoirs as foils, I explain how and why his poetic representation of his war refusal and stay in prison in "Memories" fails to provide anything but a containment vision of war resistance. Lowell's overidentification with power (both a characteristic of containment culture and his personal worldview) may help explain why he represents war resistance in prison as the strivings of othered pacifists—the insane, Jews, homosexuals, Jehovah's Witnesses. In particular, Lowell's failure to participate in, and his silence about, the conscientious objectors' 135-day strike to desegregate the Danbury Prison mess hall—an originary moment in American nonviolent direct action and radical pacifism—forces us to ask new questions about the relationship between his poetry (and Cold War American poetry in general) and political power.

Lowell's Catholic Phase

Lowell once called his refusal to participate in the Second World War "the most decisive thing I ever did, just as a writer" (qtd. in Hamilton 86). Yet, despite two exhaustive biographies and countless critical works on the poet, Lowell's conscientious objection to the war gets downplayed amid accounts of mental breakdowns, unconscionable treatment of wives and lovers, and disturbingly confessional poetry. Lowell criticism has occasionally veered into infotainment; Ian Hamilton's biography, in particular, directly conflates Lowell's objection to the war with his manic-depression; by contrast, Paul Mariani's framing of the objection within the poet's Catholic period, and Saskia Hamilton's recent editing of Lowell's letters, aid in recovering the contexts that illuminate the poet's refusal.

Lowell's 1943 letter to President Roosevelt, as the poet wrote, "refus[ing] the opportunity" of military service, and the attached "Declaration of Personal Responsibility," communicate his grounds for refusal in the Catholic tradition of Just War Theory and allude to his family's tradition of patriotic service to the country.[2] For Lowell, once the Allied forces committed to total war against Germany and Japan in 1943, they lost their moral authority and, as he told Roosevelt, "demonstrate[d] to the world our Machiavellian contempt for the laws of justice and charity between nations" (*Collected Prose* 370). He was outraged by the news that, "in a world still nominally Christian," there were "staggering civilian casualties that had resulted from the mining of the Ruhr Dams . . . [and the] razing of Hamburg, where 200,000 noncombatants are reported dead, after an almost apocalyptic series of all-out air-raids" (369). The final two paragraphs of the letter demonstrate Lowell's reasoned shift from conditional support of the war to outright objection:

> In 1941 we undertook a patriotic war to preserve *our lives, our fortunes, and our sacred honor* against the lawless aggressions of a totalitarian league: in 1943 we are collaborating with the most unscrupulous and powerful of totalitarian dictators to destroy law, freedom, democracy, and above all, our continued national sovereignity.
>
> With the greatest reluctance, with every wish that I may be proved in error, and after long deliberation on my responsibilities to myself, my country, and my ancestors who played responsible parts in its making, I have come to the conclusion that I cannot honorably participate in a war whose prosecution, as far as I can judge, constitutes a betrayal of my country. (italics his 370)[3]

Lowell's letter, in its classical rhetorical flourishes—such as parallelism and anaphora—demonstrates the poet as painstakingly reasonable in his assertion of conscience, though it is hard not to notice its failure to mention the concentration camps. Lowell may well have not known of the horrors that faced Jews and other minorities in Nazi Germany, but with our historical hindsight—however unfair—it is difficult not to see his omission as a glaring oversight.[4] Despite its epistemological limits, Lowell's letter demonstrates an articulate critique of the conduct of the war, shared by antifascist Catholic pacifist Dorothy Day and historian Howard Zinn, a Second World War veteran of bombing missions in Pilsen and Royan.[5]

Ignoring the rigor of Lowell's argument, Hamilton systematically assaults the intentionality and validity of the poet's refusal. Hamilton's narrative insinuates that Lowell's refusal was merely an extension of the poet's troubled personal relationships and lifelong struggle with manic-depression. First, Hamilton sandwiches the "Declaration" between accounts of Lowell's previous intent to serve and Lowell's mother calling his refusal "a question of poetic temperament." Second, Hamilton treats Lowell's conversion as a symptom of his mania, connecting Lowell's "follow[ing] his conscience and trust[ing] in God" (91), to a kind of mental instability, being "more Catholic than the church" (96). Third, Hamilton's insinuation that Lowell's objection may have occurred under the influence of the poet's bipolar dysfunction finally becomes, in his discussion of "Memories of West Street and Lepke," an outright allegation: "He knows too that when he was a 'fire-breathing Catholic C.O.' and refused military service, he may well have been in the grip of energies that must now, if he is to live any sort of 'normal life,' be 'tranquillized' . . . But then what are 'ideals' worth if they can only be pursued in mania?" (264). Hamilton here cedes to a simplistic notion of confessional texts—that they read simply as literal and true confessions—rather than as performative masks. Hamilton's fallacy recalls M. L. Rosenthal's coining of "confessionalism," in a review of Life Studies, "Poetry as Confession" (1959). Rosenthal argued that in Life Studies, "Lowell removes the mask. His speaker is unequivocally himself" (109). To be fair, Hamilton's conflation may actually emerge from Lowell's own poetic self-representation of his CO experience in "Memories of West Street and Lepke," which invites the reader to associate the poet's jail term with his terms in mental asylums.

Paul Mariani's Lost Puritan recontextualizes the poet's refusal to serve within a chapter aptly titled "Catholics: 1940–1943," noting the poet's "immersion in Catholic apologetics" (98) and apocalyptic antiwar poems. Indeed, just before his letter to Roosevelt, in a letter to his parents, he wrote of the need to build a Christian society, quoting Blake (*Selected Letters* 35–36), and wrote a letter to Richard Eberhart that ends, "by the way I am not a pacifist but a Catholic" (*Selected Letters* 43). The antiwar poems in *Land of Unlikeness*, including "On the Eve of the Feast of the Immaculate Conception: 1942," "The Bomber," "Concord," "Napoleon Crosses the Berezina," "Christmas Eve in Time of War," and "Cistercians in Germany" condemn the war in religious and apocalyptic terms. Later poems, such as "The Quaker Graveyard in Nantucket" and "At the Bible House," wrestle with the longings for pacifism in a violent world, a violence that Lowell enacts on the level of language and syntax.

Despite the balanced secularity of his letter to Roosevelt, Lowell's war resistance poetry foregrounds the influence of his recent conversion to Catholicism. An early draft of the poem later entitled "Cistercians in Germany" echoes Wilfred Owen's famous antiwar poem "Dulce Et Decorum Est," and foreshadows Lowell's self-characterization in "Memories of West Street and Lepke":

> . . . now the dragon's
> Litter buckles on steel-scales and puffs
> Derision like confetti from ten thousand
> Scrap-heaps, munition pools and bee-hive camps:
> "Pleasant and gracious it is to die for America." (qtd. in Mariani 102)

Underlying Lowell's metaphor of the hoarding dragon is the connection between modern warfare and capitalist profiteering; in fact, his early poems consistently critique the excesses of capitalism, if from a Christian and aristocratic point of view. In addition, Lowell introduces the disjunction between Christian pacifism and warfare, a point he underscores in his letter to Roosevelt; the Second World War, in Lowell's early mythical poems, becomes the repetition of Jesus's crucifixion, in the deaths of all the "holy innocents."

The thematic conflict between a nonviolent Christ and a violent world, so clear in this poem, repeats itself—albeit in an ironic form—in the later "Memories of West Street and Lepke." In the earlier poem, the dragon America has given birth to an army of weaponry which condemns people to "bee-hive camps." In the later poem, Lowell himself becomes the dragon, the "fire-breathing Catholic C.O." This self-critical shift underscores the fundamental changes in Lowell's politics and poetics from his early to his middle period. Alan Williamson theorizes a break between Lowell's early political poetry and his mature work; Lowell's early poems are shot through with a radical vehemence and a consciousness of evil, while the later poems tend to turn this critical gaze upon the speaker himself (84).

The poems of Lowell's early period—though occasionally imbued with the dynamic tension between his newfound Catholic belief in a nonviolent Christ and his Puritan ancestral heritage of genocidal colonialism (in particular, "Concord," "At the Indian Killer's Grave," and "Christmas Eve Under Hooker's Statue")—often rely on an accusatory, self-righteous stance. Still, Helen Vendler's Oedipal reading of early Lowell replicates the analytic of which she accuses the poet, without adequately acknowledging his radical historical revisionism. Calling Lowell "politically correct" for naming his ancestor an "Indian killer," Vendler is content to argue that the early poems largely narrate "the disaffiliated son rebuking with grim triumph his rotting ancestors" (5). On the contrary, despite their weaknesses, Lowell's letter and early poems often demonstrate an acute awareness of his vexed relationship to the history and politics of the United States, not simply reducible to his family heritage.

Revising Resistance

Ian Hamilton conflates the poet's objection to the war with his mania; however, Lowell's own work, particularly in *Life Studies*, contributes to the erasure of his Catholic phase and his objection to the war by placing "Memories of West Street and Lepke" as part of a psychological narrative of mental breakdown and recovery.[6] *Life Studies*, written ten years after Lowell's incarceration, after Lowell had abandoned Catholicism and his early poetics, marks the poet's turn from, in Steven Gould Axelrod's phrasing, "the aristocratic, traditionalist ambiance provided by [Allen] Tate" (75). Still, one cannot underestimate the disciplining power of the New Criticism on a poet as concerned with authority as Lowell.

Axelrod has effectively traced Lowell's shift toward a new poetic on the level of literary association; as Lowell's poetic allegiances shift (toward William Carlos Williams and his idea of poetry), his politics also appear to change. Alan Nadel's discussion of Salinger's *Catcher in the Rye* facilitates a new cultural reading of Lowell's "Memories" and the emergent confessional poetry. Nadel argues that Caulfield's rhetoric (and, like Lowell, his madness) works as the political unconscious of the McCarthyist period, when the ideology of containment dominated American culture—a time of intense social regulation and conformity, professional loyalty oaths, confessions of past complicity with leftist political organizations, and accusations of others' complicity. The House Un-American Activities Committee conducted 51 anti-communist investigations in 1953 and 1954 alone (Engelhardt 126). In conjunction with the HUAC, the entertainment industry produced both "televised confessionals, which were prepared, written, and rehearsed and then were performed by real-life actors" (Nadel 80) and feature films, such as *I Was a Communist for the FBI* (1951). Confession, therefore, should not be regarded as a private act but rather as a moment when the private or individual moves into the public.

Before turning to "Memories," we must consider the micro- and macroeconomics of the new poetic emerging in Lowell's *Life Studies*. "Memories" necessitates a deceptively simple question: to whom is the speaker talking? W. R. Johnson's analysis of the lyric poem suggests that analyzing the use of pronominals in lyric poetry might render visible its ideological implications; he notes that modern lyrics increasingly eschew the personal I/You lyric address in favor of the meditative poem. Lowell's "Memories" follows the meditative pattern but cannot create the transparent subjectivity upon which the meditative poem relies; Lowell's poem insists on drawing a particularized self-portrait that recognizes his past dissent. For Johnson, the meditative poem addresses itself "to himself or no one in particular, or calls on, apostrophizes, inanimate or nonhuman entities, abstractions, or the dead" (3). Despite the explicit dangers in generalizing about genre, psychoanalysis may provide a way to consider the ideological implications of a meditative lyric like "Memories," precisely because Lowell's confessional poetry explicitly invokes the discourse of psychoanalysis.

From its earliest manifestations as poems written in royal courts, the lyric has often been attended by a silent third person who authorizes the relation and for whom the lyric is ultimately performed; so-called confessional poetry also often relies on an imagined analyst or silent judge. M. L. Rosenthal, who coined the term, argues that true confessional poems "put the speaker himself at the center of the poem in such a way as to make his psychological vulnerability and shame an embodiment of civilization" (79). He fails to consider to whom this confession is addressed, as how the poet attempts to speak representatively. In a period when HUAC was terrorizing American intellectuals and artists, Lowell's "Memories" reflects and refracts that element of public confession of his political dissent during the Second World War. Lowell's disavowal of his objection in "Memories"—as naïve Oedipal rebellion, as religious zealotry, or as manic—can be read as a complex pledge of allegiance to power.

"Memories of West Street and Lepke," the poet's only published work directly dealing with his objection is, in Alan Williamson's words, "the moment of crystallization" where Lowell "uses his intense self-exploration . . . as a source of metaphors for understanding aspects of the public world" (4). At the center of *Life Studies*, the poem recounts a midlife crisis, an individual's and a country's, in the middle of the bloodiest of centuries: "these are the tranquilized *Fifties*, / and I am forty" (*CPoems* 187). Moreover, the poem creates an insurmountable opposition, in the tradition of Yeats's "Easter 1916" and Auden's "September 1, 1939," between the objector's "seedtime" experience of refusing to go to war—one of many solipsistic acts in the poem—and his present, almost infantilized position as an academic. Lowell's young self, already an "empty mirror" to the speaker, is darkly reflected in the intensely ambiguous, even sublime, figure of Czar Lepke, a kind of impotent monster with whom Lowell identified in his manic phases.

From the first word of the poem, the poet's current domestic lifestyle is portrayed as being full of extravagances, eccentricities, and infantilization:

Only teaching on Tuesdays, book-worming
in pajamas fresh from the washer each morning,
I hog a whole house on Boston's
"hardly passionate Marlborough Street" (*CPoems* 187)

Lowell is "only teaching," not "teaching only" on Tuesdays; his choice to frame his memories by his present situation speaks to a time when teaching itself was surveilled for its subversive elements, as "teachers and professors were being forced to sign loyalty oaths and/or were being dismissed because of present or past political beliefs" (Nadel 82). Characteristically, Lowell's numerous animal metaphors (here, "book-worming" and "hog," and six lines later, "sheepish") do not evoke animal power but rather a declawed domesticity, a toothless intellectualism. Moreover, the poet lives on a "hardly passionate" street in a neighborhood so well off that "the bum on the street / has two children, a beach wagon, a helpmate, / and is a 'young Republican'" (*CPoems* 187). Midlife domesticity clearly does not sit well with the poet, and causes him to look back to his earlier days.

This midlife view backwards, however, is far from nostalgic. Perhaps because Lowell has rejected the Catholicism and poetics of *Land of Unlikeness* and *Lord Weary's Castle* that propelled his decision to go to prison, the ironic hindsight of the poem represents his younger self as "solipsistic, ineffective, merely bizarre" (Williamson 80):

These are the tranquillized *Fifties*,
and I am forty. Ought I to regret my seedtime?
I was a fire-breathing Catholic C.O.,
and made my manic statement,
telling off the state and president, and then
sat waiting sentence in the bull pen
beside a Negro boy with curlicues
of marijuana in his hair. (*CPoems* 187)

It is as if Lowell were answering HUAC's question, "Are you now, or have you ever been, a Communist?" with a half-embarrassed, half-bragging, "No, I was a fire-breathing Catholic C.O." If one reads Lowell's confession as ironic, these lines have a subversive quality, because they answer the question by self-caricature—a cooked version, perhaps, of Allen Ginsberg's 1956 protest romp, "America": "I used to be a communist when I was a kid I'm not sorry" (146). At the same time, Lowell's irony is a strategy of defeatism, insofar as the self-caricature replicates dominant stereotypes of dissent. Lowell's past self now becomes the dragon from his earlier poem; Lowell also conflates his objection with mania. Williamson explains Lowell's choice of the word "manic" as a poetic failure: "a technical psychoanalytic term like 'manic' in a subtle descriptive context, however accurate it may be, suggests a complacent patness attained at some cost to richness of feeling and recollection" (80). Lowell's use of "manic" invites the reading that his Declaration of Personal Responsibility occurred while under the influence of madness, even though no biography provides any evidence that Lowell experienced mania at the time.[7] In addition, Lowell was not, strictly speaking, a CO, because CO status was a legal definition for a person who refused for reasons of conscience to serve in any war and was thus eligible for alternative service in Civilian Public Service camps. And finally, one could hardly call Lowell's politely formal letter a "telling off" of the president. Why would the poet choose to associate his mania and his war refusal?

Lowell's odd caricature of his younger, objecting self emerges against the backdrop of postwar containment culture, itself marked by the reemergence of Freudian self-scrutiny. As Kaja Silverman has argued, the Oedipal narrative, a narrative of family and private life, reemerged with a vengeance in order to repatriate (both in terms of bringing them back into the country and in terms of reinserting them as patriarchs) the soldiers into the U.S. economy. The desire to forget the war and the world and to focus on the family, as in *The Man in the Gray Flannel Suit*, fed containment culture's pathological fear of difference and led to a cultural desire to put communists in their place—and women in theirs; thus, in popular media, anticommunist detectives appeared next to idealized wives, from Mike Hammer to June Cleaver. Though the containment culture of the early Cold War would cede to "the politics of consensus" (Davidson *GLU* 56), Cold War culture required strict policing of the homefront.

The Freudian vogue that fundamentally influenced the confessional poets, however, emerged both as a symptom of the culture's retreat to the domestic and as a resistance to the narrative of forgetting; thus the confessional impulse in poetry emerges as both submissive and rebellious. Lyric poems may be written to another, but the confessional poem is written *for* the Other. Slavoj Zizek outlines the tradition from "confession to psychoanalysis," in which "the subject is compelled to attain the truth in himself . . . by way of its verbalization, of its translation into the language of an expert invested with power (theologian, psychoanalyst). . . . [This kind of truth is a] performative fiction at the service of power" (*EYS* 180). Just as *Catcher*, for Nadel, "manifests thematically and formally an ultimately theological context: appeal to an authority in touch with truths that remain opaque within the world of the text" (89), so too did Lowell's speakers appeal to an authority outside the text—the gesture of allegiance that typifies Cold War discourse and its literary handmaiden, the New Criticism.[8] By making this gesture toward the authority, Lowell, like Nadel's interpretation of Caulfield, "manifests two drives: to control his environment by being the one who names and thus creates its rules, and to subordinate the self by being the one whose every action is governed by the rules. To put it another way, he is trying to constitute himself both as subject and as object" (73). In other words, the workings of "Memories" functions as an analogue to the analytic relation; the poem allows Lowell to speak about himself as both subject and object.

Lowell performs an allegiance to political authority by disavowing what might be termed the fantasy of the absolute rebel—the *beyond* of resistance. The absolute rebel, of course, does not need to exist in reality in order to make claims on the subject. As in "Easter 1916," where Yeats's speaker experiences a fascination with and repulsion toward the Irish rebels, who "trouble the living stream," Lowell's poem exhibits a troubled fascination with the absolute rebellion of his youth. His portrait, though caricatured, also represents his "seedtime," a foundational moment. Still, this resistance is so loaded with negative modifiers that it seems always already phantasmatic, inhuman, and destined to fail.

"Memories" similarly represents other pacifists besides Lowell himself, in less than glowing terms, staging a tragicomic scene in which a fey Jewish pacifist named Abramowitz tries to convert two "Hollywood pimps" to his diet of "fallen fruit," only to be beaten "black and blue" (*CPoems* 187–188) Here, it is most clear how Lowell's poem projects onto the past the present atomism of the 1950s; all the figures in prison are *others*—ciphers of disconnection, separation, and alienation from the mainstream: his younger self, the Negro boy with marijuana in his hair, the Jewish pacifist, the pimps, the Jehovah's Witnesses, and Lepke.[9] But Lowell does more than project atomism onto the prison inhabitants; he pairs his younger self against these others as if they were foils: the more ominous or dangerous alternatives of blacks, gays, Jews, pimps, Jehovah's Witnesses, and the murderer Lepke. Nadel notes how autobiography, in containment culture, becomes testimony against the other, revealing "the Other—the subversive—everywhere but in the place he or she was known to be, even in the audience of investigators and/or the speaker" (84).

Lowell thereby stages religiosity and pacifism—and resistance itself—as ineffectual and impotent in the context of a prison society where the violent Lepke reigns:

> *Murder Incorporated*'s Czar Lepke,
> there piling towels on a rack,
> or dawdling off to his little segregated cell full
> of things forbidden the common man:
> a portable radio, a dresser, two toy American
> flags tied together with a ribbon of Easter palm.
> Flabby, bald, lobotomized,
> he drifted in a sheepish calm,
> where no agonizing reappraisal
> jarred his concentration on the electric chair—
> hanging like an oasis in his air
> of lost connections . . . (*CPoems* 188)

The figure of Lepke is complex, a complexity reflected in the sudden shift to a tighter metrical rhythm at this moment in the poem. Williamson notes that in Lowell's poetics, meter and rhyme often create "not neat rational statements, but a kind of trance . . . [s]ymbols arrive with such intensity that they threaten the usually strong tension between symbolic thought and the real world" (11). Here, too, in the lines describing Lepke, one senses the hypnotized, entranced gaze of the poet on a figure of terrible proportions. Throughout his life, Lowell had a fascination for the tyrant. Napoleon, Hitler, and Attila the Hun transfixed Lowell, particularly in his manic phases, when he experienced delusions of grandeur and omnipotence (only to be followed by intense guilt and remorse in his depressive phases). He both identified with and was repulsed by these tyrannical, monstrous figures. Lepke acts as an empty mirror, a doppelganger for Lowell. However, Lepke's special status, which allows him the trinkets of American life "forbidden the common man," dangerously nears the position of the midlife Lowell (and America itself). Because Lepke seems to embody so many oppositions, he becomes what Slavoj Zizek calls the "quilting point"—a sublime, negative position which absorbs and produces multiple, even contradictory meanings (*SOI* 95–96). Zizek's reading of the movie shark, Jaws, is also a reading of Lepke: "what one should do is rather conceive of the monster as a fantasy screen where this very multiplicity of meanings can appear and fight for hegemony" (*EYS* 133). Lepke is at once a figure of omnipotence and impotence, of cunning violence and lobotomized passivity, of patriotism and religiosity, of a nuclear America and a domesticated Lowell.

Though his seedtime self may have been "out of things," Lowell is most lost precisely when he is living the American Dream—living in a house set in a beautiful neighborhood, working and raising a family. Even his implicit call for "agonizing reappraisal" has a touch of irony, for the poet lifts the phrase from Cold Warrior John Foster Dulles. In Lowell's profoundest argument with himself—between the young rebel and the ironic midlifer, between the murderer and the pacifist, between the manic and rational man, between the lobotomized and the agonizing reappraiser—we are left, as readers, with only a bleak, disconnected oasis. In "Memories," Lowell invokes one of the most troubling aspects of the containment (and postmodern) culture—the selfish wish to repress our connections to the past and to the others. But while Lowell offers no explicit, positive image of pacifism, the negative mirror of his earlier self delivers the pang of conscience itself.

The Danbury Prison Strike of 1943

The difficulty in teasing out the traces of history from a confessional text has everything to do with its complex lyric address. As Emile Benveniste argues in *Problems in General Linguistics*, the subject's appeal to the other fundamentally alters his language, and consequently, his history: "through the sole fact of addressing another, the one who is speaking himself installs the other in himself, and thereby apprehends himself, confronts himself, and establishes himself as he aspires to be, and finally historicizes himself in this incomplete and falsified history" (67). The subject that emerges from the analytic relation always shapes and is shaped by the narrative he creates. Similarly, Lowell's "Memories" both defines and is defined by the poet's appeal to the other. But in his appeal to the other, other connections inevitably are lost; in the poem, Lowell himself is clearly wary of and fascinated by the oasis of lost connections.

In this final section, I read Lowell's "Memories" against other war resisters' recollections of West Street and Danbury—Lowell Naeve's *A Field of Broken Stones* and Jim Peck's *Underdogs vs Upperdogs*—tracking the possibilities of a poetics of war resistance, and in particular, interrogating the primacy of certain canonized texts over forgotten ones. Some striking comparisons and equally striking contrasts become immediately evident. First, the resisters' reasons for refusing to serve emerge from different circumstances: Lowell's Just War principles, Naeve's anarchism, and Peck's anti-imperialism. Second, Naeve's and Peck's depictions of West Street Jail and Danbury Prison, where all three served the tenure of their sentences, corroborate the physical details of Lowell's poem; Lowell's documentary style, however, offers the ruse of realism. Third, all three accounts describe the shocked submission that accompanied the early phase of internment; if Lowell's seems to linger in its numbed gaze, we must remember that the poem itself sets out only to consider West Street. Yet, Lowell's elision of his experience in Danbury—especially the prison strike for desegregation organized by conscientious objectors—has serious implications for how we remember war resistance during the Second World War. Fourth, each representation—whether narrative or poetic—articulates the various and differing modes and possibilities of resistance; this final point underscores the horizons of Lowell's text as not representative of CO prison resistance. Finally, and importantly, each representation implicitly comments on its own production, thereby providing a glimpse into the historical context.

Each of the writer-resisters underwent a process of coming to resistance, and comparing the three accounts sheds light on the multiple, and at times, contradictory paths that led to war resistance. Lowell's "Memories" is the most evasive, even duplicitous, as an articulation of his reasons for refusal to participate in the war; in fact, the poem deliberately obfuscates and demeans his decision as manic, "fire-breathing," and religiously motivated, when his letter to Roosevelt suggests Lowell's refusal likely resulted from his conversion to Catholicism and the changing situation of the war. In contrast, Naeve's simple refusal to register for the draft came out of a dual belief that killing was wrong and that "war was to enrich munitions millionaires, to protect Standard Oil properties abroad, etc." (6). His refusal, like Lowell's, was individual, as

Naeve was not affiliated with any political or religious organization. Peck, by contrast, had already been involved for a number of years in radical political activity. Raised Episcopalian by his Jewish parents, Peck had by 1933 attended his first demonstration (against the Nazi Party), scandalized his classmates by bringing a black woman from Roxbury to the Harvard freshman prom, and got involved in a union struggle while working on a freighter. When the Second World War approached, he began writing for the War Resisters League's newspaper, the *Conscientious Objector*. On October 6, 1940, he refused to sign his draft card and later was sentenced to three years in prison.

In light of the parallel details of West Street Jail provided by Naeve and Peck, "Memories" appears so accurate that it forces one to ask whether Lowell could be considered a docupoet, intent on cataloguing historical particulars for social effect. All three recount the anxious wait in the claustrophobic bull pen, the unholy presence of Lepke, and the exercise cage on top of the building. In addition, Peck's text, exposing the privileges accorded to wealthy or well-connected prisoners, even goes so far as to mention Willie Bioff and George Browne as "racketeering officials of the International Alliance of Moving Picture Machine Operators and Theatrical State Employees" (23); these are the prisoners Lowell sexualizes as "two Hollywood pimps." No mention of Abramowitz, or of his being beaten by Bioff and Browne, however, occurred in either of the memoirs.

But if Lowell's poem aspires to docurealism, "Memories" also clouds its details in the haze of immaturity, emotional distress, and shock. The poem jars the reader with explicitly bizarre juxtapositions and metaphors—describing, for example, the caged prison rooftop as a school soccer court, not to mention its characterization of the young Lowell as "fire-breathing," "manic," and generally "out of things." Similarly, Naeve's memoir, written in hauntingly spare prose and illustrated by Naeve's own pencil drawings, creates an effect of claustrophobic pressure. Still, if Naeve's early behavior at West Street and Danbury was marked by shock, he soon began small refusals, and on his fifth day at Danbury he stopped working. Paul Goodman's preface notes "the increasingly active character of [Naeve's] responses and his increasing participation in groups both inside and outside [the prison] walls." To mollify Naeve, the warden provided him with a studio to paint in. However, Naeve realized the warden wished to display him for visitors and, growing tired of the interruptions, he refused to let anyone visit. When the warden ordered Naeve to paint some signs for the war, he refused absolutely, and they had to carry him limp to the cell. He remained in segregation until the end of his first prison sentence; eight months later, he was arrested again for being without a draft card. He was returned to West Street, processed, and sent to Bellevue for psychiatric testing after he protested in solidarity with two hunger strikers, Stanley Murphy and Louis Taylor, who believed all refusers should be set free. There, he was force-fed and drugged until the war resistance community began visiting him in prison.

Peck also recalls the "utter monotony and aimlessness of prison life . . . [and its] considerable 'mental torment and emotional damage'" (25). Along with Naeve, perhaps as a mode of survival, he and other prisoners began striking. Here Peck's experience organizing and leading political actions came into use. Prisoners—both regular and war resisters—had a "potato boycott," a "scrap the scrapple boycott," and later a strike against a longer work week (landing them one week in solitary) and refusal to paint victory signs (giving them 10 days in solitary and 28 months' segregation).

Lowell, despite his connections, "chose to do manual labor in the mason shop to get experience in building a Catholic community which he hoped to do upon release . . . [and wore] the standard, shabby, ill-fitting overalls" (Peck 36). For Lowell, resistance extended principally to his refusal to serve in war, though he spent his prison term working and revising galleys to his antiwar first book, *Land of Unlikeness*. But one strike in particular, when all three were in Danbury Prison, highlights the chasm between Lowell and the other two resisters. According to Hamilton, "Peck and others tried to involve Lowell in a strike against the segregation of black and white prisoners . . . but Lowell made it clear he had larger matters to attend to: 'He was "spaced out"—he was only interested in one thing, Catholic communities.' Even so, Peck— along with most of the others—gradually warmed to this abstract, shabby 'man of God'; he may not have been their kind of protesting pacifist, but he was manifestly not a fraud" (93). In contrast, Peck acknowledges that though one might think that COs might be united by common goals, "the individualistic COs at Danbury found it almost impossible to agree on any common action to support their cause" (38). Yet, Lowell's declining to participate in the strike against segregation, and his concomitant silence about it in his "Memories," are a stark reminder about the epistemological limits—and potential dangers—of "getting the news" from canonized texts. Though it would be unfair to call Lowell's failure to act *racist*—given the stakes involved in prison resistance—it does compel a reconsideration of the strange portrait in "Memories" of the "Negro boy with curlicues / of marijuana in his hair" (*SP* 91). The "Negro boy" acts merely as a cipher, shorn of any possibility of identification, a bizarre mirror to the youthful Lowell's insolent rejection of his parents' social mores. From the earliest draft of "Memories," the "Negro boy" initiates the poem as part of Lowell's disavowed other half: "I am two people I confess" (Houghton Archives). The Negro boy, in this reading, is one of Lowell's "lost connections." I do not want to judge Lowell's refusal to participate in the desegregation strike, given the severe consequences that participation entailed, but rather point to the limits of the poet's religious conscientious objection, divorced from a broader vision of social progressivism, and to the limits of Lowell's "Memories" as a representation of war resistance.

Lowell's other published poem about his prison experience, "In the Cage," deals more directly with what appears to be Lowell's terror of prison life, particularly in terms of the presence of black men. The poem mentions a "colored fairy," whose tinkling song causes the other prisoners to "beat their bars and scream" and "the Bible-twisting Israelite / Fast[ing] for his Harlem," a member of an African American religious sect who believed themselves to be the chosen people (*CPoems* 55). Lowell writes that "age / Blackens the heart of Adam" (*CPoems* 55), using blackness as a symbol of Adam's (and Lowell's) degradation. Lowell's other depictions of African Americans, in "A Mad Negro Soldier Confined in Munich," "At the Mouth of the Hudson," and "For the Union Dead," all demonstrate the dynamic present in "Memories"; Lowell identifies with, but ultimately keeps distant from African Americans, who seem for him to dwell in another world.

Despite the difficulty of organizing independent-minded and diverse objectors, the strike to desegregate the prison dining hall was not the first CO strike; the first CO prison actions began with the Union Theological Seminary students in 1940 and continued with Stanley Murphy and Louis Taylor's 84-day hunger strike "to protest the imprisonment of CO's" (Peck 38). Still, the strike in 1943 to desegregate Danbury Prison holds particular significance, because no prison in the United States had yet desegregated, and the strike became an experiment in resistance against institutional racism that would later emerge to inform the Civil Rights movement in the 1950s. On August 11, 1943, Peck and 17 others struck to end mess hall segregation and were placed in segregation cells; allowed only 45 minutes per day outside, the strikers had to rely upon various means of communication and expression. Lowell Naeve began a newspaper while in segregation called "The Clink," which included articles, poems, and drawings. Naeve also made a guitar out of papier-mâché. Peck even wrote a song, which the group performed while in segregation cells and which included the following lyrics:

They say that Hitler is wicked
To persecute race in his way

But when it's done in the U.S.
It's quite perfectly o.k.

The blacks are as good as the whites
Why shouldn't they have equal rights
The warden says no
But we tell him it's so
Jimcrow must go. (49)

Even if the song's analogy between Hitler's Germany and the U.S. is somewhat strained, it nonetheless satirically points out the hypocrisy of fighting a
"people's war" for a country that had systematically brutalized black people in
slavery and segregation.

The strikers' creative methods of communicating and supporting each
other did not reduce the various stresses, personal arguments, and problems
that emerged while trying to resist collectively, as Naeve details in his account. For months, the strike seemed to make no impression on prison authorities. Only when one striker's fiancée, Ruth MacAdam, "went to Harlem
and persuaded Representative Adam Clayton Powell to organize a special
committee in support of the strike" (51) did pressure begin to form. Some 135
days later, the warden agreed to end segregation; Danbury became the first
federal prison to abolish segregation. Peck called this successful strike "one of
the most important accomplishments of CO's in world war 2" (53). Not surprisingly, some of the strikers immediately found new reasons to strike, including the continued imprisonment of COs; others, including Lowell Naeve,
went on hunger strikes. However, when their resistance got too defiant, the
hardcore resisters were all split up and sent to different prisons. Naeve and
Peck both served many years, but not without a transformed understanding of
the system of oppression at work in the U.S.

Even though Lowell's lack of participation in the strike helps explain why
it failed to appear in "Memories" (or any other of his poems, for that matter),
another important difference between Lowell's text and the others is its belated completion, under much less confining circumstances. Lowell's situates
itself in the "tranquillized Fifties," in a wealthy neighborhood, many years after his prison experience. Naeve's prison memoir, in marked contrast, contains at its core the story of the manuscript's production and escape from
prison; Naeve, with the help of fellow war resister David Wieck, smuggled out
the writing in a hollow papier-mâché frame for one of his paintings. (Prison
authorities confiscated the other two copies when Naeve attempted to leave

the jail with them). The core and title of Peck's memoir, as he notes, came from "a 15-page cartoon-illustrated pamphlet [written] in solitary confinement for striking to end messhall segregation at the Federal Correctional Institution at Danbury, CT" (5).

As Lowell went on to become the highest regarded postwar poet, many of his fellow war resisters continued their dissent and political activism. If there is anyone who might qualify as the absolute rebel, it would be Jim Peck, whom Lowell met in Danbury, and who called himself a "robot picket." Peck's list of arrests reads like a greatest hits record of protest from 1940 to 1970. Peck protested the Bikini bomb explosions in 1946; in 1947, some twenty years prior to similar protests during the Vietnam War, he publicly burned his draft card; in 1955, he participated in the first civil defense protests with members of the Catholic Worker; in 1958, he sailed the *Golden Rule* into an atomic test zone with Albert Bigelow. Peck continued his work challenging racism and segregation by participating in the 1947 Journey of Reconciliation one year after the Irene Morgan ruling in the Supreme Court banned segregation on interstate buses; two Second World War COs organized the action. Then, in 1961, the Boynton decision expanded desegregation to include facilities used by interstate travelers, and Peck joined the Freedom Ride, a bus trip made by black and white activists to test the national government's enforcement of desegregation; they traveled by bus into the Deep South and encountered serious resistance. On May 14 near Anniston, Alabama, their bus was bombed by an angry mob. At the next stop, Peck was beaten nearly to death in Birmingham. In the hospital after having received fifty stitches in his head, Peck told the national media that "I think it is especially important . . . that we continue to show that nonviolence can prevail over violence" (qtd. in Williams 149). Despite the violence of racist segregationists, the Riders helped end segregation on all interstate travel.

Lowell's "Memories" intimates that his days of dissent were done, but he soon became an active resister against the Vietnam War, publicly refusing to attend a White House gathering of writers in 1965, participating in readings, and taking part in the March on the Pentagon in October 1967. Lowell's letter to President Johnson refusing the invitation to the White House function initiated his public dissent. Hilene Flanzbaum sees Lowell's opposition as part of the poet's "yearning to find common ground with the large American audience" (47) and argues that "the growing unpopularity of the Vietnam War, and the cultural revolution spawned in the wake of protests against it, found Lowell closer to mainstream American ideology and appetites than he would ever have thought possible. Abruptly, Lowell's iconoclasm was chic" (45). However, Flanzbaum supports her thesis by arguing that "from its inception, the anti-war movement attracted large crowds, which made protesting American involvement in Vietnam both respectable and profitable" (45). But Lowell's 1965 initial refusal came at a time when the antiwar movement was still very much a marginal cultural force. According to Howard Zinn, "in early 1965, when the bombing of North Vietnam began, a hundred people gathered on the Boston Common to voice their indignation. On October 15, 1969, the number of people assembled on the Boston Common to protest the war was 100,000" (477). Lawrence Wittner corroborates Zinn's perspective, arguing that a December 1964 rally in New York City, numbering 1,500 people, "fell far short of a mass movement" (281). In addition, most Americans "thought the American involvement in Vietnam was not wrong" in late 1965 (Zinn 483).

Lowell, therefore, may have ended up a cultural sensation not because he happened to share the views of the new radical movement, but because, as a Boston Brahmin, his early public dissent anticipated the mass movement and gave cultural weight to antiwar views and arguments. According to James Sullivan, Lowell's "presence at the [1967 Pentagon] rally was a sign of the intellectual and cultural legitimacy of protest and, by implication, the illegitimacy of the Vietnam War" (199). Still, Lowell did not abandon his characteristic ambivalences in his poetry about resisting the war. His poems, including "Waking Early Sunday Morning" (from *Near the Ocean*, which is a part of both *Selected Poems* and *Collected Poems*), "The March I," and "The March II," rather than simply playing to the antiwar crowd, wrestle with the problems of war resistance and further exemplify Lowell's overidentification with power. According to Paul Breslin, in poems such as "For the Union Dead" and "Waking Early Sunday Morning," Lowell laments a lost heroism in a time which "suffer[s] public experience without being able to participate in it" (74). While Breslin sees Lowell's empathetic identification with President Johnson in "Waking" as surprising, Richard Tillinghast argues that "Lowell's portraits of tyrants and other powerful men [were] informed and energized by his own fascination with power" (35). Tillinghast's observation should be extended even further; Lowell's identification was with Great Men who were libidinal, violent, wounded, trapped in the girdings of their own power. In "Waking," Lowell feels

> elated as the President
> girdled by his establishment
> this Sunday morning, free to chaff
> his own thoughts with his bear-cuffed staff,
> swimming nude, unbuttoned, sick
> of his ghost-written rhetoric! (*CPoems* 385)

Similarly, in the final lines of his letter to Johnson, Lowell is able both to commiserate with and yield to the president, using a collective *we* in its address:

> What we will do and what we ought to do as a sovereign nation facing other sovereign nations seem now to hang in the balance between the better and worse possibilities. We are in danger of imperceptibly becoming an explosive and suddenly chauvinistic nation, and may even be drifting on our way to the last nuclear ruin. I know it is hard for the responsible man to act; it is also painful for the private and irresolute man to dare criticism. At this anguished, delicate and perhaps determining moment, I feel I am serving you and our country best by not taking part in the White House Festival of the Arts. (CP 371)

The collective we of the letter and at the conclusion of "Waking" hold a striking similarity, in its taking responsibility for the actions of the government. Here, Lowell wishes

> peace to our children when they fall
> in small war on the heels of small
> war—until the end of time
> to police the earth, a ghost
> orbiting forever lost
> in *our* monotonous sublime. (italics mine, CPoems 386)

Lowell's identification with the powerful sees its poetic obverse not only in "Memories," then, but also in "The March I" and "The March II," where protestors—and especially Lowell—are helpless against the brutal efficiency of soldiers called to break up the March on the Pentagon. "The March II" begins:

> Where two or three were flung together, or fifty,
> mostly white-haired, or bald, or women . . . sadly
> unfit to follow their dream, I sat in the sunset
> shade of our Bastille, the Pentagon,
> nursing leg- and arch-cramps, my cowardly,
> foolhardy heart; and heard, alas, more speeches,
> though the words took heart now to show how weak
> we were, and right. (CPoems 546)

Parodying Christ's words about spiritual community—"whenever two or more are gathered"—Lowell casts the protest as a tired and unmanly lot of the elderly, the aging, and women—unable to end the war; while longtime activists and many women did take part, Lowell's denigrating portrayal belies other accounts of the March. In *The Armies of the Night*, Norman Mailer details the huge and diverse crowd, the conflicts of strategy, and the partial overnight occupation of a portion of the Pentagon. Mailer went so far as to compare it to the battles fought by the Second World War generation. Though many people, especially women, were viciously beaten and trampled, Lowell admits that he fled the scene in "The March II," having failed to get arrested. Just as in "Memories," then, Lowell casts protest against war as a hopeless, but morally justified, endeavor.

Lowell's overidentification with power and reliance upon "Great Man" historiography probably lead him to represent war resistance simply as the strivings of the weak. But lest we scapegoat Lowell, we must consider the ways in which these representations emerge from both a personal worldview and from the dominant discourse's treatment of revolt as "revolting," abject, or crazy. On the one hand, the odd paradox of Lowell's overidentification with power, along with his resistance to the abuses of that power, resembles the dynamics of his bipolarity—from fantasizing being a dictator to desiring his own castration. On the other hand, in the late twentieth century, the politics of spectacle—a prevailing concern of Lowell's in "For the Union Dead—has made Americans acutely aware of their lack of agency; the Gulf War coverage offered by the Pentagon, and its missile-eye views of destruction, was designed specifically and precisely to allow for "identification with the aggressor," to use Anna Freud's term. This identification seems to target men in particular, where the patriarchal energy of society requires the disavowal of symbolic castration. Insofar as Lowell does not deny his symbolic castration in his mature phase, we might be tempted to see Lowell's depictions of resisters as antipatriarchal, and therefore oppositional to the patriarchal energies of warfare.

On the contrary, Lowell's "Memories" has it both ways, simultaneously confessing and disavowing; in presenting his present self as castrated, he can project, in classical psychoanalytic terms, "an unwanted feature of the *self* . . . onto the other" (Silverman 45).[10] In other words, even if the speaker of the poem lays himself bare as a castrated figure, the author emerges, paradoxically, with an even greater authority. Lowell's poems of resistance therefore speak to the crisis of male subjectivity, but they also point to the limits of Oedipal psychoanalysis as a progressive mode of theoretical inquiry; a myopic psychoanalytic reading could then easily argue—as many psychologists did at the time—that war resisters simply were coddled as children, or had not accepted their symbolic castration, and that war resistance itself was simply a defense against the moral complexity of the world. Such *ad hominem* attack deflects attention from the challenging beliefs, rational analysis, and subversive actions of war resisters.

Lowell's poems, far from providing a paean to war resistance, present the conundrums and crises of a privileged American male subjectivity; moreover, as *"the* poet of the American empire" (qtd. in Greiner 24, emphasis mine), Lowell articulates the limits inherent in individual attempts to resist at the center of empire. Robert von Hallberg argues that the most interesting poets are the ones who attempt to address the "center of culture" (9), because they are willing to "live with their complicity, fully aware that moments of shame go along with access to the cultural authority of a centralized culture" (4). While Lowell's poetry refuses the partisanship of other explicitly radical poetries, it also provides a shaky ground for resistance. Paul Breslin validates Lowell for his skepticism, although he admits that Lowell's skepticism is at times so problematic "as to paralyze all sympathy and judgment. Characteristic of Lowell is an ambivalence about ambivalence" (59). However, the fact that Lowell assumed he could be a prototypical "American citizen" was not necessarily an elitist assumption of birthright; rather, like the activist, Lowell allows for no cynical distance between himself and the political realm. Because Lowell overidentifies with power, he may actually provide a model for exposing power's illegitimacy. In Slavoj Zizek's formulation, the "strategy of overidentification" (*SOI* 71) involves taking the symbolic order at its word, literally undertaking the script in such a way that it threatens the required cynical distance upon which all governing systems rely.

Lowell's mature poems capture the peculiarly ambivalent American subjectivity pervasive in containment culture; but as former Secretary of State Robert McNamara's memoir, *In Retrospect: The Tragedy and Lessons of Vietnam* (1995) makes all too clear, the ambivalence built into American imperialism has not made the U.S. less willing to project its ideological and military power throughout the world. Still, even if Lowell's "Memories" reflects Cold War culture and fails to wrestle with the implications of the Danbury Prison strike, it also refuses to settle into the blind privilege and forgetfulness of the "tranquillized Fifties." Finally, Lowell's "Memories" enables us to extend the notion of history as a palimpsest between two periods; history is radically contingent, subject to the future, itself an arena of struggle.

2. William Stafford's Lost Landmarks

THE POETICS OF PACIFISM AND
THE LIMITS OF LYRIC

Though William Stafford is best known for his poetry, his largely forgotten memoir of his years as a conscientious objector during the Second World War, *Down in My Heart* (1947), anticipates the central questions of his pacifist and utopian poetry. How to resist war in one's writing and yet avoid the Manichean us/them discourse that perpetuates war? How to pledge allegiance to the nation and yet articulate an alternate vision of social connection—a poetics of nonviolent community? How to write a poetry which invites pacifist response, or interpellates a pacifist subjectivity? How to oppose a history of generals and wars on the level of poetic form? *Down in My Heart* stages the drama between Stafford's utopian poetics—manifested in an ahistorical vision of the "beloved community," where consensus decision making, accommodation, and respect for the law and for others are paramount—and the press of history, genocidal war, and outright resistance.

Stafford's memoir represents both a "lost connection," to echo Robert Lowell, in the history of nonviolent literature and a landmark by which we can reorient ourselves in the poet's massive lyric domain. The memoir is an Ur-text that informs and exposes the monological limits of Stafford's poetry; while it anticipates Stafford's lyric preoccupation with building an imagined community that respects—and even requires—solitude and difference, it also illuminates the horizon of Stafford's lyric and, indeed, the limits of the lyric as genre.

Brooding about Community in the Civilian Public Service

Of all contemporary American poets, William Stafford "broods most about community—the 'mutual life' we share" (Bly Introduction xiii). Stafford's brooding about community originates in *Down in My Heart*, a collection of stories that imagines and recounts the "beloved community" of conscientious objectors who performed nonviolent service for the U.S. during the Second World War. Despite its relative obscurity, *Down in My Heart* is perhaps the most articulate and sustained literary work to grapple with and represent war resistance during the Second World War. Both historical account and fictional representation, combining poetry and prose, *Down in My Heart* avoids the pitfalls of self-pity, nostalgia, or rebellious alienation as it inscribes a poetics of nonviolence. In other words, it consciously imagines itself, even as it represents Stafford's alternative service experience in Civilian Public Service (CPS) camps, as a model of living in communal resistance to the structures of war and violence. Such a task might seem to be a doomed literary project, caught either in ahistorical utopianism or self-righteous moralism. But Stafford's politico-literary gambit—one that may even outstrip his subsequent 60-plus volumes of poetry—succeeds precisely because the memoir remains open to, and includes, the very voice that proclaims the CPS experiment in nonviolence a failure—the voice of a "certain absolutist" named George.

A brief recap of the history of the CPS experiment will illuminate how Stafford's memoir provides a representative glimpse of pacifist action during the Second World War. In 1940, pacifist organizations had won a key victory in Congress with the passage of a law recognizing conscientious objection as a legal category; the idea of creating a civilian service program as an alternative to military service captured the imagination of pacifists throughout the country, and Stafford and other COs set out to make their lives in CPS a witness to the possibilities of nonviolent community within a nation-state at war. Their task was to "work at being a distinct society within but not removed from the larger one, at living out their convictions in the face of both natural suspicion and all the propaganda resources of our modern government" (Gundy 97). CPS brought together future Civil Rights leaders (Bayard Rustin, among others), longtime radical pacifists, and artists and writers (Stafford, William Everson, Kenneth Rexroth, and J. F. Powers). The wartime contribution of COs also was not insignificant; over six years, 12,000 COs worked eight million days fighting forest fires, battling soil erosion, building dams, planting trees, farming, raising money for war victims, working in mental hospitals, and volunteering as human guinea pigs for medical research on disease. CO William Anderson, for example, took part in medical research on the effects of starvation on human beings (see figure 1)—research that would provide data for the postwar relief effort.

Despite these contributions, many COs began to see the CPS project as a failure even before the war was over. The program had begun as a compromise project between pacifist organizations and the U.S. government; the historic peace churches provided the funding, but the government took control of overseeing the program. Not only did COs receive no money from the government—they lived on less than a dime a day—but they were often compelled to do meaningless tasks under a system of military coercion. COs had hoped to be a living witness for pacifism among their fellow Americans, but they found themselves isolated in depopulated areas, underemployed, and largely forgotten. Though some COs, including Stafford, continued to serve, others began engaging in resistance through personal protest, work slow downs, and walkouts, calling the whole program a "violation of the 13th Amendment . . . [that] mirrored the global trend toward totalitarianism" (Sibley and Jacob 261–262). Historians Sibley and Jacob recount the phenomenon of "certain absolutists," conscientious objectors who defiantly resisted state coercion; Corbett Bishop, most notably, engaged in absolute resistance after authorities arrested him for walking out of camp. In prison and in hospital, he would not eat, walk, dress, or even go to the bathroom for 337 days. The authorities finally let him go. He left with these words: "the authorities have the power to seize my body, that is all they can do. My spirit will be free" (qtd. in Cooney and Michalowski 107). Bishop's absolutist stand points to the power and the limits of conscientious objection, a resistance centered in the individual.[1]

The difficulty of building community among a diverse group of objectors in a nation engaged in total war, and of bridging the increasingly unbridgeable gap between those who toiled through their internment as a mode of war resistance and those who turned their resistance against the CPS itself, haunts Stafford's memoir. *Down in My Heart* dramatizes the fundamental conflict in CPS between those who envisioned their work in the camps as an alternative community based on human fellowship, rather than on structures of authoritarian order and violence, and those who increasingly saw their labor as involuntary servitude. In the introduction to his memoir, Stafford first underscores the radical disjunction experienced by COs from society at large, rather than from each other: "During the war years we who openly objected and refused to participate often felt alone, and said good-by and went away to camp or to prison" (*DH* 7). Stafford employs the collective first-person plural, characterizing the experience of objectors as exile from the national community. The very exercise of conscience provokes a spiraling descent into the self and away from community; indeed, the notion of conscience itself is founded upon a "fundamental antagonism," to use Slavoj Zizek's term, between the individual and society (*SOI* 3). The one who objects for reasons of conscience is situated at the point of tearing in the social symbolic; like Lacan's Antigone, the conscientious objector finds himself torn between two laws, and in between two deaths.[2]

During the Second World War, when civilian society in the United States transformed into a total war economy, and when conscription effaced distinctions between combatants and noncombatants, the objector became, in Lacanian parlance, the "*objet petit a*," the indivisible remainder that blocked national enjoyment. Stafford writes that when the Japanese attack on Pearl Harbor and concomitant fears of invasion precipitated American involvement in the Second World War, the United States also underwent a symbolic conquering from within,

> by aliens who could shout on any corner or in any building and bring down on us wrath and hate more intense than on any foreigner. The country we had known was gone, had completely disappeared, was wiped out in a bombing that obliterated landmarks which had stood for years— since long before we were born. (*DH* 7)

Though the continental U.S. remained unscathed by actual bombing, Stafford's metaphor suggests that the transformation to a total war culture itself "obliterated" the country that had existed prior to the war.

For Stafford, then, the conscientious objector's primary struggle was to orient himself in a new and unfamiliar landscape, seeking out others who were themselves "almost totally alien, proscribed, lost, tagged, orphaned, outlawed" (*DH* 7–8)—trapped and yet adrift, stigmatized and yet forgotten. Stafford writes that, despite the challenges both without and within pacifist communities, COs sought, and found, "down in [their] hearts," a common bond of fellowship and peace, "something more important—something prerequisite to—any geographical kinship or national loyalty" (*DH* 8). Stafford's belief in something that precedes, or even outweighs, regional or national loyalties is central to the politics of his writing.[3]

Recalling the complexity and burden of nurturing community, neither merely in opposition to the hegemonic culture nor in concert with the culture of war, Stafford's stories let the narrative itself—what he calls just "a series of incidents, purposely planned to give the texture of our lives" (*DH* 10)—become a literary enactment of the possibilities of nonviolent community. Stafford's articulation of collective witness, rather than suppressing or effacing differences among objectors, is founded upon an acceptance of difference. The ability to negotiate differences among the CO community becomes the testing ground from which successful negotiations with larger communities are made possible. His use of a narrative frame, in which Stafford the narrator communicates to his fellow CO George, who has left the CPS community, ensures a complicated address; Stafford must simultaneously represent the experience of nonviolent community for its most intimate critic, George, and for us, the readers, who know little of what Stafford calls this "footnote in the big histories" (DH 4).

Psychoanalysis with a Certain Absolutist

Down in My Heart situates its stories within a narrative frame in which the narrator talks to George, a fellow CO who chose to go to jail rather than continue to serve in CPS after the war had ended; George is a literary rendering of the "certain absolutist." George's subsequent hunger strike to protest prison conditions has left him, the narrative suggests, in an unresponsive and perhaps comatose state. The narrator tells his incapacitated friend that he wants "to talk through to you" the stories of their time together in CPS camps, when they attempted to create a life that resembled neither mere conformity nor outright rebellion.[4] In his introduction, Stafford implicitly criticizes the excesses of "personal rebels" who act out a solitary resistance like Sibley and Jacob's "certain absolutists," because such actions seem to be merely the inverse of the larger society's addiction to conflict: "For us a personal rebellion against other human beings became a capitulation to the forces we held to be at the root of war. We perceived the hazard poignantly, because in order to avoid participating in the large violence of our immediate society—and thus to stay true to a larger society—we found it necessary to act in such a way as to arouse the antagonism of our neighbor" (DH 8–9).

Attempting to live nonviolently and resist the energies of war, Stafford still acknowledges that sometimes the refusal to see human beings as separate nations or races requires actions that expose individual prejudice or structural violence. In "The Mob Scene at McNeil," the narrator recounts how COs were warned by the project superintendent "against saying 'Mr.' and 'Mrs.' to Negroes, [but they] continued to use these terms" (DH 14). The conscientious objectors' friendly relations with blacks aroused suspicions among the local white Arkansas residents and led to a confrontation in which COs found themselves accused of espionage for the enemy.

By situating this conversation-in-stories with the silent George, Stafford acknowledges the compelling power of outright noncooperation. Stafford's narrator vacillates, with increasing intensity, between an allegiance to the CO community and a sense of bewildered awe for the absolute resistance of his friend. Near the end of the collection, the narrator admits that his friend's vision of absolute resistance "now repelled, now fascinated, me, a life that was no longer tied to considerations of policy, personal prestige, or the endless decisions, diplomacies, and hopes of ordinary social living. . . . I learned the exhilarations of the outlaw, his personal freedoms, and his constant living with rebellion" (*DH* 91–92). The narrator's contradictory feelings of repulsion and fascination with George's decision hound him, even if he ultimately sees that decision as an abdication of the openness fundamental to living nonviolently.

The dynamic between Stafford the narrator and George replays Lowell's split subjectivity in "Memories of West Street and Lepke," between an accommodating pacifist and an (absent) absolutist other. We might be tempted to read the Stafford/George relation simply as a rhetorical ploy used by Stafford to legitimate silencing dissent within the CPS community. In other words, Stafford both invokes and then argues against those radical pacifists who call into question the heart of the experiment in nonviolent living that Stafford has chosen. However, the stories told to answer the demand of the unconscious George thus take on a compelling intensity that masks their outward rhetorical simplicity; as the work progresses, each story leans closer and closer to George's final position of dissent. In the process, the unconscious George becomes a Zizekian saint, one who "occupies the place of the *objet petit a*, of pure object, of somebody undergoing radical subjective destitution. He enacts no ritual, he conjures nothing, he just persists in his inert presence" (*SOI* 116). George cannot respond, as he is literally and figuratively beyond words. By his rejection of communication, the saintly George "puts in question the Good embodied in the State and common morals" (*SOI* 117). Stafford thus projects an imaginary figure of absolute noncooperation onto George, one who has gone beyond the rational Law, a move strikingly resembling Lowell's rejection of his "fire-breathing Catholic CO" self in "Memories of West Street and Lepke." Perhaps like Lowell, Stafford wishes to answer the charge that all pacifism is *ipso facto* anti-American or even an act of treason.

Toward a Nonviolent Community

To restate, then, the central dynamic of the memoir: even as these stories present themselves as transparent personal-historical accounts of life in CPS, we should read them as spoken by a narrator attempting to remind, or even convince, himself and his friend of the importance of the community that they forged against the enforced regimentation of a society at war. The stories attempt to recreate their community, in its small successes and failures, which rejected both the precepts of the hegemonic, war-making culture and the ideology of absolutist rebellion. Stafford's first story begins, intriguingly, with George as a main character; the narrator thus relates the creative and open-hearted George that he remembers to the alien, unresponsive George. "The Mob Scene at McNeil" opens with three objectors' disparate responses to the threat of a mob attack:

> "When the mob comes," George would say, "I think we should try surprising them with a friendly reaction—take coffee and cookies out to meet them."
> "As for me," Larry would say, "I'll take a stout piece of stove wood, and stand behind the door, and deal out many a lumpy head—that's what they'd need."
> "Well, I don't know about you all," Dick would say, "but I intend to run right out of that back door and hide in the brush—'cause I don't want my death on any man's conscience." (italics Stafford's DH 13)

George's reaction, while as comical as Lowell's Abramowitz in "Memories," exemplifies the spirit of nonviolent resistance through defying the expectations of an antagonist; if his offering of reconciliation has a certain naïveté, it also demonstrates the odd and creative courage of conscientious objectors. Larry's fight and Dick's flight responses—by contrast, the two typically animal reactions—indicate also that objection to war did not always mean objection to self-defense, when it could extricate oneself from a violent situation. These three reactions comically depict a breadth of approaches to the question of self-defense for the CO, and speak to the larger differences within the CPS objector community.

In "The Mob Scene," three COs—two poets (George and Bill) and a painter (Bob)—recreating on a Sunday find themselves surrounded by an angry gathering of the local townspeople of McNeil, Arkansas; the COs nonaggressive and accommodating response to this mob scene determines their fate. The crowd suspects that their artistic activities are "evidence" of espionage and points to one of the poets' unrhymed verses as clear proof:

> There was an implication that if it wasn't poetry it might be something else—like information for the enemy. George said he thought what he had written . . . was poetry, and that poetry didn't need to rhyme. . . . [A local] grabbed the book [of Walt Whitman poems] from under my arm

and opened it at random. He read a passage aloud to prove that poetry rhymed. He started off confidently, read more and more slowly, and finally closed the book with a snap. "Well, that may be poetry," he said, "but what you wrote ain't." The crowd was a little taken aback. (*DH* 18–19)

The townsfolk interpret George's unrhymed poetry describing the town of McNeil as "information for the enemy," as it details how "loaded freighters grumble through the night" (*DH* 19).

But the unorthodox authority of Whitman's free verse actually saves the three from immediate harm; the mob's disrupted expectations about poetry parallel the disrupted expectations of the reader about war resisters in the comic opening of the story. Rather than argue with the mob, and not "know[ing] what else to do" (*DH* 19), the three "were merely quiet and respectful." In hindsight, the narrator realizes that "almost always the tormenter is at a loss unless he can provoke a belligerent reaction as an excuse for further pressure or violence" (*DH* 19–20). Paradoxically, the COs were saved first by Whitman and then by the State—in the figure of the sheriff, whom the mob decided to call. The legal legitimacy of conscientious objection afforded the COs nominal protection under the law for their war resistance; "The Mob Scene" speaks to the importance of loyal dissent, as a mode of attempting to reform the State from within. The relief of the Law in this story, however, is necessary only because, in the words of another CO, "our government is spending millions of dollars and hiring the smartest men in the country to devote themselves full time just to make everyone act [with suspicion and hatred toward outsiders]" (*DH* 22). Stafford's story both evades easy caricatures of the pacifist and grapples with the problematics of a dissenting patriotism.

"The Battle of Anapamu Creek" reverses the dynamic of patriots against objectors present in "Mob Scene"; however, the community of COs refuses to act as a mob even though COs outnumber their "patriotic" foreman out in the wilderness. Instead, in this battle, a group of objectors offers an alternative, nonviolent mode of conflict resolution with their viciously anti-CO foreman, Eric Kloppenburg. Just as in "Mob Scene," Stafford's narrative points out how the law itself is threatened by war hysteria. Prior to an expedition into the chaparral wilderness, the forest rangers repeatedly threatened the COs with machine-gun violence. One of the rangers recounts killing a "German" somewhere nearby; to the protests of unconstitutionality and fascism, he retorts, "When it's a matter of defending my country I'll do anything—law or not" (*DH* 29). Here, in the wilderness, in the community of COs, the laws of the State and mob cede to a third law, the law of nonviolence; Eric Kloppenburg, isolated from the social supports of war hysteria, still continues his verbal abuse of the cook and the rest of the group.

When the objectors suddenly find themselves in the oppressed majority, they undertake, in addition to their spike camp project, a "reconciliation project" with their foreman. Because of continued insults, the cook draws up a list of minimum conditions under which he would work; Eric, in turn, appoints another CO as cook, who promptly refuses the order, despite the foreman's threats: "And Eric, the boss of the camp, sat down in the circle of men, the only society for miles, not one of whom would utter a harsh word at Eric, but not one of whom would volunteer, or even consent, to take Ken's job. And nonviolence began its work" (*DH* 32).

Slowly, through silence and debate, silence and further conversation, the men hash out the issues at hand with Eric. Even when Eric decides to cook for himself, no one moves; George pursues Eric's tone of discontent, saying "I guess we are just afraid you don't feel right about it. It just doesn't seem all settled to us. It isn't settled for us until everyone feels right. I wish we could figure out a better way" (*DH* 33–34). They finally come to an agreement. Days later, when another ranger joins Eric in the chaparral and asks how things have been going, Eric responds, "I was off my feed for a while, but going good again. . . . How's everything with you?" (*DH* 35). Stafford's pun, "off my feed," encapsulates this CO community's struggle to share meals at the same table with those like Eric, antagonistic to their communal identity as war resisters. Their isolated environment, the wilds of the American West, suspends the established notions of law and social norms enforced in the rest of the U.S.; that suspension of traditional law paradoxically enables both the possibilities of vigilante rule and nonviolent community.

Throughout, Stafford's stories both represent and enact the work of building community, against the backdrop of severe isolation and alienation. The choice to be a conscientious objector also affected and sometimes isolated whole families and communities. While a handful of objectors were successful in relocating their families near their CPS camp, many others (including William Everson) suffered the unraveling of marriages and families. In "Duet for Cello and Flute," the tenuous life of an impoverished CO family living near a camp, whose days are lightened by their evening concerts, is juxtaposed to the atomic nightmare on the other side of the world:

The time at Rich Bar was like that—the kids, the families, and—this time—the flute and the cello while people looked up and down, and, on the way home, evening on the river.

And at camp that night we heard on the radio that we had dropped a new kind of deadly bomb on a city of Japanese people. (*DH* 78)

Stafford's juxtaposition points to the insufficiency, the sheer smallness of CO fellowships, in relation to the devastation caused by the atomic bomb; that tone of unsparing self-critique mounts as *Down in My Heart* continues.[5]

The narrative increasingly focuses on George's intensifying alienation and anger at an American society that refuses to acknowledge conscientious objectors. In "The End of the War" and "To Meet a Friend," the narrative allows George's perspective full airing. With the celebration going on around them, George wonders, "How can we join in the celebration of the atomic bomb?" (*DH* 81), and posits an early version of Virilio's Pure War, suggesting that war is a continuous condition of society: "the war goes on every day. They fight it when the shooting begins, but we've got to fight it when the good can be done. During a war is a time of rest for a pacifist; the war itself is an incident, a lost battle in itself" (*DH* 81). Stafford knows that his attempt to make the CO experience a witness of conscience is, without question, problematized by the fact that the CPS life essentially erased COs from public view. Though being a CO sometimes brought direct antagonism, George argues their invisibility was just as alienating.

In *Down in My Heart*'s final story, "To Meet a Friend," the narrator's struggle with George reaches its greatest point of estrangement, in which both argue the importance of their kind of war resistance. The narrator visits George, just before George is due to enter prison, and learns why George has left CPS. George argues that the Civilian Public Service is a "precedent for slave labor, not a place for constructive service in crucial times, a dictatorial program administered, in spite of the wording of the law, by military men" (*DH* 89) and decides to refuse further internment. The narrator, by contrast, argues that he cannot do any good in prison, despite George's claim that only there can "you make your protest plain" (*DH* 90). George's complete refusal of conscription, for the narrator, implies that George is unable to live in the paradoxes that nonviolent living requires and "had found exhilaration of making a complete decision that ended uncertainty" (*DH* 90). Just as Yeats's Irish revolutionaries "make a stone of the heart" in "Easter 1916," Stafford's George is hardened by his sacrifice, cut off from the solace of community:

One night I was put in a cell by myself, Bill—in an empty block. There was only one light, and it was out in the corridor, a dim connection between me and the world, between me and life. And that night, the bulb burned out; I was sitting there, and suddenly it was dark. Just stones and iron around me and no light, no noise. Do you how it would be? . . . I suddenly realized where I was, what might happen—how far I was from any kind of life I had ever dreamed of living. I thought of my mother, my friends. What if no one ever got me out of there? What if it stayed dark—with bars around and me screaming—forever? (DH 91)

The light, which George and Bill read by during their evenings in the CPS camp, suddenly burns out. The scream, though of despair, is connected to all the other screams that weave through the memoir: the scream of the Negro woman in labor pains whom the COs help, the scream of relief by the people who hear of the war's end, and the unheard scream of those killed and maimed by war. Stafford's project is to thread those cries together, into something larger than their individual pain.

The narrator's estrangement from George (and George's deep alienation) does not end their communication, or their differences. George writes of plans "to try to get the warden to end racial segregation in the prison" (DH 93), but Stafford ripostes with the warden's words: "Yes, it's all right for CO's and your friends to try to make these reforms while you're here; but you won't be here forever, and when you leave I'll be left with the job of administering a nonsegregated prison with prisoners who want segregation" (DH 93).

By using the warden's words as a counterargument, Stafford here seems to be protesting too much; the successful Danbury Prison strike, discussed in chapter 1, was a great victory for conscientious objectors during the war, and members from that strike went on to become key figures in Civil Rights and Vietnam War protest. Yet, Stafford's point is that true societal reform requires a conversion of the whole of society, and cannot be gained principally through coercion. Down in My Heart ends with Stafford at the hunger-striking George's bedside; Stafford, in his story of "incidents without heroes and without villains" (DH 95), attempts to keep open his allegiances to those working for a world without war. Even if Stafford finally rejects George's decision, the narrative itself encourages one to believe that George, in fact, is the primal impetus for the book.

George's position, and Stafford's response to it, also foreshadows the divisions within the peace movement during the Vietnam War era; until about 1967, those who actively worked to end the war often came from the pacifist and nonviolent communities that had protested previous wars. The debate between Stafford and George mirrors the debate about the core of nonviolence and nonviolent action; for some, like Stafford, nonviolence works through conversion, while for others, like George, nonviolence is a tactic of coercion. Increasingly, anger at the government's continued policies of bombing and counterterrorism gradually led antiwar groups to advocate, and engage in, acts of violence. In *You Must Revise Your Life*, Stafford recalls participating in readings and rallies at "Kent State, Stanford, Berkeley, Madison, all over the country," but he always felt out of place, as "most activists were not pacifists but . . . political partisans . . . ready for violence. That violence, it seemed to me, helped to bring on the Nixon reaction. Both sides spread out leaving pacifists where they usually were, alone" (18–19).

Down in My Heart, then, enfolds within its own witness of war resistance in CPS camps—that "loyal dissent"—the drive for more extreme modes of absolute resistance. Even though "certain absolutists," to borrow Sibley and Jacob's pun, endanger the more compliant, legal mode of conscientious objector service, Stafford recognizes the limitations inherent in all forms of resistance and the implicit dangers of romanticizing individual acts of rebellion. Stafford's paean to collective resistance, through the formation of an alternative community of nonviolence, refuses to reduce the ethical complexities and sacrifices of the CPS experience and finds its greatest strength in confronting its own complicities and failures. Stafford's choice of the memoir as a form allows him to let the community speak for itself through multiple characters and narratives, in essence, to make the community itself the main character.

Down in My Heart also points to the fact that resisting war in contemporary America necessarily includes grappling with the difficulty of representing resistance. In a country that tolerates a modicum of dissent, even as mass media journalism distorts and subverts that dissent through its coverage, outright resistance requires artistic and literary self-representation, to tell its stories to itself and to the larger social orders—the community, the nation, and the world. Stafford's poem, "How It Is," speaks to the voiceless position of the CO, who is indistinguishable from the military conscripts on the departing train:

It is war. They put us on a train and
say, "Go." A bell wakes up the engine
as we move along past the crowd,

and a child—one clear small gaze from all the town—
finds my face. I wave. For long I look
back. "I'm not a soldier," I want to say.
But the gaze is left behind. And I'm gone. (WI 191)

The exchange of gazes is a moment of paralysis for the CO, for revealing his identity as an objector might provoke disdain from the child, the only "clear small gaze" that mirrors the speaker's own gaze. The speedy departure of the train, and the muting behind the window, make communicating his witness impossible. He is gone, then, not simply in the sense that his train has departed, but that he has become an object, a text to be read by others, rather than one who can testify.

Toward a Pacifist Poetic

With the republication of *Down in My Heart* (1985) and the publication of *You Must Revise Your Life* (1986), *The Darkness Around Us Is Deep* (1993), *The Way It Is* (1998), and finally, *Every War Has Two Losers: William Stafford on Peace and War* (2003)—which includes daily writings, poems, talks, and selections from interviews on Stafford's lifelong commitment to nonviolent war resistance—Stafford's pacifism claims such a central role as to become an irrefutable literary fact. Robert Bly, Judith Kitchen, and Kim Stafford point to Stafford's conscientious objection as the ground from which all his future writing grows. His "fixed vision," as Kitchen calls Stafford's consistent (if unchanging) poetic gaze, "seems to have solidified during the four years spent in . . . camps during World War II" (10). The criticisms leveled at Stafford's poetry—the veneer of rhetorical simplicity, called by Paul Zweig "strained simplicity" and "deliberate naiveté" (qtd. in David Young 263), and poetic fecundity—fail to take into account how these excesses emerge in light of Stafford's vision of writing developed as a conscientious objector.

In *You Must Revise Your Life*, Stafford explains his unorthodox approach to writing: "people have told me that my way is spineless and slovenly . . . but there are considerations deriving from my way of writing. Each piece comes to me as a crystallization of its own, and preferably without my thinking of its effect on others" (17). Stafford's answer to his critics uncannily reverberates beyond the bounds of poetry; his conversation about writing is implicitly one about living nonviolently. Pacifists have long been called "spineless and slovenly," while military discipline is lauded as an antidote to teenage rebellion. Further, Stafford's ambiguous use of the term "others" suggests both other poems and other people; the poetic act, thus, is an act of independence, of momentary suspension of the pressures of the social. Stafford's refusal to toe the poetic line is not an act of laziness, but of principle; poetry is both a radical freedom in its creation and a radical potentiality. Because poets are "not committed to something settled beforehand . . . [but to] something that may show up ahead of them," Stafford suggests that the poetic act involves the suspension of ideological constraints, though the poetry itself can be "dedicated" to some "principles" (RL 59).

Yet, for Stafford, poems are also "nothing special" (RL 58). In fact, Stafford actively resists the self-conscious attempt to create universal work: "I don't want to claim that one should assume that one is creating something worthy of the ages. Not at all. So the product is expendable, but the process is precious" (RL 81). Peter Stitt argues that Stafford forgoes authorial mastery and becomes instead the "eternal analysand in the psychoanalytic process, one who refuses to act the role of the analyst to any meaningful degree" (165).[6] Stafford thus makes the claim for a kind of authority that is a form of self-erasure: "Imposing my will on language—or on a student, or on the citizens of a country—was not my style. I wanted to disappear as teacher, as writer, as citizen—be 'the quiet of the land,' as we used to designate ourselves in CO camps" (RL 21). What does Stafford's desire to disappear as a writer, as critic, as citizen, mean for his work? A "leave no trace" ethic makes sound ecological sense, but it did not stop Stafford from publishing sixty volumes, or from signing his work. Nor did it cause him to abandon the authorial I of the lyric.

Stafford's Communitarian Lyric

Despite the centrality of Stafford's poetic obsession with peace and war—
The Way It Is (1998) includes at least twenty-five poems meditating on the culture of war and the culture of peace—and in contrast to his dialogic memoir, Stafford's poetry tends to avoid addressing the antagonistic other. With few exceptions, Stafford's lyric poetry resists the press of history and the problem of otherness; to read a Stafford poem is to enter into an ahistorical space, where a single lyric voice explores the mysteries of existence and imparts some hard-won wisdom. In contrast to the dialogic or serial modes employed by other war resister poets, Stafford's poems tend toward the brief and undialogical— that is, the mainstream lyric tradition, in which the lyric poem gambles on

universality by reaching beyond its sociological, cultural, and even linguistic horizons; however, that act of reaching beyond has often led to an effacement of history and of the other, in favor of the apotheosis of the lyric moment and the I.

At the same time, in "On Lyric Poetry and Society," Theodor Adorno has argued against an easy sociological critique since poetry's essence lies in "either not acknowledging the power of socialization or overcoming it through the pathos of detachment" (37). A sociological approach, therefore, must attempt to ascertain "in what way the work of art remains subject to society and in what way it transcends it" (39). Adorno rigorously resists collapsing the boundary between literary production and ideology, even though he notes that that boundary is permeable. However, Adorno's lyric manifests utopian possibility: "lyric expression, having escaped from the weight of material existence, evoke[s] the image of a life free from the coercion of reigning practices, of utility, of the relentless pressure of self-preservation" (39). Because the lyric is utopian, it is fundamentally a "protest against a social situation that every individual experiences as hostile, alien, cold, oppressive" (39), and an expression of "the dream of a world in which things could be different" (40). The lyric I, for Adorno, "expresses itself as something opposed to the collective" (41), and bears witness to alienation from the masses.

This notion of the lyric is perhaps overly Romantic in orientation—that poetry, part of a high culture tradition that explores true subjectivity, is inherently oppositional, and that the poetic subject is a rebel protesting against the status quo. Poets have been both marginal rebels against and apologists for empire; in particular, the best poets located in the ascendant American empire often find themselves negotiating their position between privilege (often both cultural and economic) and marginality (in relation to their biographical circumstances and the dominance of mass culture and the marketplace). Still, Adorno's notion of the lyric as utopian possibility enables a rethinking of Stafford's poems, insofar as they go underground, away from the history of governments and newspaper headlines, and formulate parabolic alternative lyric worlds. Because Stafford's pacifist poetics attempt, at least obliquely, to address American history and American militarism, he does not rest in easy utopian generalities; the tension between the desire for community and the temptation to withdrawal and isolation, between history and the moment, persists in Stafford's lyric poems of war resistance.

If Stafford's memoir Down in My Heart represents through its narrative the collective witness of conscientious objectors living an experiment in nonviolence, Stafford's poems tend to constrict any such collective statement in favor of parabolic lyric. However, reading Stafford's poems as simple homilies would be to miss what might best be termed his *quaint cunning;* like Robert Frost, Stafford presents a deceptively simple narrative in deceptively plain language as a way of addressing the reader and creating, through parable, a way of living that has been "forgotten by everyone alive." In the poem "Watching the Jet Planes Dive" (1960), the speaker issues a series of directives to the reader, in the vein of Frost's "Directive," as a result of witnessing "jet planes dive." It is typical of Stafford's poems; we have no indication of the historical specificity of the event, nor do we know the literal situation of the speaker: whether he is watching an air show, watching an air raid on television, or being bombed himself. In addition, as is the case in most Stafford poems, we find ourselves in what Stafford himself calls, in *Writing the Australian Crawl,* "an always arriving present" (18). This generalized literary present has certain poetic advantages and disadvantages. In this poem, the ambiguousness of the situation leads one to consider all three simultaneously—that each possible literal situation (whether at an air show, watching a bombing, or being bombed) is less different than one might first expect. Certainly, in the era of Pure War, the air show or watching a bombing on television are both integral aspects of the culture of war that precedes actual war. Yet, because the poem's directives insist upon discovering a lost way of being in the world, Stafford's poetics are founded upon an internal tension. Since Stafford tends to invoke history (cf. "History Display," "Entering History," "Not in the Headlines,") as the history of generals and wars, the poet can only assert the lyric present as a defense of the particular; yet, that lyric present always points to a reality somehow not contained entirely by the present. It is a poetics of utopianism.

The second internal tension in Stafford's lyric—also an extension of utopian thought—is between his meditation on the communal and the solitariness of the lyric I. Bob Perelman has critiqued Stafford's use of the first person persona as a disingenuous act that pretends to be sensitive to the communal and yet actually is repressive and "suppresses dialogue" (*MP* 113). That lyric poems are often monological should not be dismissed as simply a limitation of the genre, but as a limitation in their deployment of the genre.[7] Stafford's utopian poetics, therefore, are often framed by their generalized history and their use of the lyric I. But Stafford's lyric I is far less meditative than conversational; an imagined audience is central to Stafford's communitarian poetics. "Watching the Jet Planes Dive," for example, begins as a Thoreauvian exhortation to return to the ethics of the wild:

We must go back and find a trail on the ground
back of the forest and mountain on the slow land;
we must begin to circle on the intricate sod.
By such wild beginnings without help we may find
the small trail on through the buffalo-bean vines. (WI 68)

The impulse to return to "wild beginnings" and the "slow land" is a defensive move, whether it is defending against the fearsome powers of military-technological endocolonization or actual attack. The regular meter and slant rhyme establish a veneer of human artifice in tension with the longings for wild beginnings.

But the neoprimitive desire for escape from human orders suddenly evaporates in the middle of the second stanza, replaced by a larger need to make connections: "if roads are unconnected we must make a path / no matter how far it is, or how lowly we arrive" (WI 68). The sudden compulsion for making paths is both literal and metaphoric, a "climb[ing] over the map" that necessitates "l[ying] down wherever there is doubt." The final stanza suggests that the speaker sees in uncivilized spaces the resources for a future culture freed from the oppression of war. Stafford sees in the penitential rites of rural Mexico something that has been missed in accounts of history:

some fabulous gesture when the sun goes down
as they do by custom in little Mexico towns
where they crawl for some ritual up a rocky steep.
The jet planes dive; we must travel on our knees. (WI 68)

Stafford's final juxtaposition places two different kinds of movement against each other—the jet attack and penitents crawling on knees. In light of the heritage of spiritual resistance to the Second World War, Stafford's use of a symbolic analogue of resistance—the religious act of crawling on one's knees—seems particularly apt. Stafford's image condenses two kinds of resistance—resistance to technology and resistance to warfare—that hearkens back to Thoreau and anticipates the cooperative living experiments of the 1970s. Like Lowell's protesters, Stafford's penitents are full of doubt, lowly, and contrite—in essence, symbolically castrated; unlike Lowell's March poems, though, Stafford's poem employs the collective we throughout, opening outward rather than narrowly defining a group of war resisters. The final striking disparity of power presented by the juxtaposition of the final line renders the jet planes as obscenely, inhumanly phallic.

Though like "Watching the Jet Planes Dive" in its historically generalized landscape, "Peace Walk" particularizes the collective we as a group of war resisters on an "un-march," marked as other by the gaze of the social orders. But more important, the poem offers two elements typically missing in poems about antiwar protest. First, the poem attempts to represent a specific kind of demonstration, a peace walk, one that defies the conventions of protest and collective action. Second, though the poem clearly situates its identification with the demonstrators, its overall sense of ambiguity and self-critique renders it an acutely Yeatsian "argument with ourselves," thus working against the monological lyric. The poem begins, unstridently, with an open question— "we wondered what our walk would mean"—and instead of answering it, immediately observes the various interpretations thrust upon it by the gazes of bystanders:

Men by a tavern said, "Those foreigners . . ."
to a woman with a fur, who turned away—
like an elevator going down, their look at us.

Along a curb, their signs lined across,
a picket line stopped and stared
the whole width of a street, at ours: "Unfair." (WI 59)

The first bystanders, "men by a tavern," immediately identify the demonstrators as "foreigners," people outside the national identity. This association is deeply imbedded in a culture that has frequently quelled dissent on the grounds that it "helps Hanoi." The wealthy woman's response, more ambiguously, is simply to "turn away," to refuse to recognize the existence of the demonstrators. And, in an even more ambiguous exchange of gazes, a local labor picket line "stop[s] and stare[s]." Their signs of "unfair" seem to read like rebukes of the peace walk, rather than as a public message about a new labor contract. In sum, the whole social world, to the speaker, levels its judging gaze at the protest, so that even in the first stanza, the sun itself, Stafford writes, "gazed at our signs."

Opposing the gaze of the other, a voice, seemingly from out of nowhere, emerges with an interpretation of the walk. If the gaze of the other renders people into objects, the voice, as Lacan has suggested, acts as the primary locus of subjectivity, as the act of speech brings the speaker into the realm of the symbolic. The importance of speech as act is particularly clear in the case of dissent, where the subject is defined by her public linguistic disagreement.

However, though the speaker clearly sympathizes with the reading of the walk, he also self-effacingly points to the limits of demonstrators' vision (both physical and metaphorical) and of the walk itself. Amid the silent stares, "the sound truck blare[s]":

that love could fill the atmosphere:

Occur, slow the other fallout, unseen,
on islands everywhere—fallout, falling
unheard. We held our poster up to shade our eyes.

At the end we just walked away;
no one was there to tell us where to leave the signs. (WI 59)

As in "Watching the Jet Planes Dive," "Peace Walk" cages the specificity of the demonstration—that is, against the nuclear arms race and of testing—in generalized language; the islands, of course, refer specifically to the Bikini Atoll, where a native people was exposed to fallout and nuclear radiation, but here take on a broader meaning to imply the archipelago of human communities isolated or powerless as subjects in the nuclear experiment. At the peak of lyric, however, Stafford deflates the language with the humbling action of a demonstrator "hold[ing] our poster up to shade our eyes." The activist's attempt to put his message between himself and the world, Stafford implies, blinds even as it shades him.

Despite the fact that any ideological placard narrows a person's perception, Stafford does not condemn ideology itself; in fact, the final lines contain in their lonely description of the protest's dispersal a vision of egalitarian society. It would be easy to read the final couplet simply as the failure of the demonstration, of Stafford's poetic skepticism of a public protest. Yet, the fact that "no one was there to tell us where to put the signs" forces the individual demonstrators and not some authority figure to decide what to do with the "signs"—not just the physical placards but also the things that they signify: the dangers of nuclear testing, the resistance to warfare, a vision of human community based on love.

In the 1990s, Stafford's poems dealing with the Persian Gulf War abandoned his previous indirection and grappled with the problematics of complicity. The poem "Entering History" materializes the simulated participation of Americans, watching missile-eye views of the destruction of Baghdad. The absent-presence of American civilians at the scene of conflict is possible because we underwrite the military through our taxes:

You were there, on the telly, part of
the military . . .
Where was your money when the tanks
grumbled past? Which bombs did you buy
for the death rain that fell? Which year's
taxes put that fire to the town
where the screaming began? (WI 10)

"Entering History" depicts military conflict as the apparatus of the state, a total war economy into which the ordinary citizen is conscripted, thus blurring
the distinction between civilians and military. The poem also echoes
Thoreau's "Resistance to Civil Government," one of the crucial literary works
in the nonviolent tradition to link the payment of taxes with complicity in war.
But Stafford's accusatory tone in this poem is more an act of self-flagellation
than an accusation of others, given its speaker's clearly antiwar stance. Perhaps
the difference in tone between these poems and *Down in My Heart* speaks to
one crucial difference between the Second World War and the Persian Gulf
War—namely, the present existence of a professional army and hence the lack
of possibility of demonstrating one's loyal dissent through alternative service
to the state. In a sense, the screaming also threads back thematically to
Stafford's memoir, when the poet first worked to transform and connect the
individual cry into something larger than its individual suffering, something
based on more than power.

Despite the accomplishments of Stafford's poetry of pacifism, his voluminous and relatively uncensored output has placed the onus on his editors to
choose his best work. Because a collection of his poems rarely builds from
poem to poem, Stafford's poetics limits sustained meditation. His vigorously
miniature approach, while reflective of his politics, occasionally amounts to a
privileging of the lyric over history, of the individual voice over collective
chorale. Still, Stafford's claims for poetry, "essential kind of breathing," are
small but by no means paltry. In "Poetry," he calls it "a shrine / by the road / it's
a flower in the parking lot / of The Pentagon, it says, "Look around, / listen. /
Feel the air" (WI 169). Perhaps poetry can do no more than make present the
natural world around us. But it does do more than that. Stafford's poetry, born
out of his time working in the internment camps of the Second World War,
constitutes resistance as attentiveness. Attention to his present amounted to a
reclamation of time itself—of the span of moments—from the claims of the
state; this freedom could last Stafford at least for the span of composition.

In the end, Stafford's poems do advocate a politics. In "Something to De-clare," he writes that "They have never had a war big enough / to slow that pulse in the earth under / our path near that old river" (WI 251), and continues:

> They say that history is going on somewhere.
> They say it won't stop. I have held
> one picture still for a long time and waited.
>
> This is only a little report floated
> into a slow current so the wind will know
> which way to come if it wants to find me. (WI 251)

History, for Stafford, may be not unlike Lowell's conception of a drama of Great Men and tumultuous events. But while Lowell embraces and even enters into the drama of History, Stafford opts for a smaller chronicle of for-gotten ways. Stafford's "little report," drowned out by the machinations of "great people" and the tide of history, is like a message in a bottle, an anti-epic, waiting for someone observant enough to notice it.

3. William Everson and the Fine Arts Camp

FROM UTOPIAN HOPES TO A CHRONICLE

OF DIVISION

In its February 1940 issue, *Poetry* magazine published "The Sign," with a note from the author, a migrant worker named William Herber: "I am writing from a camp fire near a small town between Bakersfield and Tulare, Calif. I have had no address in three years . . . have just finished working the fruit in Imperial Valley and am on my way to Oregon. . . . Before I became a 'fruit bum' I had a couple of semesters in college and got interested in poetry there" (qtd. in Bartlett 25).

After accepting a second poem from Herber, *Poetry*'s editor George Dillon learned, from a letter by a young poet named William Everson, that he had been duped. Everson confessed to writing the poems and to assuming the false identity after repeated attempts to place his poems in the prestigious journal using his own name. Everson wrote, with considerable vitriol, that he did not understand "the consistent stream of material entering the magazine on no other discernable grounds than that it dealt with the class struggle . . . [so he] sat down and scrawled a facetious, hurried scrape with a social message, concocted a fantastic letter," (25) chose a different name, and the rest became literary history.[1]

The story of Everson's literary masquerade summons a host of questions. Why had Everson's poems been accepted under the assumed name? Perhaps the story of Everson's literary masquerade shows the degree to which proletarian poetry had, at the time, some degree of poetic capital, and also how that capital presented obstacles for other poets. On the other hand, perhaps it suggests that Everson's poetry, written by "William Herber," was superior to the work he submitted under his own name (which was, indeed, Dillon's claim)—and that the performed identity granted the poet an aesthetic opportunity that writing under his own name had not. But why did Everson send them in the first place and then retract them in such a violent way? In the end, the story—and the tenor and substance of Everson's confession—illuminates the contradictory personality of arguably the most important American pacifist poet during the Second World War. Everson performs a marginalized identity and then comes clean, admitting his deception; at the same time, he can't help but condemn the editor with colorful invective for failing to maintain the aesthetic standards of the journal. Driven by his own conscience, fueled by an arrogant rage, Everson presents a decidedly different image of the pacifist poet than does Robert Lowell's Just War rationalism (in his letter to President Roosevelt informing him of his refusal to serve) or William Stafford's nonconfrontational "smoke's way" memoir and poems.

The CO poetry of World War II exists in that liminal space between modernism and postmodernism, between the socialist proletarianism of the 1930s and the anticommunist reaction of the 1950s, representing both a departure from, and a continuation of, the radical poetry of the 1930s. Poet, printer, and organizer, William Everson played a leading role in creating a pacifist poetry community that would act not simply as a cultural arm of war resistance but as a minor civilization, a "seed-state," from which heretofore unimaginable futures might be possible—ones which, in terms of experimentation both in poetry and in daily life, have yet to be fully realized. Everson's struggle to maintain artistic independence in the face of internal pressures in the conscientious objector community, as well as from the external pressures of the war, does not represent a repudiation of the politics of the 1930s; rather, it amounts to an argument with the ossification of radical poetry practices.

However, in his work for personal and societal transformation through poetry and in his representation of CO life in Civilian Public Service camps, Everson proves the relevance of the autobiographical lyric sequence as a poetic mode and as an essential aspect of the cultural work of war resistance poetry. Equally important, the movement from the self-lacerating collective subjectivity of his early poems to the crisis poems of *Chronicle of Division* parallels the larger trajectory in CPS life from initial utopian promise to discontent and gradual dissolution. Everson's experience in CPS will later inform his poetry and poetics, as he becomes an important figure of the San Francisco Renaissance, itself an important branch in the larger tree of the experimental New American poets.

Theory and Practice in the Fine Arts Camp

Of all CO poets, William Everson most actively integrated his conscientious objection as an extension of aesthetic and ethical principles, through writing, publishing, and organizing artists during his tenure in Civilian Public Service camps. During his first two years serving as a conscientious objector, Everson worked to propose, found, and lead the Fine Arts camp in Waldport, Oregon—an artist commune and "network of cultural production" dedicated to the production of art in the service of peace. Everson's Fine Arts Camp at Waldport provides a direct link to the rise of the San Francisco Renaissance and its countercultural project. Recovering the Fine Arts, then, is a crucial step to describing a tradition of war resistance and dissent poetry with which the Beats would later become associated.

The Fine Arts at Waldport—what Glenn Wallach calls "a footnote to a historical footnote" of the CO experience (15)—would not have existed at all had Everson not proposed it. The Civilian Public Service, begun to accommodate a loyal but pacifist alternative to military service, did not have any intention of setting up a camp for artists. Everson's letter arguing for a "school for the arts" within the CPS system convinced Harold Row, the national director of Brethren CPS, that "the most imperishable part of any collective activity was its aesthetic ingredient" (Wallach 18). Everson's prospectus details the importance of harnessing all the powers of pacifists, including their "cultural yearnings," and the crucial position of the artist as promoter of pacifism:

> The intellectual element of any society is always profoundly swayed by
> the caliber and manifestation of the art product within it. . . . What the
> powerful artist believer espouses, the world will hear. . . . It is because of
> the inherent sympathy between the purposes of pacifism and the
> purposes of art that a pacifist artistic movement seems capable of wide
> influence. . . . Given the articulation of an earnest and serious artistic
> movement, a movement that could make whole and poignant the
> longing of the people, what might not be accomplished?
> ("The Fine Arts at Waldport" 20)

Everson's argument rests on the pragmatic sense that artistic production, more than political writing, will transmit pacifism more convincingly to the wider society, because of the rhetorical and identificatory possibilities of art. But Everson does not call the Fine Arts a propaganda arm of the Civilian Public Service; quite the contrary, he praises English poets who are not writing "pacifist propaganda, but the ideology of pacifism, its conception of human nature, its values and attitudes which are being drawn upon and exhibited in their work" (Wallach 18).

Everson's distinction between an art that refuses to be propaganda yet still emerges from an ideological position develops against the backdrop of the radical poetries of the 1930s and attempts a third way between "engaged" poetry and the apolitical poetry trumpeted by the New Critics. The word "propaganda" originally comes from the seventeenth-century Latin name for the "committee of Cardinals of the Roman Catholic Church having the care and over-sight of foreign missions" (*Oxford English Dictionary* 632), and so emerges from the Church's history of evangelization and is linked to the histories of institutionalized colonization and imperialism. Recent definitions of propaganda emphasize the spreading of information for institutional purposes, with particular reference to war propaganda. Jacques Ellul suggests the degree to which modern propaganda—spanning fascist, communist, *and democratic* regimes—includes not merely psychological action but also a whole range of educational methods, including brainwashing, public relations, and human relations (xiii). The material history of propaganda is inextricably linked to the material history of information production and dissemination in general, controlled by ruling classes and nation-states. Everson's usage suggests that propaganda can come even from a marginal ideology like pacifism. Perhaps Everson's experience within the institutional framework of CPS suggested to him the potential danger of all institutional affiliations; Everson suggests that art ensures its integrity as a nonpropagandistic medium only when it has no affiliations that constrain it to a party line.

Everson's distinction between ideological poetry and propaganda was not intellectual hairsplitting; he consistently fought attempts merely to propagandize through poetry. In 1944, the War Resisters League advertised in the camps a call for submissions for an anthology of CPS writing. The Fine Arts group, headed by Everson, rejected the WRL approach and retorted with a broadside: "There is an issue at hand. We've been facing issues, as pacifists, ever since we came to the camps. We have not often faced them as artists. This one, then, is unique. We are not letting it by" ("An Indelicate Commission"). They argued that the anthology was "so limited in conception, so questionable in method, and placed in such inadequate hands for selection . . . that we consider its value not only negligible, but of actual danger to the incipient creative movement forming in American pacifism" (AIC). Their fear that the anthology, being "strictly political in concept," and thus limited to antiwar poems, would lead to a serious debasement of pacifist poetry. Their vocal resistance to the WRL anthology forestalled its publication.[2] Such an anthology would have been an invaluable addition to the literary production of pacifists during the Second World War; at the very least, it would allow one to test the

Fine Arts group's claims regarding a "strictly political" poetry. However, its absence is almost equally interesting, because it speaks to the fierce independence of the Fine Arts group, who saw the need for a poetry that would *embody* pacifist subjectivity rather than simply argue for it, in the mode of the rhetorical poetry of the 1930s.

This debate, framed here between the Fine Arts group and the War Resisters League, between an activist-centered poetry and a poetry-centered cultural production, recurs throughout the cultural history of war resistance; it is precisely the irreducible tension between these viewpoints that makes the poetry of war resistance so various and rich. In light of their initially strident rejection of the WRL proposal, the Fine Arts group's follow-up broadside, *An Importunate Proposition*, in a move reminiscent of Everson's earlier retraction and apology to *Poetry*, attempts to make amends for the harsh tone of their initial broadside and introduces a counterproposal. First, it would "establish and maintain a central clearing house of creative writing" for historical purposes of preservation; and second, it would "select from this body of work . . . [and] publish" the best of it. In other words, the question for Everson and the more practiced poets was how to encourage the greatest possible range of poetic creativity and yet publish only the most successful of these works.

What survives of CO literary publication suggests that the Fine Arts group succeeded in balancing encouragement for voluminous production with support of excellent writing, as is proven by the range of genres, talents, and aesthetics demonstrated in the CO archive. COs produced numerous publications—including *Illiterati* (a literary journal for which William Stafford worked and in which his first poems were published); *Compass* (the CO "Time Magazine"); *Tide* (the official camp newsletter); and Untide Press (Everson's printing project)—as well as art exhibitions, musical performances, and plays, including Millay's *Aria da Capo*, Shaw's *Candida*, and Ibsen's *Ghosts* (Eshelman "EFAW" 16). Everson's experience as a printer's apprentice aided his establishment of Untide Press, which published his own writing—including the striking *X War Elegies* (illustrated by Kemper Nomland, 1944) and *Waldport Poems* (illustrated by Clayton James, 1944)—as well as fellow CO poets Glen Coffield (*The Horned Moon*, 1944); Jacob Sloan (*The Generation of Journey*, 1945); and Kenneth Patchen (*An Astonished Eye Looks Out of the Air*, 1945).[3] Consider, for example, the range of the following excerpts from CO poets:

As in a man, a nation's breath moves hard,
But the nerves are sensitive as the radio-mind control;

The brain knows when the foot is hurt, or the hand,
And the pain cries out for the soft, unspoken cure.

Unlike a nation, the world, more loosely strung,
Is a given being, with disproportionate cells,
And the pain more slowly felt, destroys the sense,
As when wild horses stampede on broken hooves.
—Glen Coffield, "Indivisible"

Silenced. We cannot answer
Ringring-ring of phone:
I hear the sound of water, dripping
From a leaky faucet
Into basins buckets, spilling
(Nights our love lay spilling)
Our mouths and ears
Months years.
(And a voice sang down the alley)
Our wires are down
(my love . . .)
—Jacob Sloan, "From New Hampshire"

O the soul of the world is dead . . .
Truth rots in a bloody ditch;
And love is impaled on a million bayonets.

But great God! the stars go to sleep so peacefully.
—Kenneth Patchen, "Untitled"

Of these poets, only Patchen did not serve time as a CO. Even though he
was the most well-known antiwar poet of his time, Patchen here resorts to
pedantic generalities (soul, truth, love), while Coffield and Sloan write a lyric
poetry that articulates a range of possibilities, both in terms of conceit and in
terms of subject. Clearly, Coffield directly addresses the war, writing through
a more restrained, and perhaps more stark, image of world conflict. Sloan, on
the other hand, chooses to focus more closely, on the absence of his beloved
as a result of his internment; his letter-poem only obliquely suggests the wider
context of the war, yet comes closer to embodying a pacifist poetry not reliant
on argument alone. Sloan's autobiographical impulse, in the context of war
resistance, becomes more than a cramped self-narrative; instead, it opens out

into a representative experience of the trials of objection. William Everson's poetry unites the seemingly polar modes of Coffield and Sloan into a meditation on the struggles of a pacifist to maintain his fragile web of connections to the world outside the camps.

X War Elegies

Everson's X *War Elegies* and *Waldport Poems*, considered in counterpoint, foreground and represent the vexed experience of objection, providing us with a picture of the pacifist experiment that is at once utopian and self-critical. X *War Elegies* offers Everson's pre-CPS experience, his articulation of a poetics of conscience, and the promise of a collective pacifism; they are utopian lyrics, a minor literature produced in conditions of marginality and often addressed to a marginalized community. In contrast, *Waldport Poems*, which ends up as a section in the longer sequence *Chronicle of Division*, chronicle the divisions that question the possibilities carved out by the early *Elegies*. In fact, the later sequence is itself an elegy to the utopian vision of the early poems. Considered together, they articulate the polarities of the experience of objection—from the early hopes, to the gradual disillusion—and finally point to life beyond the camps, where objectors would reenter American society with a tempered utopianism.

X *War Elegies*, originally published by mimeograph in 1943 as the first Untide publication, according to Everson, was "the one that scored . . . [selling] hundreds and hundreds of copies" (Bartlett 47). Hand-printed and bound by Everson, illustrated with abstract ink originals by Nomland, the second edition ran 975 copies in November 1944. Because the elegies were written between 1940 and 1942, and later published in internment, they demonstrate Everson's poetics and experience prior to serving in the CPS camps. The poems most keenly echo Robinson Jeffers's antiwar verse, as well as the apocalypticism of modernist poetry; however, Everson sought to avoid the First World War's "poetry of disillusionment." Instead, Everson begins his pacifist lyric poetry—relying upon a highly alliterative and assonantal line—with a lyrical I declaring not only his refusal to fight but also his complicity in the wider violence of war. Everson's early poems oscillate between declarations of faith in pacifism and admissions of guilt, as if attempting to convince himself of the rightness of his conscientious objection. For Everson, a pacifist poetic never ceases to delve into the heart of human compulsion toward violence and destruction.

The first elegy manifests this oscillation between declarations of nonviolence and complicity with violence in his search for peace. Though Everson
exhibited a pantheistic delight in the natural world in his prewar poems, solace in nature evades him now that war looms:

> And I kneel in the grass,
> In the sere, the autumn-blasted,
> And seek in myself the measure of peace
> I know is not there. (X *War Elegies* unpaginated)

The near rhymes, grass/blasted/peace, render the sense of incompleteness
and establish Everson's war with his own impulses toward violence. Further
in the poem, the poet encounters a dream-vision of battle, in which "flyers
high on the rising rivers of air / . . . loose [their] cargo" on the town below.
Everson's employment of assonance (the long "i" of "high" and "rising") and
metaphor ("the rising rivers of air") causes us to see both the awe-inspiring
beauty of flight and the apocalyptic flood that the bombers will rain down.

Rather than simply disidentifying himself from the bombers and seamen,
the poet envisions sailors as they float on rafts after their ship has gone down,
and sees all too clearly his connection to them and to an ancestral history of
warriors:

> And I dream the delusion of men twisting in death
> Without honor or love;
> I feel the unresolvable tension forming within me,
> Knowing myself of the same breed,
> And I shatter the hollow weeds. . . .
> I, the living heir
> Of the bloodiest men of all Europe,
> And the knowledge of past tears through my flesh,
> I flinch in the guilt of what I am. (*XWE* unpaginated)

By identifying with the soldiers, Everson is forced to confront his own violent
forebears and his own "unresolvable tension." Even if he merely "shatter[s]
hollow weeds," the poet knows that his blood contains "those who endured
crazy with hate." The poem begins and ends with the poet on his knees, as if in
prayer, like Stafford's penitents in "The Jet Planes Dive," and ends with a series
of vows, "not to wantonly ever take life," as an attempt to "atone in my own soul
/ What was poured from my past." Still, despite the self-condemnation, by the

end of the poem, he can "lift up [his] eyes, / And they find the bearing that swings the sky."

If the first elegy exhibits Yeatsian self-argument, the second elegy confidently incants in a collective voice the refusal to participate in war—despite Everson's having written this poem prior to entering the CPS camps. Unable to "resolve in the wrestling soul / The old intractable contradiction" (the interminable violence in oneself despite the desire for peace), the voice of the collective objector nonetheless speaks, aware of the consequences of his pacifism:

> we are the ones
> Who, outside the narrows of nationalism and its iron pride,
> Reject the compulsion;
> Who stamp our allegiance
> Only at last on a concept wider than it can hold . . .
>
> We would wait in these rooms
> And watch them go down,
> The raiders hawking the low sky,
> And see all about us the forms we have loved
> Blasted and burned, nor rise against it. (XWE unpaginated)

Everson calls the war the result of both social and human flaws: the compulsion to violence by both state and individual soul. Despite his confident declarations of rejection, Everson shows awareness that his pledge of allegiance to something that is "a concept wider" than allegiances means that he must face the destruction of everything he loves. In light of our knowledge of Nazi concentration camps, it might be tempting to believe that conscientious objectors either were naïve or simply did not adequately assess the threats of fascism; in this poem, Everson almost perversely attempts to imagine total nonresistance against the enemy, refusing to "rise against" the raiders "blast[ing] and burn[ing]" the "forms we have loved."

Our retrospective desire to protest against and even abhor such nonresistance in the face of fascism might distract us from the audacity of the rejection itself and from the sources where the poet finds the strength to resist war. Everson's collective is not composed of war refusers alone but of an imagined community, a shared history in literature of moral heroism: "in our books and hear in our music / The high morality of those dauntless men / Who could never be bought." Everson's collective voice is audacious, considering that his decision to object did not have the support of a faith community, as many COs had. Yet Everson's romantic imagination of a collective resistance does not blind him to how the very will to resist can, as Yeats proposed in "Easter 1916," render hearts into stone; though pacifists "are not to be wooed," they also "draw . . . the detail to one iron focus / They watch with eyes wide, and they wait." Everson imagines pacifists "with eyes wide"—i.e., not blinded by their ideology—but they are "iron focus[ed]." As if frozen in place, Everson's pacifist can only act as the agonized, impotent witness in the face of certain destruction. Interestingly, in these poems, Everson uses the image of "iron" to describe both the nationalist (with his "iron pride") and the pacifist; how quickly, the image suggests, might these strengths turn into a paralyzed rigidity?

The final poem of X War Elegies, the only elegy written while in the Waldport CPS camp, deserves attention because of its placement in both X War Elegies and Waldport Poems. In X War Elegies, the poem acts as an initial consideration of CPS life; even if it represents the bleak existence of labor on the rock crusher, it also adds a note of grounded sobriety against the earlier, more stentorian poems of the collection. In Waldport Poems, however, it is buried in a longer meditation of division and breakdown, and will be discussed below. In X War Elegies, though, the COs' hard labor breaking rocks becomes a metaphor for the toll that war resistance takes on the objectors' lives:

> To sunder the rock—that is our day.
> In the weak light,
> Under high fractured cliffs
> We turn with our hands the raw granite;
> We break it with iron.
> Under that edge it suffers reduction.
> Harsh, dense and resistant,
> The obdurate portions
> Flaw and divide. (XWE unpaginated)

In the futility of the labor, the poet half-empathizes with the stone itself, as it "suffers reduction" under the workers' iron blows; the COs who hammer the rock seem to replicate the violence of the war—they are both killer and killed, hammer and "obdurate" stone. Again, Everson's typical employment of alliteration seems to recreate the hardness of the work, in its repetition of the "k" sounds ("rock," "weak," "fractured," "cliffs"). That the portions of rock "flaw and divide" foreshadows the larger motif employed by Everson of war as "division"—between nations and between people.

Even as they work, the COs never forget that they are simply biding their time, away from their true lives. Everson's objectors "wait, suspended in time; / locked out of our lives, / We abide, we endure . . . / Confronting encroachment the mind toughens and grows." The Waldport COs, for Everson, must resist by enduring separation from everything they knew. The poem ends with the sense that the earth itself cries in pain: "We perceive our place in the terrible pattern, . . . / The loss and the utter desolation / Howl at the heart of the world" (XWE unpaginated). Here, Everson's bleak portrait of CO life, in contrast to the earlier elegies, embodies the contradictions of the objectors' war resistance. The conscientious objector has found a sense of place, but it is only "in the terrible pattern" of a world that is wounded by war. Everson's subsequent poems turn from that momentary solace of connection to a larger meditation on the divisions that emerged as a result of war.

Chronicle of Division

Waldport Poems, written and published while at Waldport, became the first part of the long sequence called Chronicle of Division, the most accomplished work by Everson about his CPS experience and the concomitant breakup of his marriage to Edwa Poulson. Thomas Parkinson writes that Everson's breakup "hardly seems adequate to serve as a prototype for an entire world in the agony of the greatest war in human history" (30), and yet the sequence demonstrates—in ways that no other account of CO life does—the trajectory from utopian hopes to disillusionment that haunts the Civilian Public Service project. Chronicle of Division—his third poetic sequence, after Sides of a Mind and The Masculine Dead—enables Everson's lyric tendencies to stretch out into a complex narrative. Anticipating Lowell's lyric sequences in Life Studies, Everson's Chronicle articulates the inextricable web of connections between the lyric self and history, between promise of pacifism and the subsequent breakup of his marriage and of CPS. Chronicle of Division distills the best impulses of Everson's earlier poems—his highly wrought alliterative line, his faith in pacifism in conflict with self-accusation—into a broader and more sustained and consuming meditation on the price of war resistance. By focusing on a dissolving marriage, paradoxically, Everson succeeds in writing his most poignant elegy to war resistance. The costs of sustaining resistance to war manifest themselves from the first sections; the self-evident motif of the work, division, pervades all the levels of social connection—between nations, between communities, between individuals, between gender, and even within individuals—as a result of the war. Everson's poem, therefore, situates itself against the official myth that the Second World War was a "good war" that brought unity to American society. In contrast, the war functions in *Chronicle* precisely as the impediment to unification; the war hangs over the poem as an absent-presence, only emerging once in the bodies of wounded veterans riding the bus with Everson on his way to visit his wife.

Chronicle progresses temporally, beginning with Everson's departure from his wife and home to return to the camps, and ending after his breakup, at the seashore. Time itself plays a crucial role in *Chronicle*, and not for any traditionally poetic reason but because of the unique position of the objector during the war. According to the Selective Service Act of 1940, objectors would pursue alternative service for at least the duration of the war, and would be released proportionally to the return of soldiers from the fronts. Because no one knew how long the war would last—some predicted as long as twenty years— objectors experienced their tenure as suspended time. The third *Waldport* poem, while it captures this sense of suspended time, also universalizes the objector's situation as one that parallels the fundamental unpredictability, tenuousness, and poverty of human existence:

> This, then, is our world.
> Having entered the gate,
> Who is there to measure the length we stay?
> The factors that manage that endurance have yet to be formed.
> This much we know:
> Blood will be poured.
> The world in constriction must loosen, unlock,
> The tides withdraw,
> And all the wide chaos,
> That dwarfs our meager participation,
> Must have its great way.
> Yet the impassive calendar governs our minds.
> And the gate remains. (WP 151)

The "world" here refers principally to the microcosm of the internment camps, but it also invokes the larger world, where no one can know their "length of stay" or govern the "wide chaos." The reality of the war remains without question, even though it does not physically harm the objectors. The "impassive calendar" and "gate" does not stop anyone from departing from this world, but those who "openly ask the consequent hurt" choose to remain.

In sharp contrast to the *War Elegies*, whose confident declarations of paci-fist community belie their epistemological limitations, *Chronicle* weighs every perception with a retrospective "knowledge of loss" (150). Even those first impressions of a newcomer, marveling at the pacifists whose faces "wear its look like an open hand" (151) and at the camp that appears as the speaker's "glimmering vision" (152), will slowly dissipate like the mirage of an oasis:

> And here he would hold it,
> Till time taught him less,
> Revealing the brittle bias,
> The unseen error that makes human the saint,
> Thwarts the idealist,
> Marks the martyr,
> For none is immune.
> What the soul strives for is not to be had.
> That too he would learn.
> But here for a time it is true. (152)

The possibility of utopian connections in the CPS experience is slowly ground down in the extended parataxis of the sentence. Even though the speaker grants the momentary truth of those first impressions of unity among the objectors, the passage of time soon reveals the "brittle bias" of any imag-ined unanimity.

In fact, the speaker soon realizes not only that the saint is human but that the objectors enter camp with only a common rejection — "thou shalt not kill" — rather than a shared and coherent alternative vision of the world:

> The pacifist speaks,
> Face to face with his own kind,
> And seeks to fashion a common course
> That all may mark.
> But whatever he offers,
> Finds already framed in another's thought
> A divergent approach.
> The binding belief that each allows
> Is cruxed on rejection:
> *Thou shalt not kill.* (152)

Despite the poet's dream of a unified pacifist community, there was no single binding vision of the world shared by COs. Everson's use of the alliterative "binding belief" suggests the way in which the beliefs of the COs (most of them from the historic peace churches) may bind them together (the root of "religion" being *religio*, to bind) but also constrain them from movement (whether physical or intellectual). As Everson later states in the poem, "no man is alone," and yet, the experience of internment forces the mind to "erect its own defenses" (*CD* 155). The "divergent approach" of objectors paradoxically may be their defining characteristic. Although most conscientious objectors came from the Mennonite, Brethren, and Quaker churches, the range of ideologies and practices of COs made a certain level of difference impossible to avoid. Everson himself struggled against the conservative elements of the camp that were scandalized by the artists' open hedonism.

Successive sections of part I depict the inner struggles of those Everson once called "the Holy Joes" to endure their internment. The Holy Joes become, however, a cipher for those entranced in a certain worldview, one that both blinds and provides sustenance. Even if, "for most, there is prayer,"

> by night they implore.
> The bodies, doubled beside the beds,
> Invoke redemption.
> The faces, knotted in need,
> Thrust up toward attainment.
> The eyes that have wept on a fabulous vision
> Pierce rafter and board of our circumscribed lives. (153)

When Everson describes the vision like "the violent coupling of lovers" (154), from which the others must turn away, he clearly invokes the religious theme of annunciation, that erotic penetration of the god into the human. The bodies are "doubled," meaning both "doubled over" in prayer (as if from a blow) and somehow divided. The faces are "unaware," "knotted in need," and they "thrust up" and "pierce rafter and board" in a phallic gesture of ecstasy. The Holy Joes, like the pacifists in general, provide a stark vision of the masochistic economy of belief (whether ideological or religious). Their refusals, even while they cause pain, also yield some kind of pleasure. In psychoanalytic terms, jouissance is only accessible to the Holy Joes insofar as they accept the terms of their belief—their refusal to know war. For Everson, "engrossed in that vision they are saved and lost / Are indeed transfixed, / Who abjure the sanction of doubt" (154).

The internment of men without their spouses, loved ones, and families, represented for Everson the inhumane divisions rendered by the war itself.

And in reality, Everson's forced separation from his wife, Edwa, led not only to their isolation from each other but to marital infidelities, lasting emotional wounds, and their eventual breakup. In the poem, their relationship becomes a symptom of the larger cuts exposed by the war. Everson phrases the splitting of him and his wife as if a violent blade were cutting an umbilicus:

> The man struck from the woman—
> That is the crime.
> As the armies grow
> So gathers the guilt,
> So bloom the perversions,
> So flower the fears,
> So breed the deep cruelties and the secretive hurts. (155–156)

Because the war had such a distant reality to the objector, and because resistance to the war often caused objectors to abandon the mass media representation of the conflict, even the radio becomes an "abstract voice that spills from the box / [that] Cannot bring [the war] clear" (158). Without any institutional affiliation within the camps, and estranged from his extended family, Everson had only his wife. Their split, their painful attempts to reconcile, and their eventual divorce, recounted in the succeeding sections of the poem, force the poet to confront his own fundamental disconnection from society around him. In the city, after release from the camp, he finds himself "given again to the indifferent world" (179), where he loiters in a café and gives a blind veteran a "guilty coin" that he knows will be "found insufficient" (180).

The final section, after the breakup, turns from the narrative of breakup to a lyrical confrontation of the "divisible self" at the shores of the Pacific. In the attempt to find again coordinates to map his life, the poet meditates upon the sea and its "vast withholding," increasingly interspersed with an italicized command from an unknown voice to "*Dip down!*" Emphasizing the sea's unity in disunion, the poet writes how the sea's "breakers" form a "plumed piling" which drops on the shore "split up and spilt" (181). The sea's perpetual movement of waves breaking on the shore is evoked in repetition of "the same" and points toward a more healing sense of time. Still, his wife's letter of infidelity in his coat reminds him that he cannot simply abandon the past while attempting to piece together his shattered self. When he asks himself, "what is he?," it is a question he must answer in relation both to his violent anger at his wife and the dropping of the atomic bomb:

Now that the old volcanic hurt,
In its black upheaval,
Buried the civilization of the past?
Now that the Peace,
Breached in the air over Nagasaki,
Lays its ash on the world?
The myriad fragments that make up a war
Come asking home,
Like the unanswerable letter,
In from the islands,
Back from the reefs,
With the foreign sun on their faces,
With the foreign blood on their hands;
Back from that blind insouciant sea,
That sulks and champs and is unconcerned,
Self-caresser,
Forever involved in its own immolation. (182)

In his constant struggle to temper his pacifism with a sense of his own violence, Everson places the "old volcanic hurt" of the self alongside the American use of the atom bomb in Nagasaki. Here, at the shore, Everson seems to envy the sea's ability to carry the veterans back from the bloody theaters of war with blind unconcern, being "forever involved in its own immolation." Everson sees himself, at this moment, like the bloodied veterans.

When he hears in the sea's mumble to "dip down," he moves into an archaic vocabulary of violent invasion and piracy, as if attempting to regress into the past and into the unconscious. First, he attempts to sink into the recesses of the self, to invade "the storehouse of the breast, / Where the old acquisitions / Lie heaped in its hold" (184), but it's not far enough, for the command to "dip down" returns. If this first raid yields "the rapturous body, / Its naked divestment, / Its total request" (185), he finds he has not dipped far enough. Below, he finds "like a human skin / Peeled from the flesh and stretched up dry, / The raw map of the world" (185):

Who made it, the map,
Skinned from the torn flesh of the world,
Hung up in the heart
To blanch the face and blind the eye?
Is this his own handiwork,

Who grubbed out the years in the squalid camps
With the men who denied. (186)

This dream-vision of a map constructed out of skin transforms the abstract
Cartesian map of blank space into an embodied construction of human in-
habitation. At the same time, the image inevitably echoes that of the lamps
comprised of the skin of concentration camp victims; it is as if, at the bottom
of the self, this pacifist self must confront this map of human skin.

By the end of *Chronicle*, the poet has refused the metaphor of the sea as
the self, even as he wonders whether the self is also "oceanic, / A central flux
and a surface trouble" (189). Though Everson has not moved geographically
from his initial poem of resistance (at the coast's edge), his oscillations between utopian pacifist beliefs and his experiences of violence, and disillusionment have moved him, and us, into a broader understanding of the trials of
war from the standpoint of the objector. Further, Everson's poems suggest the
way in which the lyric sequence propels the poet away from the self—even if
those orbits return to the self—and create a map of the world.

The Fine Arts Legacy

Just as Everson's poems demonstrate the complex and contradictory experience of conscientious objection during the Second World War, Everson's
feelings about the Fine Arts Camp also vacillated between utopianism and
disillusioned pragmatism. Everson noted in a 1946 letter, evoking the images
of rock crushing, that the Waldport COs "saw to the heart of the pure creative
substance, the rock, and they began cutting into it, and they hewed off layer
after layer of incidentals, and they got to the heart of it, stripped it down, made
it shine" (Eshelman 512). In the same letter, Everson considers how the Fine
Arts functioned as a kind of "minor civilization," where people "penned out
of their lives" created a new life: "You only have to walk into this kind of camp
to realize what we had there, the thing we fashioned, and nourished, and
brought to bear. For this is the society of manners, where people, penned out
of their lives, fashion another, a kind of minor civilization, with emphasis on
the social graces, and the social concerns, for they have little else" (Eshelman
THUF 511–512).

In later life, Everson even saw the camp as "like a religious order . . . a total
dedication and involvement in some ways more than a religious order. . . . It was

a real seed state" (26). Everson also saw how the Fine Arts Camp—like the CPS system at large, and the world at war—always threatened to tear itself apart from contending elements: "There were some real snobs, pains in the asses . . . misanthropes . . . difficult people, temperamental, artistic, normal run-of-the-mill artistic, difficult people. The less talent they had, the more problematical they were. The ones who were really creative and productive created their way through and kept it together. But trouble was never very far away" (Bartlett 66).

On the one hand, then, we have Everson's utopian image of the Fine Arts as a seed state of pacifist artistic production, and on the other, the most prosaic image of Fine Arts as a group of petulant poseurs. This oscillation, visible at times in Everson's individual poems, emerges most clearly and richly in his longer narrative sequences, representing the contradictions of CO war resistance.

Despite the contradictions in the Fine Arts experiment (and in CPS more generally), the Fine Arts CO experience provided the seeds to a flowering of arts on the West Coast. The utopian image of CPS articulates that the fruits of the CPS experience fundamentally altered the postwar cultural landscape of the Bay Area. Indeed, the Fine Arts group, with Kenneth Rexroth, funneled its energies after the war into what became known as the San Francisco Renaissance. Rexroth, another CO who served time in mental hospitals, saw the COs as a moral wedge in his anarchopacifist assault on the cultural establishment: "The men from Waldport . . . were also living proof of a moral revolt that could be staged against the establishment while still holding true to individual principles" (Wallach 29). What would come to be called the first "San Francisco Renaissance" in the late 1940s—with its "new poetics . . . [of] formal innovation . . . [and] discovery of alternate social forms" (Davidson SFR xi)—included poets such as Muriel Rukeyser, Robert Duncan, Jack Spicer, Everson, and Rexroth, and yielded to the second San Francisco Renaissance, with the influx of the East Coast Beats.

The Beats emerged as a legitimate foil to conformist culture in the early 1950s. But even though Rexroth promoted Everson as the first Beat, in a 1959 Time magazine article, "The Beat Friar," Everson (who by then had converted to Catholicism and changed his name to Brother Antoninus) situates himself as alternative to the alternative Beats:

> The beat [sic] is different from the other generations of revolt. Other
> generations have wanted to set up a counter-institutional world; even we
> anarchists wanted to do that. But the beat sees all these movements as
> being entrapped in the world of the square. The word square means four-
> cornered, or lacking flexibility. Of course, we all have some element of

squareness in us. But the point is that the beat refuses to have any real dialogue with the world of the square, and to me this is fatal. ("The Beat Friar")

The fruit of Everson's experience as a CO in the Second World War was the recognition that no revolution (or refusal, for that matter) can occur without both a vision of utopia and a conversation with the world. Everson saw the Beats' refusal to dialogue with squares—a characterization which no doubt flattens the heterogeneity of Beat writing—as "their fatal flaw, refusing, as they do, to illuminate their explorations of the unconscious to the collective mind, thus frustrating their role of poet as prophet by keeping their illuminations imprisoned in their own egos" (Rizzo 163). The Beats, at least in Everson's stereotypical view, refuse the fundamentally social function of prophecy and merely follow the fantasy of uninformed radical individualism, without ever recognizing the need for collectivity and for dialogue with the institutions of the square, the hegemonic authority.

Everson's "central flux" of identity led him from Herber, to Everson the CO, to Brother Antoninus. And though in 1969, he would finally take off his robe and leave the Church for married life, Everson's permutations of identity always performed in the tension between poetry and belief, between the safety of institutional affiliation and the ecstatic but more dangerous effusions of the unconscious. Even though after *Chronicle*, Everson abandoned pacifist ideology in favor of erotic and devotional love poetry, his decision to follow new paths belies the recalcitrance typically associated with pacifism and war resistance. His move away from narrowly defined pacifist poetry speaks to the divergent paths of conscientious objectors in general and of the CO poets in particular, who continued to revise their poetic personalities.

In an introduction to a selection of Everson poems, William Stafford casts the poet as a rebel with a cause, and argues that Everson's poetry

> flourishes because it expresses many impulses which practical, politic life coerces most of us to avoid. . . . [T]here is another way to live, a way to stay honest without staying silent. . . . [Everson] demonstrates this other way—it is a shock and a delight to break free into the heart's unmanaged impulses. All literature lives in one way or another with this freedom, but . . . [Everson's] poetry lives openly—even flagrantly—by continual recourse to shock . . . [and] exemplifies the exhilaration of rebellion. (*ABA* 5)

It may be true that Everson's poems reject the accommodating tendencies of the New Critical poem—eschewing political engagement to accommodate to the poem as an expression of universality. However, Stafford projects onto Everson the image of one who resists the coercion of "practical, politic life" and who refuses to internalize the mechanisms of self-repression, "break[ing] free" into the less predictable impulses of the heart. Stafford thus recasts Everson as George from *Down in My Heart*, an "absolutist . . . the principled rebel" (*ABA* 9). Stafford's admiration of, but evident discomfort with, Everson's marginal position demonstrates the importance of the "absolute rebel" in the poetics of Stafford, Lowell, and Everson, even as a mode of self-differentiation. Ultimately, the CO poets demonstrate that the rapprochement between poetry and war resistance is a provisional one, worked out by poets in their own idiosyncratic ways, uneasily harnessed to the singularity of aims required by activist movements.

PART 2.

Vietnam

THE WAR ON THE HOMEFRONT

FIGURE 2: *Tom Melville, Philip Berrigan, and Dan Berrigan burning military draft files with homemade napalm, Catonsville, Maryland, May 17, 1968*

Somewhere my body goes taut under the deluge, somewhere I am naked behind the lines, washing my body in the water of that war.

—ADRIENNE RICH, "SHOOTING SCRIPT"

4. Bringing It All Back Home
▪ FROM ANTHOLOGY TO ACTION

In a 2003 TV advertisement for Tommy Hilfiger, the rousing opening line of Creedence Clearwater Revival's "Fortunate Son"—"Some folks are born to raise the flag / Ooo they're red white and blue . . ."—is sliced away from its subsequent irony: "And when the band plays Hail to the Chief / Oh they'll point the cannon at you." With that revision, the advertisement reduces the blistering protest song from 1970—so full of bile at class inequity and the cynical patriotism of the well-connected—to a patriotic flag-waving celebration of nubile youth. In another ad, the National Football League amputates the opening of Edwin Starr's anguished "War"—"War / Good God y'all" from its subsequent cry, "What is it good for? Absolutely nothing." These advertisements, for those who know the songs, cannot but resurrect the Vietnam era, in which protest was at once massive and even mainstream and yet also regularly distorted by mass media. In the ongoing struggle over the meaning of the Vietnam War, these protest anthems' beheadings for the patriotism of commodity consumption is a traumatic repetition of the loss of dissenting voices.[1] One of the great fantasy screens upon which the partisans of the culture wars project their versions of the past—and therefore frame our visions of the present and imaginings of possible futures—the Vietnam War persists in the various framings and reframings not only by writers and critics but also by the architects of mass culture.

What I will argue here is that the consensus view of literary criticism that the antiwar poetry produced during the Vietnam War—that it was forgettable, lamentable, or even dangerous—misses the cultural work which the rich archive of war resistance poetry contributed to and constitutes.[2] This "potential archive," to adapt Alastair Fowler's notion of the "potential canon" (213–216)—the sum total of war resistance texts that could be included in such an archive—consists of more than a catalogue of protests or statements against the war; rather, it is an ongoing poetic engagement with and window into the movement's identificatory investments, its conflicted rhetorical address, its resistance to co-optation and commodification as *war story*, and its attempt to overcome its own conditions of marginalization (both from American political culture and from the war itself). These works, to echo the title of Bob Dylan's transitional album (half folk, half electric), "bring it all back home"—rendering the war abroad visible on the homefront. Taken as a whole, the massive corpus of war resistance poetry from the Vietnam War challenges long-held assumptions about the literariness, authority, and truth claims of poetry about war. First, it dramatizes the ongoing engagement of American soldiers and civilians alike to understand their material and psychic relationship to the war in Vietnam and to articulate a poetics of resistance. Second, it demonstrates how poets confronted their own experiential and ideological limitations to speak representatively about a conflict that exposed the deep fissures between Americans. Finally, it speaks to and confronts the increasingly technologized and bureaucratic formation of modern warfare itself, as most Americans witnessed the war principally through mass media lenses.

This poetic archive, this corpus of the possible, is more than a body of material texts within books and magazines; it reaches outside the bindings into the public sphere, including symbolic actions of all sorts. Robert Lowell's notorious letter (subsequently co-signed by numerous writers) declining the invitation to the White House Festival of the Arts (1965); the antics of Ed Sanders and the Fugs in "Levitating the Pentagon" during the March on the Pentagon (1967); Ginsberg's pleas for peace by chanting "aum" for seven hours in Grant Park during the tumultuous moments before the police riot broke out at the Democratic National Convention in Chicago (1968); "Jackson [Mac Low] the concrete poet at Bryant Park . . . reading his 'non-political poem,' which he explained 'expressed no attitudes or opinions or ideas of a political nature,' and nearly causing a riot with a single litany of names" (qtd. in Mac Low ix); the Catonsville Nine's destruction of draft files as a linguistic act (1968); Robert Bly's acceptance speech for the National Book Award (1969), in which he lambasted the National Book Award Committee, universities, and book publishers, extolled acts of civil disobedience, and then gave the award monies directly to the draft-resistance movement; Levertov's speeches and readings throughout the country, and particularly in Berkeley; such moments in the archive propose a counterargument to the oft-quoted lines of poetry's ineffectuality in the face of historical events. Thus, this potential archive demonstrates the range of strategies that poets undertook to overcome both their own marginality as poets engaging in the public discussion of the war and the constraints of lyric poetry as a single voice meditating on direct or imagined experience, destined for library immortality.

In this chapter, I will examine anthology production, poetry readings against the war, and participation in demonstrations by poets as producers of language. The debate between Denise Levertov and Robert Duncan, carried forth in their personal correspondence, frames the larger debate between an occasional protest poetry bent on speed, information, and message and a more long-lasting, but less immediate protest as witness to nonviolence. Further, I will articulate a typology for a war resistance poetry that grapples with its own homefront conditions, distant from the scene of battle; along a continuum of physical proximity to the battles in Vietnam, poets attempted visionary, documentary, first-person witness poems, and translation and other cross-cultural poetic collaborations—all to make visible and audible their own narrative of war resistance, so refracted and distorted by mass media representations focusing on extremist elements within the antiwar movement itself.

Gathering Voices of War Resistance

An obvious place to begin investigating the material archive is with the anthology, itself a mini-archive, a gathering of voices. The dizzying number of titles, published during the span of the war—A *Poetry Reading against the Vietnam War* (1966), *Where Is Vietnam?* (1967), *Poems of War Resistance* (1968), *Out of the War Shadow* (1968), *Campfires of the Resistance: Poetry from the Movement* (1971), *Winning Hearts and Minds* (1972)—render the developing sense of a collective consciousness, of a countercultural nation, and also propose in themselves an invention of a war resistance tradition, stretching back, for editor Scott Bates at least, to the beginnings of human history. They both represent resistance and become in themselves a script for future readings and resistance, as Bly and Ray hoped A *Poetry Reading against the Vietnam War* would become. When Bly and Ray, initiating American Writers against the War in 1966, began doing a series of readings, others wanted to host their own. According to Bly, "The main problem was that people . . . didn't have the material. So I gathered up some of the things that seemed to be most effective in our given readings, and I got a guy in New York who would help find cheap printers" (Bly interview). From this anthology, one notices that a page has been blacked out; one can discern, from the table of contents, that it was cummings's notorious antiwar poem from the First World War, "i sing of olaf." Apparently, cummings's widow refused to grant her permission to publish the poem and threatened to sue—causing Bly and his publisher to hire a bunch of people to spend all night blacking out the offending pages. The blacked-out page itself is suggestive of the wider censorial frameworks that occluded Vietnam War coverage; mass media tended not to transgress what Daniel Hallin called the boundaries of "legitimate controversy."

The samizdat work of antiwar veterans Jan Barry, Basil Paquet, and Larry Rottman, who founded their own press (1st Casualty Press) to publish antiwar veteran poets in *Winning Hearts and Minds* (WHAM) after the Winter Soldier hearings in 1971, conceived their project as a script for readings:

> Read it aloud
> Recopy it
> Dramatize it
> Give it as a gift
> And sing it!
> Poetry is a human gift.
>
> Use it. (*WHAM* 118–119)[3]

The editors' principles of inclusion, like Bly and Ray's, allowed space for quotes from a broad range of text and photographic sources, not just poems, and pushed the bounds of polyvocality already implicit in the form. Consider, for example, the amateur soldier-poem from the follow-up anthology to WHAM, *Peace Is Our Profession*, collectively written by "GI's of the 1st Air Infantry Division," a succinct analysis of why the U.S. war policy was not simply ill advised but often criminal:

> We shoot the sick, the young, the lame,
> We do our best to kill and maim,
> Because the kills count all the same,
> Napalm sticks to kids. (*POP* 22)

James William Gibson's analysis of Technowar articulates how the Pentagon imported corporatist logic whereby a certain number of kills, measured through body counts and kill ratios—in which all Vietnamese deaths were typically counted as Vietcong deaths—would determine American victory. The pilot-poets, in their mass-produced assembly-line verses, rife with self-consciously idiotic rhyme ("maim"/"lame"/"same"), foregrounds the painful way in which their job was to produce deaths—enemy or otherwise.

If Vietnam veteran poets played a crucial role by lending their authority as ex-soldiers to war resistance—not only in WHAM but also in their activism, their witness, and their testimony—African American and Chicano poets (both veteran and civilian) clarified the ways in which the homefront itself was, to quote Barbara Harlow, "an arena of *struggle*" (italics hers 2). Though there were real differences between the movement of racial minorities for empowerment and the movement to end the Vietnam War, the anthology *Vietnam and Black America* (ed. Clyde Taylor 1973) decisively shows how, as the war dragged on, the struggles for racial justice and against war were inextricable. African American intellectuals frequently framed their cause in relation to the revolutionary struggle of the Vietnamese, against U.S. imperialism. The Student Non-Violent Coordinating Committee believed that "the United States government has been deceptive in its claims of concern for freedom of the Vietnamese people, just as the government has been deceptive in claiming concern for the freedom of colored people in such other countries . . . and in the United States itself" (258). Eldridge Cleaver saw "a structural relationship between these two arenas of conflict [in Vietnam and at home]" (273). Huey Newton went so far as to address the National Liberation Front of South Vietnam "to assist you in your fight against American imperialism" (290). Even Martin Luther King Jr., who entered into the antiwar movement late because of the potentially deleterious effects on the Civil Rights movement at home, went so far as to say that "the greatest purveyor of violence in the world today [is] my own government" (82).

That *Vietnam and Black America* is replete with poems, even featuring a section entitled "Home Front" composed entirely of poetry (by such poets as Amiri Baraka, Askia Muhammed Touré, A. B. Spellman, Sonia Sanchez, and Etheridge Knight), also demonstrates how poetry functioned as a central mode of resistance and an articulation of radical African American subjectivity on the homefront. Manning Marable concurs, arguing that "Black poets were among the most effective critics of the war" (102). Though none of Baraka's poems in "Home Front" explicitly addresses the war—which in itself suggests the way in which war resistance moves beyond depictions of military engagement—other poems directly address how the struggle for racial justice redraws the line between "war" and "homefront" itself. Touré's poem attacks Dionne Warwick's entertaining the troops on a warship as a kind of sex slavery, while Sonia Sanchez in "the final solution/the leaders speak" articulates how immigrants and blacks, welcomed by this "land of free/dom," will be allowed to fight:

> we will make responsible
>   citi/zens
>
>   out of them or
>   kill them trying. (169)

Interestingly, the anthology both begins and ends with poems. Nikki Giovanni's "The Great Pax Whitie"—which connects the history of Roman empire and its Pax Romana with the so-called Pax Americana—opens the anthology and speaks to Hardt and Negri's observation that Empire summons the language of peace in order to justify its wars and oppression. It ends with Margaret Walker's "The Ballad of the Free," incanting the names of revolutionary rebels against slavery—Nat Turner, Gabriel Prosser, Denmark Vesey, Touissant L'Ouverture, and John Brown—as models for the work of freedom (310–311).

After the war ended, anthologies with Vietnam War poetry continued to reassess and recirculate permutations of the resistance: *Peace Is Our Profession* (1982), *Carrying the Darkness* (1985), *Visions of War, Dreams of Peace* (1991), *Voices from the Ho Chi Minh Trail* (1993), *Against Forgetting: Twentieth Century Poetry of Witness* (1993), *Writing between the Lines: An Anthology of War and Its Social Consequences* (1997), *Mountain River: Vietnamese Poetry from the Wars, 1948–1993* (1998), *From Both Sides Now* (1998), and *Aztlán and Viet Nam: Chicano and Chicana Experiences of the War* (1999). These anthologies range in emphasis from civilian verse to soldier poetry, from protest poems to witness poems, from American poets to Vietnamese poets. The new anthologists have discerned the danger in privileging only the voices of American soldier-poets—and the danger in treating the Vietnam War as an exceptional case, disconnected from all other wars. Major anthologies from the 1990s include the work of American women poets, Vietnamese poets, Chicano and Chicana poets, and poetry from other conflicts. While some anthologies perpetuate the tradition of soldier poetry (*From Both Sides Now*), and others privilege the Vietnam War as the archetypal conflict (*Writing between the Lines*), they collectively succeed to create a broader, more inclusive field of voices.

Aztlán and Viet Nam—to examine a recent addition—makes visible Chicano war resistance during Vietnam, and how it had to confront its own community's tradition of military service, its cultural drive for assimilation, and its machismo in the process. Despite the fact, as George Mariscal relates, that Rodriguez is the second most common surname on the Vietnam Memorial in Washington (3), and that Chicanos themselves engaged in their own struggle on the homefront, Chicanos did not produce "highly visible anti-war activists" as the African American community did (6).[4] Yet Mariscal details how Chicanos and Chicanas overcame internal and external cultural resistances to organize "some of the largest anti-war demonstrations of the late 1960s and early '70s" (187), especially in California. Chicano and Chicana poets included in *Aztlán* commingle English and Spanish to speak out against the war as a manifestation of white American privilege (Adrian Vargas's "Blessed Amerika" 236), as a rejection of César Chávez's nonviolent movement (Luis Valdez's "Pensamiento Serpento" 230–231), as the inevitable outcome of machismo (Ben Reyes's "Juan Carlos González"), in this prose translation by Mariscal:

> Juan Carlos González was very macho. He liked the army a lot THE CUT OF HIS UNIFORM and he was a big hero to the kids of the neighborhood when he came back with his red, white, and blue ribbons. He told them in great detail the process by which a man becomes a SOLDIER. First, you delicately adjust the buckle in the middle of your stomach. And then the bayonet. It's important to sharpen it scientifically. One day, on a holiday, we got the news that Juancho had died and nobody asked how. But we know that HE WAS VERY MACHO. (238–239)

The use of capital letters, the description of how to become a soldier, and the repetition of "macho" in the framing lines of the poem all undercut the masculinity proffered by military service. The poem subverts the heroism that war service proposes and suggests that the military uses Chicano machismo against the best interests of Chicanos. Further, despite the fact that the antiwar movement of the period was male dominated, this poem articulates an intriguingly feminist critique similar to Dorinda Guadalupe Moreno's "La niña Lina en East Los Angeles," written in 1973, about a three-year-old girl who gets lost during a demonstration when police tear gas the crowd: "Lina sleeps while people riot in the streets. / Smashed windows, like smashed hopes, dignity reclaimed in rebellion" (250). Such poems give voice to the rarely heard experience of activists who throw off the burdens of race, ethnicity, language, gender, and class to speak out against the war at home—a war that may manifest itself "over there" but is felt on the bodies of those on the homefront.

Talking Back in Poetry and Action

The potential archive of war resistance necessarily moves outside of the spatial bounds of material text into ephemeral, time-bounded events such as poetry readings, demonstrations, and other symbolic actions. Bibby's recovery of GI samizdat poetry during the Vietnam War, and Sullivan's analysis of antiwar broadsides, suggest how the reception of poetry outside of books requires us to move beyond a static, nonmaterial understanding of poetry into a more nuanced reading of its cultural materiality. Reading the ephemera produced by activists enacting the essential and daily work of resistence requires recovery, in both senses of that word—both retrieval and analysis; through pamphlets, broadsides, graffiti, poetry, songs, speeches, or bodily actions, a movement inscribes itself in the public space, transmits itself into the public ear. In their materiality, these texts offer themselves as concrete evidence of resistance, or in James Sullivan's words, become "a material sign to be touched and seen, engaging the senses rather than, as is conventional, passing transparently through them to the literary intellect" (1). Ephemeral literature operates on the most immediate and visceral levels by intruding into the alleged neutrality of public spaces, where the dominant ideology reigns. The time-bounded events of war resistance demonstrate not only the way in which poets actively participated together in bringing war resistance poems to audiences, but more interestingly, how poets actively worked through the praxis of poetry and war resistance—by interacting with audiences and in public spaces, in ways that generated material texts and symbolic actions. Further, these time-bounded, poetry-inflected events implicitly carry forth Kenneth Burke's notion of language as symbolic action, as "a species of action" (15) and extend its implications, by illuminating the ways in which certain species of actions are themselves a kind of language. First, insofar as poets foreground the way in which language constructs reality, poetry itself can become an inoculation for the wider public, who tend to read language as transparent, against the abuses of language in political discourse. Second, as Burke suggests that language's symbolic action is not merely rhetorical but identificatory, the poets' embodiment of a certain way of seeing invites their readers or listeners into similar modes of seeing.

Poetry readings became opportunities not only to foreground the crisis of language and embody a new way of seeing but also to dissent publicly, to connect with local activists and connect them to the national movements, and even to raise money for war resisters. In a December 1967 letter to RESIST, Denise Levertov reports how her recent two-week poetry reading tour enabled her "to tell potential sympathizers what is going on, to activate the apathetic, to encourage isolated activists, and to alleviate their isolation by helping to put them in touch with one another" (qtd. in Bertholf and Gelpi 597). Her opening thesis, the subsequent narrative of her report, and her appendix of "tips" suggest that Levertov meant the letter to provide a road map for theorizing how poetry events can work for war resistance.

The tips given by Levertov illuminate how war resister poets sought to make connections between their poetry work and their peace work, between their own activist communities and the ones that they visited, and to negotiate the particular localities where they found themselves:

1) Contact peace people beforehand so that they can make best use of you when you come.
2) Try to find out local conditions so that your remarks will be on the most useful and appropriate level.
3) Wear a peace button of some kind while traveling.
4) Perform whatever you are being paid to do with extra zeal—it will give more weight to your peace activities.
5) If you can arrange to give a benefit performance of some kind, try to have them use "local talent" too. It gives more feeling of solidarity—and at the same time takes a bit of strain off you. (qtd. in Bertholf and Gelpi 602–603)

Levertov's desire to connect with, address, and cultivate the local through her daily activities as guest lecturer and reader emblematizes the struggle of war resister poets to think through the rhetorical conditions of their utterances and to integrate the labor of war resistance into their poetry readings. Rather than simply using poetry to further her own agenda, or conversely, rather than using politics to further her poetry career, Levertov sought to become both an embodiment of war resistance and a conduit for the work of local resistance groups.

More than offering merely rational argumentation, readings became events in which poet and audience could summon together an affective response to and argument against the war. Insofar as the principal architects of the war conducted it as a rationalistic exercise and legitimated it with reasoned argument, poetry actively counternarrated the war by addressing missing elements in public discourse; according to Robert Bly, a teach-in on the war in Mankato had addressed the political aspects of the war but failed to address the students' affective experience:

[S]tudents were feeling a tremendous emotional upset. And so when we came in doing poetry, it was like hearing someone scream onstage. Which was important for them to hear. And that's one reason that the reading became so powerful, because it isn't quite proper to talk in a calm, rationalistic way. So in the poetry there was much more yelling and feeling and screaming. Emotions came in, and a little bit of insanity. (Bly interview)

Still, Bly's claim for poetry as affective utterance was ripe for manipulation by mass media; it's difficult to imagine what the average television viewer would have made of, for example, Allen Ginsberg's *"hare om namo shiva"* chant (now immortalized in the documentary *Berkeley in the Sixties*) in response to a television reporter's question about what Ginsberg thought of the rally. Perhaps that viewer might have laughed off the antics as mere clowning or worse, the onset of the end of civilization. Yet, Ginsberg's chant poem—which Barrett Watten argues is an empty signifier, given its untranslateability for most Americans—asserts the impossibility of representing war resistance using typical journalistic modes of representation; as a symbolic action, Ginsberg's performance of the mantra embodies the ethos that the counterculture attempted to bring into being—however incomplete or halting.[5]

In contrast to the community building and affective strategies of Levertov, Bly, and Ginsberg, veteran poets, such as Jan Barry or W. D. Ehrhart, lent their cultural authority as former soldiers to readings. At times, these presences not only lent credence to the war resistance but also provided it with a crucial dissonance. Unaccustomed to participating in public readings, Ehrhart recalls reading his antiwar poem, "A Relative Thing," and getting cheers. His response set everyone aback: "I got really angry and shouted something like, 'What do you think this is, a goddamned football game? It's a war, and millions of people are dying, and I just want it to stop.' The place was like a tomb when I walked off the stage" (Ehrhart interview).[6] Ehrhart's anger interjected a crucial element of self-questioning into what may have been a raucous affair of the like-minded. Relatedly, Levertov's poetic account of her May 8, 1970, reading at Goucher College, entitled "The Day the Audience Walked Out on Me, and Why," recounts how the poet's call to active resistance in memorial to the murdered students at Kent State and Orangeburg results in the audience's retreat from the reading:

> Yes, it is well that we remember
> all of these, but let us be sure
> we know it is hypocrisy
> to think of them unless
> we make our actions their memorial,
> actions of militant resistance. (*Poems 1968–1972* 220)

At the same time, affective readings, ritualistic happenings, and dramatic performances—particularly of avant-garde poets and such groups as the Living Theater—according to Jerome Rothenberg, participated in the larger "breakdown of the distinction between audience and artist . . . returning us to ritual and ceremony in a big way. These were rarely political in any agitprop sense, but convertible, like the poetry readings, to political action and protest" (Rothenberg "Chanting" 55). Others, such as David Antin, in his talk poem "the fringe," recounts his own relationship to protest as an essentially boring act, and how poetry readings might be a way to obviate the circularity of address and repetitive ennui of street marches:

> [W]e lived on the fringe and we came out something like termites   and
> at first we marched or really walked and that was nice but pious and
> boring   and lots of us thought we should do something more interesting
> so we organized readings and held them in places where mostly   people
> who agreed with us came to hear them   and that was only a little more
> interesting (22)

Throughout, Antin's talk poem cantankerously ruminates over the problem of being part of a fringe—and that war resistance itself constituted a fringe; and yet, the piece ends with a long recollection of the organizing and performance of a huge reading at the Fillmore East, called the Three-Penny Reading against the War in Vietnam, at which poets as different as Antin, John Ashbery, Mac Low, Rothenberg, and Andrei Vosnesensky participated.[7]

Not only did poets bring poetry into reading halls and demonstrations, but reading halls and demonstrations brought poetry to poets. Responding to the audience and to the moment became a mode of composition, as Bly recalls how his poem "The Teeth Mother Naked at Last"

> was written spontaneously on stage during those times. I would take
> newspaper articles and read a bit on stage, composing lines to fit the
> horrible news. I would check the tape of the reading and in that way
> find out what I had said. Sharing it with an audience, the give and take
> between poet and the audience would bring things that would never
> arrive if you were just sitting down composing alone. "The Teeth
> Mother Naked at Last" is the only poem I have created with that
> ancient relationship between poet and audience. The dark times of the
> Vietnam War gave us that bond, the union only poetry could give us.
> (Gonzalez 3)

The generative interaction between Bly and the poetry audience suggests the ways in which war resistance poetry, at moments, pushes the lyric mode from a private and privatized act of expression to one of communal voicing, visioning and embodying a shared reality.[8]

The archive of poetry events, or events which deployed language in symbolically charged ways, demonstrates the way in which poetry and other modes of symbolic action married with the expressivist politics of the increasingly countercultural New Left. After all, the New Left was born in part in the poetry of activists such as Mario Savio, whose exhortations summon the ghost of Thoreau in its critique of the machinery of war: "There is a time when the operation of the machine becomes so odious, makes you so sick at heart, that you can't take part; you can't even passively take part, and you've got to put your bodies upon the gears and upon the wheels, upon the levers, upon all the apparatus and you've got to make it stop" (qtd. in Gitlin Sixties 291).

Savio's penchant for extended metaphor (the machine as authority run amok), repetitions of phrases ("take part," three "upons"), internal rhyme (heart/part), and assonance (gears/wheels/levers and got/stop) demonstrate a strong oral rhetorical sensibility in this pithy explication of New Left politics: that the government was perceived as a kind of inhuman machine against which the rebelling youth must use their very bodies to foul up the operations.

However, implicit in the debate about war resistance poetry is whether such poetry should ultimately retain its own self-identity or stretch into some rhetorical amalgam of poetry and ideology. The argument that manifested itself in the correspondence between two poets and friends, Robert Duncan and Denise Levertov, suggested the incompatibility between these two polar positions. In Duncan's admonishment of Levertov's adoption of revolutionary language and didacticism, we see articulated the first position; for Duncan, poetry might function as true protest as long as it does not become political agitprop. Referring to Levertov's poem, "The Altars in the Street," in which she describes the 1967 Buddhist demonstration in which children built altars in the streets of Hue, Duncan proposes that "the protest is only true when it is such an altar, an expressive act. When it is directed toward a *means-ends*, it is either futile or, succeeding, belongs to a complex of political meanings that can have no 'truth in itself'" (qtd. in Bertholf and Gelpi 558). For Duncan, a true poem can become a true protest insofar as it becomes a thing in itself, insofar as it has a form that retains its own *altarity*.[9] By contrast, Levertov's own poetry actions suggest the possibility of the latter position, how poets can deploy language in ways that might be useful to war resistance. In a letter to Duncan, Levertov notes that she had written "a 'street ballad' in rhymed couplets (a 'come all ye') about the Fort Hood 3—not a good poem but something the Greenwich Village Peace Center may be able to use as a leaflet I hope" (qtd. in Bertholf and Gelpi 555). Levertov and others saw the possibilities of agit-poetry that might aspire to be both "good" poetry and useful to the movement. In the tension between Duncan's and Levertov's positions, poetry events during the Vietnam War demonstrate the wide range of tactics and poetic languages employed for war resistance. From Jackson Mac Low's early performances of "Jail Break," to the self-consciously hippie spirituality of the exorcism/levitation of the Pentagon, to the earnest Catholicism of the Catonsville Nine, from the Buddhistic aums of Ginsberg to the hectoring of Bly or the guerrilla theater of the Vietnam Veterans against the War—poetic language-events pushed the bounds of political speech into wider areas of consciousness.

Jackson Mac Low—a IV-F who protested on behalf of COs in prison during the Second World War—points to another lost connection of war resistance poetry and maps out another way in which creative action and political resistance could dovetail.[10] The standard bearer for anarchopacifist poetry, Mac Low's particular poetic achievement involved his employment of chance operations—whereby the poet composes by means of elaborate, often mathematical systems based on chance—to undermine the authority of the narrative, the lyric poem, and the self. Mac Low's poetic production avails itself of multiple writings and readings, thereby creating a model that breaks down the poetic ego and allows for free association. For Mac Low, the poet is "'a loyal co-initiator of action'; in & in which performance together establishes a new social bond or serves as model for 'the free society of equals which it is hoped the work will help bring about'" (ix). Mac Low's work is "a score" to be performed rather than a text whose meaning is to be dredged or unearthed.

The poem "Jail Break"—performed in various demos, beginning with protests of the continued imprisonment of COs in Danbury Prison after the Second World War—provides textual evidence of the way in which Mac Low worked out the problems of anarchopacifism simultaneously through the praxis of language and action. It is a simultaneity, that is, a performance piece meant to be read by multiple people, overlapping voices. In the directions provided for a later version of the poem, Mac Low instructs that the poem needs "five [people] who speak clearly, listen closely to each other & all environing sounds, & let what they hear modify how they speak" (195). Two alternate ways to perform the poem are provided; the first involves the five in a line, holding signs, and the second involves the five facing each other. In both cases, the poem involves 120 "readings" of the singular line: "TEAR DOWN ALL JAILS NOW" in each of its permutations. Read aloud, "Jail Break" rapidly moves from message-driven protest to an incantatory language event. More than a protest statement, and more than a lyric poem, this simultaneity opens out into community and is only realized by communal participation; such a poem has cultural use-value, perhaps despite its avant-garde pedigree, as a protest chant that itself is subject to nuance, listening, alteration, change. That is, it is a protest that refuses the dogmatism of protest, one that enacts an alternative community within the protest, rather than simply presenting itself as an oppositional image for the Big Other.

Poetry events came not only in performed vocalizations but in material signage. Take Ginsberg's poem-placard, which he composed for his first demonstration in 1963, outside a speech by Madame Nhu:

Name hypnosis and fear is
Enemy!—Satan go home!
I accept America and Red China
To the human race.
Madame Nhu and Mao-Tse Tung
Are in the same boat of meat. (qtd. in Schumacher 399)

Ginsberg's poem reflects his own unresolved poetic dialectic, vividly apparent in "Howl" and "Kaddish," between an embrace of the world and the Gnostic rejection of it; he wishes, at once, to make a statement of protest and a statement of affirmation and human oneness. Later, Ginsberg embraced the theater of protest, trying to work through the problematics of protest as positive peace: "given the situation, the best kind of theater would manifest the Peace that we were protesting. Pro-test being 'pro-attestation,' testimony in favor of something" (qtd. in Schumacher 453).[11]

By late 1967, poets and poetry readings had begun to cede to rock and roll and other more theatrical modes. This was due, in part, to the impression that poetry was too quiet, too solitary, too Staffordian, for a radical generation about to revolt. Writing about the poetry scene in San Francisco, Stephen Vincent argues that after 1967, "*to say that you were a poet was like assuming an unevolved, or reactionary position* . . . [and] was now considered too personal, too indulgent, and too divorced from collective callings" (italics his 33). Even if poetry in its traditional modes seemed passé, the poetics of resistance was fully engaged. Paralleling Ginsberg's dance between acceptance and rejection, this section from the leaflet that circulated prior to the Pentagon exorcism suggests the contradictory dance of resistance: "We are demanding that the pentacle of power once again be used to serve the interests of GOD manifest in the world as man. We are embarking on a motion which is millennial in scope. Let this day, October 21, 1967, mark the beginning of a suprapolitics. . . . By the act of reading this paper you are engaged in the Holy Ritual of Exorcism" (qtd. in Mailer 120–121).

The leaflet, alternately serious and clowning in tone, collages the grammar of political petitions ("we are demanding"), legal and political language ("embarking on a motion"), and religious rite ("GOD manifest in the world as man"). Norman Mailer's description of the march in *The Armies of the Night* underscores *the entire event as poetry* by peppering it with references to Allen Ginsberg and his reading of "Pentagon Exorcism" at the rally and to conversations with Robert Lowell, as both poets participated in the event. Finally, the leaflet proposes, as in a spell, that the very act of reading is constitutive of the process of exorcism.

In stark contrast to the carnivalesque hippie happening of the exorcism, but no less a theatrical symbolic action, the Catonsville Nine event ought to be understood both as an act of war resistance and of poetry, self-consciously *exscribing* (writing not in, but writing out) in the public sphere material symbols of the devastation of the war. On May 17, 1968, nine people, many of them priests and nuns, broke into the Selective Service draft office in Catonsville, Maryland, and burned draft files with homemade napalm; members had also conducted other such actions pouring blood over draft files. The visceral imagery replicates, in an uncanny way, the circular logic that underlay the infamous statement made by an American official during the war: we had to destroy the village in order to save it. Further, it moves war resistance from acts of legal political dissent (petitions, marches, and the like) to acts of civil disobedience and destruction of property. Destroying the draft records with napalm, suggests, on the one hand, a protective gesture to spare a young American from having to fight and perhaps die in an unjust war, and to protect those that soldier might kill. For Cargas, and for the Nine, the act was "a demonstration of love" (97). Still, that the resisters employed napalm also suggests, on the other hand, an aggressively self-inflicted destruction, an intimation of what the war itself could do to that young American. The fact that these men and women were part of the Church added to the dissonance of the symbolic event; in one famous photograph (fig. 2), Father Philip Berrigan holds what looks like the small shreds of draft papers with two hands in the gesture of Eucharistic transubstantiation—as if those pieces of paper were the body of Christ. What would it mean, indeed, to burn the Eucharist?

The written statement—itself a poetics of the demonstration—that Father Daniel Berrigan (Philip's brother and noted poet) read during the burning emphasizes the tonal doubleness of the act and employs poetic alliteration, rhyme, and phrasal repetition to underscore the poetry of the act: "our apologies, good friends, for the fracture of good order, the burning of paper instead of children, the angering of the orderlies in the front parlor of the charnel house" ("A Meditation" unpaginated). We cannot help but reread the "good friends" as a kind of bitter sarcasm, when we get to the description of the draft law (and the war, for that matter) as "good order." Unless, of course, this poem primarily addresses other war resisters and not "the orderlies" themselves working at the draft office. Though what follows this poetry is a religiously inflected call to end the war, to recognize the universal family of humankind and to "redeem the times," this moment in the statement embodies the simultaneity of anger and serenity, of humor and earnestness, of arrogance and humility, which constitutes the poetics of war resistance. Finally, the act itself parallels the Pentagon exorcism and Ginsberg's "Wichita Vortex Sutra," as each of these three poetic acts—in their own ways—declare the end of the war. For Berrigan, in the act, "we have chosen to say, with gift of our liberty, if necessary our lives: the violence stops here, the suppression of truth stops here, this war stops here" ("Meditation"). These language-events in themselves do not (and cannot) end the war, but they are powerful performative acts that demonstrate not only how language can enact resistance but also how resistance is always already a kind of language.

Finally, the Vietnam Veterans against the War—a group cofounded by poet Jan Barry—engaged in a number of symbolic actions that dramatized the inescapability of the conflict on the homefront. In 1970, Operation RAW (Rapid American Withdrawal), a set of guerrilla theater actions between Morristown, New Jersey, and Valley Forge, Pennsylvania (which thus reenacted one of the battle routes of Washington during the Revolutionary War), was "designed to dramatize the war by simulating actual combat conditions" (Nicosia 56). In 1971, the Winter Soldier Investigation hearings, in which soldiers testified to war crimes committed by themselves and other U.S. military, attempted to circumvent the media silence around U.S. conduct in the war by bringing first-person testimony directly to mass media. Later, Operation Peace on Earth involved fifteen VVAW barricading themselves inside the Statue of Liberty and flying the American flag upside down, a signal of distress. Finally, the 1971 Dewey Canyon III action—named after the illegal incursions of the U.S. military into Laos, in which wounded GIs were abandoned so that the media would not know about the attacks—involved a weeklong protest in Washington DC, culminated by the now iconic images of veterans throwing their military service medals over the barbed wire fence surrounding Congress.

Ultimately, the poets who exscribe the language of resistance into the homefront cannot control the representations of these events in mass media; however, insofar as resisters become self-conscious of their own employment of event-language and language in events, they at least can change the terms through their self-representation. The historical trajectory of the relationship between resisters employing symbolic actions and the media who cover them, at least according to Gitlin's research on media and the New Left, suggests that the danger of the dramatistic is that, in order to court media attention, more and more extreme actions would be required to gain the same media interest. Perhaps the Catonsville Nine action, the VVAW guerrilla actions, and those of the more violent Weather Underground exemplify this dilemma.[12] This presupposition, however, rests on the notion that symbolic actions themselves are aimed at and through media coverage and not at, as Duncan proposed, creating an act which stands alone, testifies to another way of human relation. In other words, despite Duncan's apparent victory over Levertov in the poetry wars, his privileging of unmediated poetry seems oddly disconnected from the spectacle society in which resisters found themselves.[13] In order to reconstruct a poetry that witnesses — that is, as both testimonial and specular embodiment — we must look to the poems of this period.

Imaging the War

All poets, not just war resister poets such as Denise Levertov, struggled against their distance from Vietnam; this distance was geographical, but it was also cultural, historical, and linguistic. In *Backfire*, Loren Baritz recounts how the tendency of Vietnamese men to hold hands in public disgusted many American GIs and led them to wonder why they were fighting "in defense of perverts" (22). In one instance:

A marine's truck was stopped by South Vietnamese soldiers who wanted the Americans to take a South Vietnamese soldier to a hospital. His leg had been shot off. One of the marines said, "Fuck him. Let him hop." But the commander of the truck told the wounded man to climb in. "The fucking little slope grabbed my leg." The truck commander said that he had been in Vietnam long enough "to know that most of them are queer. They hold hands and stuff." One of the Americans "wacked" the wounded soldier and told the driver to get going. They threw the wounded man out of the moving truck: "The poor fucking bastard was screaming and crying and begging us. 'Fuck you, you slope. Out you go.'" (23)

The inability of these American soldiers to understand their South Vietnamese allies emerges against a broader backdrop of a U.S. foreign policy in Vietnam that acknowledged only those elements in South Vietnam that reflected its own interests. The incident above, therefore, might be read not simply as a soldier's cultural intolerance but as a symptom of a broader gap between American policy and Vietnamese reality, and in a war that was "conducted in such a way as to ensure the separation between most American soldiers and most Vietnamese" (Christopher 2).

Yet, the soldier's experience continues to dominate the literature emerging from the Vietnam War. Jeffrey Walsh has noted how the dominant poetic viewpoint espoused "is that of the soldier whose poems recall the time he spent in occupied Vietnam" (141), often moving along the dramatic arc of a coming-of-age narrative. Vietnam War soldier-poets "suffered an ethical disorientation related to the ideological confusion over the rights and wrongs of fighting the war" (142). At the same time, according to Walsh, because these poets lack a sense of historical consciousness, "the poets tend to rely upon a kind of committed experiential poetics which does not seem commensurate to the task of representing either the physical actualities of the conflict or the underlying moral and political values at issue" (142). Divided by language, history, culture, and ideology, even the most sympathetic pro-Vietnamese poets have tended to view the Vietnamese as "passive victims, as napalmed girls or strafed farmers" (143). Given the difficulty of even those soldier-poets who lived and fought in Vietnam, one might go so far as to argue that proximity itself might be as problematic as distance.

Just because poets may not have been close to the scene of battle, however, does not mean that they were distant from the war. On the contrary, the war constantly made its presence felt through mass media representations of battles abroad and at home. The war, increasingly, became inescapable as absent-presence in the cultural and political life of the nation; war resistance poets approached the problem of their own marginality from the battlescene by rendering visible again the invisible battle and its connections to the homefront through a number of different approaches. Broadly speaking, these approaches form a continuum of proximity, from (1) a visionary mode that relies on imaginative leaps; to (2) a documentary mode that employs found evidentiary materials to mediate between the imagined and the experiential; to (3) an experiential mode, for those whose proximity to Vietnam and to the war was physical and immediate; and finally to (4) acts of translation and cross-cultural collaboration, which offer the possibility of global solidarity against war.

VISIONARY POETRY

The visionary mode of poets such as Robert Bly, Robert Duncan, W. S. Merwin, and Adrienne Rich renders visible—through associative leaps, mythopoetic figures, surrealistic dream imagery, or the tropes of bodies, respectively—a war which for many Americans remained confined to televisual or journalistic frames (at least until soldiers returned, carrying the war with them, in stitches or wounds or latent in their cells). The imaginative work of poets employing a visionary mode, therefore, engaged in the cultural and political work of drawing out the implicit connections between American life and American citizens. While their strategies of rendering visible the latent differed dramatically, these poets contributed to the cultural project of bringing the war home.

Take, for example, how Bly's "The Teeth Mother Naked at Last" proposes an implicit and even logical relationship between American capitalism and the war in Vietnam:

It's because we have new packaging for smoked oysters that bomb holes
    appear in the rice paddies.

. . .

It's because taxpayers move to the suburbs that we transfer populations.
The Marines use cigarette lighters to light the thatched roof of huts
    because so many Americans own their own homes. (*Teeth Mother*
    14–15)

In these lines, a first readerly response might be that the poem operates through a profoundly illogical set of connections; however, a second—but equal—readerly response might be that the poem is too logical, too didactic in its critique of capitalism as essentially the engine for warmaking. In either case, Bly's poem employs the rhetorical structures of logic for contradictory ends. First, these syllogisms bring the Vietnam War and the American homefront into the same space and suggest that American prosperity somehow inexorably leads to devastation in Vietnam. Second, and in contrast to the first, the syllogisms themselves function in a way that appears perilously analogous to the rational argumentation used by the administration to argue for the importance of American involvement in Vietnam, and thus they force the reader to question the structures upon which Bly's argument relies. Whatever its limits as a poem, "The Teeth Mother" yokes together these two spaces and invites new ways of reading the intent and meaning of the American presence in Vietnam.

If Robert Bly sutures the space between America and Vietnam in a vision of American puritanic self-hatred and capitalistic expansion, Adrienne Rich dissolves the apparent distance by linking the violence of patriarchy at home to the war abroad. As Michael Bibby has shown, feminist, African American, and veteran poets mobilized the tropes and images of bodies to make connections between the Vietnam War and racial and gender oppression at home. In "Newsreel," Rich employs the televisual frame in a way that suggests the war abroad perilously resembles the war at home:

> This would not be the war we fought in. See, the foliage is heavier, there were no hills of that size there.

> But I find it impossible not to look for actual persons known to me and not seen since; impossible not to look for myself. . . .

> Somewhere my body goes taut under the deluge, somewhere I am naked behind the lines, washing my body in the water of that war. (*The Will to Change* 62)

This snippet from section nine of this serial poem dramatizes the collapse of the boundary between the place over there and the one right here; even though the speaker asserts some lack of resemblance, we are not sure if she is looking at a newsreel of Vietnam or one of America. The deictics "here" and "there" are impossible to map as different. Further, the speaker finds herself at first overwhelmed by a flood (probably the flood of images of war), but then later—like Lady MacBeth—she washes herself *in* those images. In other words, her life and her body are inextricably connected to the war. Likewise, Sharon Olds's "May 1968"—though written in the mid-1990s—demonstrates how resisters placed themselves—and their future children—at risk in acts of physical obstruction and occupation of buildings; Olds juxtaposes the overbearing power of the mounted police to her own vulnerable, newly pregnant body prone on the street, as she and other students refused to give up their ground, literally and figuratively. This is the cultural work of visionary war resistance poetry: to render through poetic language the essentially inescapable relationship between the nation's war and the physical and psychic distance of the civilian at the homefront.

DOCUPOETRY

While some poets made the war visible through visionary modes, others adopted docupoetry, a poetry that documents events (whether battles in Saigon or demonstrations in Washington) and employs evidentiary texts (whether government records or oral testimony) to challenge, deconstruct, or simply lay bare the dominant narrative promulgated through journalistic media, which typically stayed within the bounds of legitimate controversy and often distorted war resistance. If, in Gitlin's words, "the people *as producers of meaning* have no voice in what the media make of what they say or do" (WWW 3), then docupoetry functioned as a producer of meaning, an "alternative media." Radical poets from the 1930s, such as Muriel Rukeyser—one of the great visionary poets of war resistance—saw poetry both as a medium to "extend the document" (qtd. in Davidson GD 135) and as a mode which could "participate . . . directly in the writing of history by exposing the institutional venues through which history is written" (Davidson GD 139) while incorporating voices that those institutional venues would routinely ignore.

Daniel Berrigan's *The Trial of the Catonsville Nine*, a drama taken from the transcripts of the legal proceedings against the Catonsville Nine, crosses genres into poetry, hearkening back to the Greek choral mode. Berrigan's version has those involved in the legal proceedings speaking prose, while the Nine— who give witness by telling the stories that led them to this act—speak in poetic lines. Berrigan uses poetry as an authorizing discourse; poetry, in his usage, is a mode of speaking the truth to power, a prophetic utterance of those whose lives witness to something beyond the dramatic form. Yet, the language is so plain and unadorned, it functions as prophecy and documentary, visionary and eyewitness. The words of the defendants trace their experiences of radicalization that led up to their act. And that is the defense's only tactic—to allow the Nine to tell their stories, in order that the judge and jury witness the reasons for committing their act of civil disobedience. All of the Nine, through their religious or service vocations, had traumatizing experiences of witnessing gut-wrenching poverty in ghettos and in the Third World. Berrigan's adoption of the poetic line imbues the Nine with a lyric authority that their metaphorical language and honesty already suggests. Take, for example, the following, in which Berrigan recounts how the image of the burned draft files brought to mind a memory from his trip to Hanoi:

When the burned draft files
were brought into court yesterday
as evidence

I could not but recall
that I had seen in Hanoi
evidence of a very different nature
I saw not boxes of burned papers
I saw parts of human bodies preserved in alcohol
the bodies of children   the hearts and organs and limbs
of women (89)

Like the visionary poets, then, docupoets like Berrigan make visible and evident what they see as the true atrocity of the war. Simply on the level of form,
Berrigan's choice suggests that these activists are essentially poets, speaking
their truth to prosaic power. Such an employment of poetry in this way no
doubt suggests a Romantic distinction between the poet (resisters) and the society (the legal system). For J. W. Fenn, the lacunae in the text function as "the
defendants' individual spiritual freedom as opposed to the rigid structure and
organization, in both a legalistic and a linguistic sense, of an authoritarian society" (76). More than marking merely the freedom of the Nine, the lacunae
also suggest the unspeakability of their traumatizing witness—both what they
have witnessed and what their act itself constitutes. In this way, the poetic line
and its lacunae also reflect the painful schism that the Nine and other war resisters felt between themselves and their society.

Other poets, such as Allen Ginsberg and John Balaban, inheriting William
Carlos Williams's own version of materialist modernism, extended the lyric
poem into a docupoem where one might not simply "get the news" but become a medium through which the news from mass media could be revealed
as part of the noise of language that obfuscated about the war. Ginsberg's "Wichita Vortex Sutra," a poetic jaunt through mid-1960s America, threads descriptive imagery of Kansas, mass media news and advertisements, and
prophetic utterances; Ginsberg bridges the vortex, the infinite, from Wichita
(the West) to Sutra (the East), in yet another leap between American life and
the Vietnam War. Composed on a reel-to-reel tape given to him by Bob Dylan, Ginsberg's "auto poesy" foregrounds the contamination of language:

McNamara made a "bad guess"
"Bad Guess?" chorused the Reporters.
Yes, not more than a Bad Guess, in 1962
"8000 American Troops handle the
Situation"
Bad Guess (398)

More than mere bad guessing, political and economic forces threaten to drown the poet's own voice, in the swirl of headlines and language:

Put it this way on the radio
Put it this way in television language
           Use the words
                language, language:
                    "A bad guess"

Put it this way in headlines
    Omaha World Herald—   *Rusk Says Toughness*
                             Essential for Peace (399)

Ginsberg thus foregrounds the paralyzing force of language—language that anesthetizes feeling, language that blocks identification and understanding— by documenting it and then by attempting to dispel that very force through the use of prophetic speech. That he *discovers* the poem by "writing-through" as he listened back to the taped version suggests how poetry becomes not simply a way of writing but a way of listening, through mediating technologies, through to some organizing self-utterance.

Unlike Ginsberg's use of omnipresent mediaspeak to critique the abstractions of the war, Balaban employs less accessible texts in "The Gardenia in the Moon." Interspersing reports from the International Volunteer Services (the organization with which Balaban worked as a conscientious objector to the war in 1967), Balaban creates a documentary lyric that elegizes the life of David Lane Gitelson, an American friend who had entered completely into Vietnamese peasant society, and who Balaban believed at the time may have been killed. Balaban's use of prose points to the insufficiency of lyric to document the secret history of the war, to educate and inform. The covert nature of what he wishes to narrate forces him to use official IVS reports, in order to substantiate—even authorize—the unwritten history of U.S. counterterrorism.

"Gardenia" juxtaposes the lyric with the historical, the poetic with the prosaic, to create a poem at odds with its own impulses to elegize or to blame, alternating between prose sections of IVS memoranda that detail Dave Gitelson's work with Vietnamese peasants victimized by U.S. and North Vietnamese bombing missions and poetry sections that articulate a lyric identity transfixed by the collage of beauty and ugliness in Vietnam. The poem begins in Pennsylvania, where the speaker gazes at the moon, and cinematically jumpcuts from the Pennsylvania moon to the lunar landing, to pornographic filmmaking, to the jungles of Southeast Asia: "Men had landed on the moon. / As men shot dirty films in dirty motel rooms, / Guerrillas sucked cold rice and fish" (AOW 26). The dizzying leaps of movement heighten the sense of dislocation of a speaker, living, as it were, in multiple places simultaneously but at home in none of them. The juxtaposition between American techno-logical achievement—encapsulated artfully in the sweep from the lunar land-ing to pornography—and Vietnamese revolutionary asceticism captures the distance between the realities of American and Vietnamese culture. It also an-ticipates the paranoiac Captain Willard of *Apocalypse Now* (1979), who feels himself withering in the city while "every minute Charlie squats in the bush he gets stronger." But here, the poet negotiates distance in order to remember the loss of his friend Dave Gitelson, whom he recalls as if in flashback: "In a puddle's moon eye I saw a shape: / A machine gun was cracking like slapping sticks, / A yelling man smacked into the smooth canal" (AOW 26).

The first prose section, Gitelson's report on treating fruit tree disease and "possible ways to reduce civilian war casualties" (AOW 27), establishes how Gitelson's involvement with the Vietnamese peasantry conflicted with a pol-icy of free-fire zones, which defined anyone caught in that area as enemy Vi-etcong. Gitelson, instead, gave voice to the peasants' desire that they should be warned before a free-fire zone was hit. The policy of "free-fire zones" ex-emplified the U.S. refusal to distinguish between civilians and guerrillas, and was part of the larger Technowar. As mentioned above, the quest to produce the results requested by the military establishment encouraged U.S. forces to count civilian casualties as Vietcong casualties. Gitelson's advocacy for the peasants represented a complication to the numbers game.

But instead of simply allying himself with Gitelson's heroism, Balaban fol-lows this first prose section with "A Cyclo Ride to Town," which implicates the poet as a privileged American. As he takes a ride into town, he characterizes the Vietnamese with animal metaphors; his cyclo driver "hoots," his head "bobbles / on a rooster's neck," as he and his cyclo driver pass "fishermen, / anonymous as jellyfish tracing the shore" (AOW 28). Later, they come upon a crowd "gawking at the farmer hauled in like a pig: / riddled dead, blood-splotched, trussed to a pole" (AOW 28). But they don't stop until they reach what was the French governor's colonial mansion, where the Americans now hold court:

The gate guard salutes, then grins with history
as an American strides the pebbled walkway

to the garden at the rear of the elegant house,
whose formal paths, boxwoods, flower beds
—laid in helplessly exact geometry—
have been tank-tracked by the armored unit
bivouacked beneath the high, threshing palms. (AOW 28)

Balaban's self-distancing—as "an American," rather than "I"—exacerbates
the poem's feeling of dislocation, as if he looks upon this figure from the time
and distance of Pennsylvania some years later.

In the fourth section of the poem, another Gitelson report further documents the civilian casualties, the aftermath of attacks, and the absolute unconcern shown to the survivors. For Gitelson, "perhaps the essence of the matter
is that the Vietnamese and American military don't feel that any mistake has
been made" (AOW 32). The peasants, according to one American official, are
"just so much foliage to shoot through" (AOW 32). After another short lyric, a
final IVS report from Dan Whitfield to Roger Montgomery details the strange
circumstances surrounding Gitelson's death, which Balaban returns to in his
memoir. According to Whitfield, Gitelson "was onto something that was extremely sensitive . . ." (AOW 36). A message Gitelson delivered to a CORDS
(Combined Operations Revolutionary Development Services) operative to be
handed to a visiting Senator Kennedy never reached the senator's hands.
Though this poem does not explicitly mention it, Balaban later suggests that
Gitelson's advocacy of the Vietnamese peasants and his documentation of the
increasing civilian casualties experienced in remote villages may have led
him to be an early casualty of the CIA's covert Operation Phoenix. Under Operation Phoenix, the CIA carried out a vicious program of counterterrorism in
Vietnam, whereby, according to Howard Zinn, operatives "secretly, without
trial, executed at least twenty thousand civilians in South Vietnam who were
suspected of being members of the Communist underground" (468).

By incorporating Gitelson's documentation into the poem's structure, the
poem attempts both to pass on Gitelson's work and to implicate the speaker
in the broader culture of war. Moreover, by using Gitelson's words, Balaban
becomes a medium through which his dead friend can speak. But as the poem
ends, Balaban asks himself: "Am I a Christer and your corpse-monger? Dead,
I am your father, brother. Dead, we are your son" (AOW 37). In his revision
of the poem, however, he changes the "and" to an "or," thus accentuating the
difference between the Christian "resurrection" of his friend and the more
morbid option that he simply obsesses over, or even sells—the original
meaning of "monger"—the corpse (*Locusts* 26). In Balaban's poem, then,

the elegiac and the documentary mutually sustain a narrative of loss that retains political meaning and functions as evidence of the unseen but nonetheless real human costs of war.

FIRST PERSON WITNESS

Though few American poets ever visited Vietnam, Balaban's unique position as an objector serving his time in Vietnam enabled him a proximity to Vietnamese people and culture that the antiwar movement increasingly fantasized about, one that allowed Balaban to be less susceptible to representing the war as one simply of American brutality or Vietnamese liberation; moreover, it forced the poet to recognize his own implication in the war. Paradoxically, then, Balaban's distance from the United States did not produce an alienated lyric poetry but rather one that continues the address of CO poets of the Second World War. Balaban's writing provides an antidote both to the traditional *war story* narrative, told from the soldier's perspective, and to the antiwar narrative that Levertov constructs. At the same time, perhaps because Balaban did not have deep affiliations with the antiwar movement, he came to rely on a poetics of elegy that situates him in a humanist tradition; that perspective leads to a lyric subjectivity at times paralyzed by a telescopic view of history that renders political agency as ineffectual.

More than providing "a distinctly original sense of experiential perspective" (Beidler 47), Balaban's poems approach the war literally and metaphorically from a distinct terrain. In *Remembering Heaven's Face: A Moral Witness in Vietnam* (1991), Balaban recounts opting for alternative service as a conscientious objector in Vietnam, first teaching linguistics for International Voluntary Services (IVS) and later working with the Committee of Responsibility to Save War-Burned and War-Injured Children (COR). He gained a working knowledge of Vietnamese language, which aided a third trip to Vietnam on a fellowship, in which he gathered and translated Vietnamese poetry, particularly the Vietnamese folk poems known as *ca dao*.

Because he had to negotiate his own Americanness amidst the war and the contradictions of alternative service, he always perceived his own implicatedness as an American in the conflict in a broader historical perspective than the one offered typically by the experientially heavy accounts of soldiers and the image-heavy accounts of antiwar poets. The opening of his memoir recalls his first time walking around Vietnam without guidance: "I was seeing the place for the first time without American intermediaries. For the first time since leaving the United States three weeks earlier, I felt I was really in Vietnam" (*RHF* 15–16). While such a moment echoes typical narratives, when the Westerner first traverses the boundary between his quarters and "Indian country," as the GIs often called Vietnam, what follows breaks the pattern. Rather than "passing" as native, Balaban bumbles into a hostile village and gets captured by the Vietcong. He can barely communicate with them, but they decide to release him after a short debate. Balaban tells no one, and a couple of days later two marines are killed outside that village. He wonders: "How did they have the nerve to release me? How could they know that I would not report the incident? Had I become a part of the ambush. . . . How was I not a part of this war?" (*RHF* 26). Balaban's sense of his own implication in the war, of the contradictions of witness, counter the sense of moral superiority that mars some resister accounts.

The complexities of his moral witness are not limited to his contacts with Vietnamese; they extend to his relations with fellow Americans. He befriends a CIA operative, a man who cannot discuss his work but nonetheless seeks out Balaban's friendship. Another friend, the drug-abusing Erhart, who says he wanted nothing to do with what he called the "burned baby business," ends up "leaking the actual construction plans [for the infamous tiger cages used by the South Vietnamese as a mode of torturing prisoners of war]" while he was working for that company (*RHF* 231–232). Outside a bank in Hawaii, Balaban gets between a man and his girlfriend whom he is abusing; Balaban beats the man until he almost dies; he later would wonder how he could "*take pleasure—take power*—from letting [the boyfriend] know that just as I did it?" (*RHF* 224).

Even his work as a CO, in both the IVS and COR, offers its own contradictions. IVS, it became increasingly clear, was "more politically important than any of us had guessed. Though volunteers might effect good work on behalf of individual Vietnamese and their families, our real force was in propaganda" (*RHF* 69). A representative for the National Liberation Front (what the Americans and South Vietnamese called the Vietcong) suggested that "by doing good works, you are doing wrong, for you confuse the people about the aim of the American imperialists" (*RHF* 69). Regarding his work with COR, Balaban recalls how his radical friends accused him and the IVS of "creating a cruel, war-perpetuating illusion of American concern and responsibility . . . [and] helping to save these kids' lives only to corrupt them culturally in the United States and so make it impossible for them to live happily in Vietnam again" (*RHF* 189). Though he came to believe his work with COR had been worthwhile, he does not absent himself from his vexed position as an American war resister.

Balaban's poetry demonstrates a keen awareness of the vexed problems of war resistance writing, in particular of address, of (geographical, historical, and linguistic) distance, and of the generic regulations of war writing. All his writing about the war—from his first chapbook *Vietnam Poems* (1970) to *After Our War* (1974) and more recently, *Locusts at the Edge of Summer: New and Selected Poems* (1997)—consistently avoids the tunnel-vision focus on the war and its casualties; instead, Balaban asks us to confront our expectations of war resistance poems because he refuses to write simply about the war. In doing so, Balaban's Vietnam poems refuse to elide "Vietnam" with "war"—an elision typical in American literature and film. Perhaps because of Balaban's work in Vietnam, his first full-length collection, *After Our War* (1974), avoids the conventional limitations of both soldier and antiwar accounts. By turning away from the narrow experiential lens of the war story, focused through the eyes of a GI, and the broad rhetorical critique of war provided by the antiwar poem, Balaban's poems repudiate an image of Vietnam as simplistic cipher of Communist savagery or of American imperialism. Instead, the poems work by emphasizing the poet's personal relationships (elegizing or honoring particular lives) and recording the human and natural life along the rivers where the poet lived.

The poems about Vietnam demonstrate that Balaban's approach to writing the war is to address, give tribute to, or elegize Vietnam and the Vietnamese that he knew while working there. In fact, eight poems from his first collection explicitly address residents of Vietnam, both Vietnamese and American. In contrast to Levertov's Vietnam poems, Balaban's move beyond the impulse to witness—whereby the one witnessed is frequently reduced to an object of pain—into the impulse to speak to or elegize. The war, always present in the background and occasionally breaking through the surfaces of the poems, becomes the matrix in which the people try to survive. It is as if writing to friends in Vietnam enables the poet to contain or at least fend off the surrounding unnarratable violence. The war does appear, but it is not allowed the last word. This does not mean his poems deliver Vietnamese life absent of American perspective, but the poems demonstrate a consciousness aware of the limitations of its own perspective. In "Along the Mekong," for example, Balaban begins the poem by juxtaposing the tropical river and the cover of the *New Yorker* magazine that he is reading:

Near mud-tide mangrove swamps, under the drilling sun,
the glossy cover, styled green print, struck the eye:
trumpet-burst yellow blossoms, grapevine leaves,
—nasturtiums or pumpkin flowers? They twined
in tangles by our cottage in Pennsylvania. (AOW 12)

On one level, the magazine's cover, artfully twining native American flowers, reminds Balaban of home; on another level, the cover's artifice of nature
also points to the interplay of human technologies and the natural world. Yet
surfaces—even natural surfaces like the river—don't reveal their hidden poisons immediately. In fact, the magazine contains an article about the hidden
devastation of the war, even in the river over which he glides: "2, 4, 5-T, ter-
atogenicity in births; / South Vietnam 1 / 7th defoliated; residue / in rivers,
foods, and mother's milk" (AOW 12). The chemical poisoning, a result of
American military use of defoliants, now infiltrates the very sources of life.
Though he cannot prove that the chemicals have caused the birth defects of
"hare-lipped, tusk-toothed children" that the poet "usher[s] to surgery in
Saigon," he wonders:

> what did they drink
> that I have drunk? What dioxin, picloram, arsenic
> have knitted in my cells, in my wife now carrying
> our first child. (AOW 12)

Balaban's status as an American allows him access to information and hospitals; it does not spare him from sharing in the common fate to thirst and thus
consume poisons.

The poem persists for two more sections, "River Market" and "Waiting for
a Boat to Cross Back," and thus undermines the dread of war and its hidden
casualties (the constricted apocalyptic vision of the conflict offered by the
American narrative) in favor of a tentative vision of survival. In "River Market," food detail piles upon detail, as the market's cornucopia of sights and
smells overwhelms, causes him to exclaim "why, a reporter, or a cook, could
write this poem / if he had learned dictation" (AOW 12). The carnage of the
food, "all this blood fleck," itself contains the violence of war and yet also "glit-
tery scales, fine white grains, fast talk, / gut grime, crab claws, bright light,
sweetest smells," mirroring "a human self" in all its contradictions (AOW
12–13). In the final section, the poet observes the market gossip and the pos-
turing of turkey cocks. Still, the violence of human and animal interactions
does not provide the last word. As in Lowell's "Skunk Hour," where the poet
watches resourceful skunks plunder a trashcan, here the poet finds a dog
"mottled with a grease-paint grin / [who] laps up fish scales and red, saw-
toothed gills / gutted from panfish at the river's edge" (AOW 13). Thus, Balaban concludes the poem with an image of a survivor, a "mottled cur" lapping
from the remains, rather than with a casualty of war.

Other poems attempt to articulate how the war separates people both from each other and from their customs. In "Mau Than," Balaban addresses To Lai Chanh, a fellow instructor at the university with whom the poet once traded language lessons. Chanh, a silenced dissident who disappeared as popular resistance to Thieu increased in South Vietnam (*RHF* 65–68), becomes the absent addressee for the poet. Following in the Vietnamese tradition of writing an occasional poem on Tet to celebrate the coming of a New Year, Balaban's poem remembers the past year and then looks forward. However, the poem cannot simply celebrate the occasion; at every turn, the poem dramatizes the failure of Balaban and Chanh to enact the traditional occasion as a result of the increasing conflict around them. Written in slant-rhymed couplets (echoing Wilfred Owen), the first section places the poet on his friend's doorstep, unable to enter. Chanh has since been drafted, and his formerly manicured garden "is now / stony, dry, and wanting a trowel" (*LES* 14). The year itself, anthropomorphized, has not simply passed on peacefully, but rather has been brutalized. The poem begins,

> the Old Man that was last year
> has had his teeth kicked in; in tears
> he spat back blood and bone, and died. (*LES* 14)

After the deformed formalism of the first section, rendered on the poetic level by the slant-rhymed couplets, the next three sections move into an Anglo-Saxon alliterative line characteristic of Balaban's early poems.

Balaban's conversation with Chanh asserts their connection to each other and his distance from how other Americans experience Vietnam. The poet describes the past year as one "of barbarities / each heaped on the other like stones / on a man stoned to death. One counts the ears on the GI's belt" (*LES* 14). The GI's war trophies become a kind of perverse way of marking time, and typify the distance between Balaban and other Americans. Balaban wonders to his friend, in another instance, how Americans

> could snap flash photos of the girl whose
> vagina was gouged out by mortar fragments?
> One day we followed in a cortege
> of mourners, among the mourners, slowly walking,
> hearing the clop of the monk's walking stick. (*LES* 15)

Balaban's juxtaposition between the two scenes speaks to his solidarity with Chanh, walking "among the mourners" and his distance from the Americans photographing the mutilated genitals of a Vietnamese girl. The juxtaposition also underscores a preference for the verbal and auditory over the visual and specular, and points back to the ears on the GI's belt. Still, even though he situates himself within the mourning ritual, the juxtaposition implicates Balaban as witness to both events.

If the poem were to end here, it might exemplify the failure of American antiwar verse to overcome the excesses of its own violent imagery. Over the next two sections, however, "Mau Than" undermines that violence by providing an alternative vision of continued existence. The third section describes a man and women fishing in the rain. The river, both in Levertov's "In Thai Binh (Peace) Province" and throughout Balaban's poems, provides another trope of time passing, one which, while not exempt from the war's devastation, offers an alternative to counting ears on a GI's belt. In other words, "If there were peace, this river would be / a peaceful place" (*LES* 15). The final section marks his own journey, as the war escalates, from Vietnam to "safe haven" in Japan. After a climb of Mt. Hiei in which Balaban experiences "Moses meeting God in the clouds," Balaban pronounces his reason for returning to Vietnam: "Friend / I am back to gather the blood in a cup" (*LES* 16). The humble cup is a perfect microcosm of Balaban's poetics, one that doggedly asserts the particular human costs of the Vietnam conflict and his attempt to assuage those wounds.

Thus, *After Our War* always places Vietnam and America in communication, juxtaposing poems set in each land against one another. Organized thematically rather than chronologically, the book's structure emphasizes the relatedness rather than the separateness of the two worlds, referred to in GI parlance as "The World" (America) and "Indian Country" (Vietnam). The Vietnam War is a constant thread in the poems, but not the *raison d'etre* of the book. Contrasted with the apocalyptic poems about the war written by war resisters, Balaban's poems maintain a more level, even sane tone, balancing the human suffering in war with a sense of the survival of people and the land; the emphasis on Vietnamese life—its fishing and rice industries, its weather, its daily and seasonal rhythms—renders the war (and hence, the American metanarrative of events) less vital.

TRANSLATION AND CROSS-CULTURAL COLLABORATION

In *After Our War*, Balaban also moves beyond the limits of his own voice and perspective by interspersing his translations of Vietnamese folk poems, as if his own voice were not enough to speak of "our" war. By translating, and including translations among his own poems, Balaban enacts a conversation between cultures, and his voice becomes a conduit not merely for his own impressions and experience but for Vietnamese culture and experience as well. The act of translation is itself an act of war resistance, according to Balaban, for "the best thing I could do now to help stop the war was gather the poetry made by ordinary folk in Vietnam and bring it before Americans. However insignificant this effort might be, the more human Vietnamese seemed to Americans, the harder it might be to slaughter them" (AOW 225).[14]

Translation itself can be an act of war resistance, particularly insofar as it renders the other more human. In addition, cross-cultural translations, collaborative acts of poetic cocreation, demonstrate the possibilities of extending solidarity beyond national boundaries. Wendy Sue Larsen and Tran Thi Nga collaborated on *Shallow Graves: Two Women and Vietnam* (1986), a novel-in-verse that alternates the autobiographical poetic narratives of the two authors; Larsen, an American expatriate living in Vietnam during the war, and Nga, a Vietnamese social worker who would later escape as a refugee to the United States, braid their stories in ways that suggest first the abyss between their experiences, and then slowly, the subtle similarities, as each negotiates the minefields of life at war. Though some might criticize that Larsen's admittedly more touristic experience of war gets as much space as Nga's, by juxtaposing them so precisely, we can read the differential experiences of Americans and Vietnamese more clearly—thus avoiding the pitfall of effacing too quickly the differences between the war at home for Americans and the war at home for Vietnamese.

Thus, American war resistance poets during the Vietnam War employed a number of strategies in order to render visible the distant war. Far from limiting themselves to the individual and individualized page-bound lyric, these poets collaborated to create multivocal works in anthologies and other print publications, in reading halls and in demonstrations. Their work—visionary, documentary, eyewitness, and translation—contributed to the project of war resistance to bring the war home, by concretizing the abstract and bureaucratic language of official sources through counternarratives, images, and linguistic play in ways that created afterimages as powerful as the photographs that would begin to alter public opinion about the justness of the war. Perhaps because these works also demonstrate the limits of war resistance argument during the period—a reliance on didacticism, a tendency to work from outrage against authority, a romantic idealization of and identification with the revolutionary North Vietnamese—they constitute an essential resource for war resisters to come to terms with its past epistemological frames, ideological investments, and rhetorical aims, in order to reimagine its possible futures.

5. Denise Levertov's Distant Witness

THE POLITICS OF IDENTIFICATION

I wanted (& want) to keep my participation in the Peace Movement (minimal
though it is) in a real relation to my feelings.
—QTD. IN BERTHOLF AND GELPI 532

"Tell Denise to wear a helmet," Joe Dunn wrote from Boston: "she's our Joan of
Arc and we can't afford to lose her."... Denise Levertov has put her
life over there on the picket line.
—QTD. IN BERTHOLF, "Duncan's Notebooks" 43: September 21, 1971

Perhaps no poet during the Vietnam War era experienced as steep a
rise to notoriety, and then such a precipitous fall from critical grace, as Denise
Levertov. Levertov, the most persistent and voluminous poetic documenter of
war resistance during the Vietnam era, may owe this turn of fortunes to the
way in which her poetry relied so heavily on the specularity of postromantic
lyric, and how such specularity incites the processes of *identification* and
disidentification.[1] Identification, after all, inheres in the lyric poetic process—
in terms of the production and reception of the lyric I, the metaphorization
of self and other, and the representation of the other as potential locus of readerly identification. Because her antiwar poetry felt its allegiances so strongly
with the Vietnamese victims of war and with the American antiwar movement, and concomitantly, against the U.S. government, military, and silent
majority, Levertov occasionally lost sight of how a lyric resistance poetry—
whose strength we have seen in the CO poetry from the Second World War—
courts blinding self-righteousness. In particular, Levertov had to confront how
the imagination of the other can also lead to the erasure of that other; and further, how a dialectic of lyric address, negotiating between addressing those
who share one's (political) vision and those who do not, might offer an opportunity that addressing the converted alone might not. The critical response to
her war resistance poetry, however, ought to be seen not only as an aesthetic

or political critique of the poems but also as a critique of the dangers of identificatory poetics and the lyricized politics of the New Left: how a poetry (and a politics) generated from and working through identification frequently blinds itself to its own libidinal investment in the drama of the lyric self. What the critical consensus regarding Levertov's Vietnam War–era resistance poetry has overlooked is how Levertov herself gradually adjusted her poetic attentions and strategies of identification, and how these shifts parallel the shifts in the war resistance ideology of the time—from a politics based on dissent to one based (however fallibly) on revolution. Beyond the two modes—what we might term, after Gitlin, "years of hope" and "days of rage"—Levertov makes subsequent poetic moves to rethink and recreate a new resistance vision, based on nonviolent witness.

In this chapter, I trace the complex dynamics of identification in Levertov's war resistance poetry as they relate to the politics of the movement, and how those identifications alter fundamentally how and for whom Levertov deploys her poetic address. I mark how four distinct stages of identification dramatized in Levertov's war resistance poetry may even instigate Levertov's gradual shifts in poetic address, from the nation at large to the resistance movement itself, and then out again; these shifts suggest the poet's increasing self-awareness about the dangers of writing through identification rather than staging identification through writing. Still, because Levertov began as a poet of immediate experience who had relied on a mystical celebration of a palpable and harmonious world, her poetry of war resistance succeeded most often when she focused on those immediate experiences. It was in the mirror of the war resistance movement that Levertov saw her poetic project take on political valences; she identified with it and became identified with it, and became one of its most exemplary chroniclers.

Four Ways of Looking at Disaster

Levertov provides a paradigmatic case for the representative war resister poet during the Vietnam War, because her poetry and its identifications so closely parallel the antiwar movement's identifications with the Vietnamese. The perils of identification were strong during the Vietnam War, in part because of Vietnam's geographical and cultural distance. For the Students for a Democratic Society (SDS) and the New Left, this identification began with Paul Potter's famous speech about the Vietnam War in 1965, in which he called for activists to "name the system" of oppression at work in Vietnam and in Mississippi; for Todd Gitlin, "Vietnam was a screen onto which [Potter] projected the New Left's political culture, its struggle for self-definition against managerial power" (*Sixties* 185). The notion that oppression at home and abroad were the same—and that there could be one revolution that spanned both—was a dangerous logic that potentially effaced the differences between Vietnam and the United States. Privately, Potter worried about "a situation in which the movement of people in SDS depends on their identification with movements outside of the country which they cannot participate in or develop through" (qtd. in *Sixties* 189). Finally, moreover, the late sixties brought a shift in the antiwar movement's affiliations from "sympathy for slaughtered Vietnamese to identification with powerful Vietnamese whose victory would surely come" (*Sixties* 248). This shift is clearly registered in Levertov's poetry—the movement from dissent to resistance. Levertov's close connections with the movement make examining her poetry an act of cultural excavation of the antiwar movement during the late 1960s as much as an act of poetic analysis.

In each of four poetic stages, then, Levertov struggled to create a war resistance poetry that represented the war abroad and the war at home in ways that would incite dissent and cultivate resistance. First, Levertov's early antiwar poems from *The Sorrow Dance* evoked the Vietnam War primarily through graphic images of atrocity and portentous warnings, as she addressed the nation in the first person plural; the poet's identifications with Vietnamese suffering often led her to represent only destroyed bodies. In an unsettling way, the poet reenacted the killing of the Vietnamese in poems such as "What Were They Like?" and "Life at War." Second, the poet underwent a crisis of poetics and turned to the "notebook" mode of representing war resistance. Instead of focusing on representing the Vietnamese, she turned her identifications toward the Berkeley student movement, compelling her to write beyond the lyric I into the lyric we representing the radical movement, thus narrowing her address to the resistance itself. Third, as a result of Levertov's trip to Hanoi, the poet became a witness, and her identifications "unfroze." This unfreezing, or "identification with a difference," like Kaja Silverman's notion of "excorporative identification," moves beyond idealization of the other and acknowledges, rather than attempting to assimilate, the embodied other. Fourth, I suggest how in poems responding to the Gulf War, Levertov circumvents the pull of identification itself by focusing on marking the absence of the Iraqi in the national narrative of the war promulgated by mass media representation.

LIFE AT WAR (1964–1967)

Levertov's first war resistance poems emerge not *ex nihilo*, but from a life-long involvement in the peace movement. Though Levertov devoted little energy in her poetry to political matters until *The Sorrow Dance*, Levertov's first peace activism dates from the early 1950s, when she participated in civil disobedience actions in New York organized by the War Resisters League and the Catholic Worker, defying the nuclear-preparedness drills. These demonstrations became increasingly large, until the city had to quit the drills entirely. In her words, ". . . our slogan used to be, 'Peace is Our Only Shelter.' We wore buttons that said, 'Stop the Testing' and 'Strontium 90 Builds Bones'" (*PW* 121). While her early activism didn't lead to explicitly political poems, Levertov considered the pursuit of peace central to her poetics. In her statement for *New American Poetry* (1960), Levertov wrote that she "d[id] not believe that a violent imitation of the horrors of our times is the concern of poetry. . . . I long for poems of an inner harmony in utter contrast to the chaos in which they exist" (qtd. in Kaladjian 7). Levertov's words prophesy the crisis that the Vietnam War would cause for her writing; her early antiwar poems, dating from 1966, ironically commit the very poetic acts that she steadfastly wished to avoid in 1960. At the same time, this statement also provides the foundation to which she would later return—a war resistance poetry based upon a vision of peace, what she would later call "an energy field more intense than war" (*MP* 58).

By 1966, as a result of increasing news stories about the human costs of the war, and during the early phase of the antiwar movement, Levertov spoke out against the atrocities, in language marked by a sense of guilt and anxious terror:

> I am absolutely opposed to the U.S. war of aggression in Vietnam. Not only is it an unjustifiable interference hypocritically carried on in the name of "freedom" while in fact its purpose is to further the strategic ends of a government whose enormous power has destroyed the morality of its members, but it is being waged by means of atrocities. This is a war in which more children are being killed and maimed than fighting men. . . . [The magnitude of this violence] promises a dreadful future for America, full of people tortured and distorted with the knowledge (conscious and unconscious) of what we have done. One does not need to be a bomber pilot to feel this; one need only be an American who did nothing to stop the war, or not enough; one only has to be a human being. (*PW* 119)

Her rhetoric closely follows the war resistance movement's characterization of the Vietnam War as a "U.S. war of aggression." Echoing the arguments of Robert Lowell's letter to President Roosevelt during the Second World War, Levertov contends that the U.S. bombing atrocities of civilians (particularly women and children) render immoral, not only the war but also the American people who do nothing to try to stop it. Similarly, Levertov's feelings of dread, powerlessness, and self-torture over the atrocities haunted her early poems, as she first ingested the indigestible images of the war. Her first antiwar poems in the prize-winning 1967 *The Sorrow Dance* appear at the end of the collection. In the book they seem, paradoxically, both peripheral and fundamental, both marginal and the last word.

Perhaps because she felt witness to the war, but not directly involved in attempting to end it at this juncture, she began writing the kind of political poem she would later theorize about in "On the Edge of Darkness: What Is Political Poetry?" which "demonstrates active empathy—the projection of a nonparticipant into the experience of others very different from himself" (168). The poet's "empathic projection," the psychic process of imaginative identification, compels a circuit from world to self and back again. Identification, after all, to paraphrase Jacques Lacan, is the (mis)recognition of the self in the other. Freud's discussion of identification, Diana Fuss notes, works from three separate metaphorizations: ingestion, gravity (pregnancy), and infection, each of which corresponds to a shift in Freudian thought. In general, we see two primary movements of identification; the first is that of the self incorporating the other (ingestion), and the second is that of the other overcoming and challenging the self (pregnancy and infection). The physicality of these metaphorizations of a psychic process suggests the way in which the identificatory process registers in the body itself, and Levertov's "Life at War" articulates that selfsame process, in order to make real a war that few Americans could register through their own proprioception.[2]

The most well-known poem of the collection, "Life at War" locates the disaster of the war within the domestic sphere, uncovering the literal meaning of the cliché of homefront, and foregrounds the inescapability—even inside one's physical self—of the trauma of the war. In the act of identification with the Vietnamese, in her attempt to imagine the war, suddenly, the war is not "out there," but, as Levertov writes, is "numb within us / caught in the chest" (*Poems 1968–1972* 121). The imagery of physical inhalation—as in the lines "we have breathed the grits of it in, all our lives, / our lungs are pocked with it"— alternates with imagery of digestion, echoing Freud, when Levertov compares the disaster to "lumps of raw dough / weighing down a child's stomach on baking day" *Poems 1968–1972* 121). The weirdly domestic and childlike image feels inappropriate, but it makes manifest how this internalization of war invades even the most innocent spaces.

For the poet, the war brings the realization that humankind—and, clearly, the humanistic vision that underwrites it—is fundamentally and radically split between bodily knowledge and rational self-distancing:

> delicate Man, whose flesh
> responds to a caress, whose eyes
> are flowers that perceive the stars,
>
> . . .
>
> still turns without surprise, with mere regret
> to the scheduled breaking open of breasts whose milk
> runs out over the entrails of still-alive babies,
> transformation of witnessing eyes to pulp-fragments,
> implosion of skinned penises to carcass-gulleys. (*Poems 1968–1972*
>   121–122)[3]

These lines, which have been repeated like a mantra by critics from Robert Duncan to Cary Nelson as proof of failed political poetry, establish the problematics of identification in Levertov's poetry. Levertov's failure, for Duncan, lies in her anger, a deepening rift between the poet "and her opposition, the amorphous 'they' who are in one way or another to blame for Vietnam" (Mersmann 111). It is precisely because Levertov's poems reflect the excesses of the antiwar movement that they remain of interest. On the one hand, her identification is with children and civilians subject to atrocity—she imagines the bodies eviscerated, turned inside out, unsexed. The images of abject bodies in the poem are meant to shock and disturb. Yet, on the other hand, the representation of the bodies, in their abjection as body parts, monumentalizes the bodies into a kind of traumatic sculpture, without particularity, without history—and thus the effect the poet aims for is obviated by their abstraction. We do not know, as Nelson has pointed out, how the poet is privy to these images, or even the conditions around which these bodies were torn apart, only that "burned human flesh / is smelling in Vietnam" (*Poems 1968–1972* 122). In fact, they become, most of all, an emblem of American moral decrepitude. In a strange way, then, this identification has her symbolically "killing off" the Vietnamese.

Still, indicative of her war poems of this early period, and paralleling CO poets' self-critique, the poem acts as a self-admonishment as much as a critique of American complicity. The poem employs the collective subject "we" throughout, a revision, it turns out, of an earlier draft which used "they" (see Levertov's Letter 371 in Bertholf and Gelpi 532). She later shares, in a letter to Robert Duncan, a quote from Ernesto Cardenal, in which he proposes that all of us carry within us the conditions of oppression and violence that we can see in human societies: "The dictators are inside of us, the h Bomb is in ourselves, it is from out of us that it burst. All the evil done by man we carry in us, political regimes are only objectivizations of what we are" (qtd. in Bertholf and Gelpi 540). Again, Levertov works through the problem of the war's distance by locating the war inside each of us. This sense of self-admonishment, as we shall see, gets attenuated as Levertov's alienation from mainstream America increases.

The poem "What Were They Like?" intensifies the dilemma of identification and representation at work in "Life at War," prophesying the extinction of the Vietnamese. Written in the form of a question-answer dialogue between two people, presumably Americans, the poem imagines a people whose hearts are "turned to stone" and a land whose trees no longer bud. As to whether "they distinguish[ed] between speech and singing," the poem ominously ends:

There is an echo yet
of their speech which was like a song.
It was reported their singing resembled
the flight of moths in the moonlight.
Who can say? It is silent now. (*Poems 1968–1972* 123)

Levertov's rendering of the "silent voices" is not an attempt to recover the words of the Vietnamese, nor is it an attempt to mark their silence, as the subaltern historian might attempt to do. The representation, while effective as a kind of prophetic warning, does not move beyond its image of the Vietnamese as reified victims of torture. The trauma of secondary witness—that is, of a person removed from the scene but still witness to it—creates a kind of poetic freezing.[4]

In both these poems, then, the poet's identifications with the Vietnamese are in danger of reproducing the Orientalist framework, whereby the other exists only insofar as she manifests our fantasy version of her—in this case, for the poem, as a pure victim of our bombing; the poems speak to Americans in a way that both shows American sadism and erases the particular bodies affected by it. Yet, both these poems, despite their limitations, bear out most importantly the impossibility of maintaining a safe voyeuristic distance from the war, because the war has found its way inside: inside the poet's very body, inside the nation's body, inside the body of knowledge known as "humanism." The infiltration of the war into privileged American subjectivity was not simply a slogan of war resistance (i.e., "Bring the War Home!") but rather an already existing reality that Levertov had confronted within herself, and thus dramatized for her readers. Even these first uneven experiments with war resistance poetry manifest the potential of identification to destabilize the distinction between inner and outer spaces, between American subjectivity and the Vietnam War.[5]

The poem "Enquiry" anticipates the direction which Levertov's poems would take her—away from addressing the nation and toward a more divisive and particularizing exhortation to war resisters. Based on a *New York Times* story reprinted in the Bly and Ray anthology about a Vietnamese woman who has lost both arms and her eyelids from a napalm strike, the poem is an address to U.S. soldiers, explicitly connecting the gaze of a wounded Vietnamese woman with the gaze of the judging other. Whereas other poems by Levertov mark the infiltration of the war into her own ways of seeing, this poem imaginatively identifies with a wounded Vietnamese woman. The end of the poem emphasizes the paradoxical power of the woman's loss of her eyelids as a gaze that will haunt the soldier:

> She is not old,
> she whose eyes
> know you.
> She will outlast you.
> She saw
> her five young children
> writhe and die;
> in that hour
> she began to watch you,
> she whose eyes are open forever. (*Poems 1968–1972* 126)

The Vietnamese woman—who is powerless to stop the soldier—as dramatized by Levertov renders the bare process of watching into an act of witness and judgment. As in "Life at War" and "What Were They Like?," Levertov's

"Enquiry" focuses on the casualties of war against women and children. In contrast to masculinist war narratives, the imaginative identification of the poem moves from woman to woman, demonstrating a sensitive portrayal of and act of solidarity with the Vietnamese woman who has lost five children; yet, Levertov's words simultaneously erect and erase the agency of this other, whose words remain beyond our hearing. Such ethical conundrums remain at the heart of such identificatory poems, written by civilians who cannot directly communicate with those living with war.

One might argue that the *you* in the poem is not just the soldier, but Levertov herself, in the position of the soldier. Such a reading makes the poem more interesting, insofar as Levertov is forced to inhabit three subjectivities simultaneously—the Vietnamese woman, the soldier, and the American civilian (herself). Yet if we do read the direct address of "Enquiry" as primarily directed at the soldier, then "Enquiry" suggests Levertov's shift from a poetry attempting to convince the nation of the wrongs of war (as in "Life at War") to one whose identification has crossed over to Vietnam. Levertov will argue, *only after the war*, that poetry matters in a pragmatic way because it can influence citizens and their political leaders, calling for poetry to address those not directly involved in war resistance; she will write, in "On the Edge of Darkness" (1975), that poetry "can indirectly have an affect upon the course of [political] events by awakening pity, terror, compassion, and conscience of leaders; and by strengthening the morale of persons working for a common cause" ("*OED*" 174). Both by awakening conscience among those in politics and by creating solidarity amongst "persons working for a common cause," Levertov will call for a poetry that is Janus-faced: one face that speaks to the world at large, and one face that speaks to an inner circle.

Her call for a poetry that would address itself both to the mainstream and to a resistance movement is something that she struggled toward and often failed to create; both "Enquiry" and "Tenebrae" signal the shift away from addressing those people that the poet believes live without concern for the "bitter" war and toward the resistance. The poem begins in the *we*—"We are at war, / bitterly, bitterly at war"—as if acknowledging the collective, if invisible, complicity of a militarized society. However, what draws the poet's ire are the people whom she imagines returning from the beach in their "million station wagons" who are "not listening" (*Poems 1968–1972* 127) to the sound of war. Critics have noted how this poem does little to convince the people whose "sequin plans / glitter into tomorrow" (*Poems 1968–1972* 126) and who refuse to be moved by the horror of the war. But she is not addressing those people— only those who have contempt for unapologetic privilege. Levertov's choice to put "Tenebrae" before "Staying Alive" suggests a turning away from convincing the mainstream and toward articulating an alternative resistance culture. "Enquiry" and "Tenebrae" are just small steps from Levertov's docupoem of the radical antiwar movement in "Staying Alive," in which Levertov turns her poetic gaze away from Vietnam to the community of resistance around her and witnesses to the struggles of war resisters, from de Courcy Squire's hunger strike to Norman Morrison's self-immolation, to the more mundane work of organizing and sustaining a revolutionary way of life.[6]

THE POETRY OF THE RESISTANCE (1968–1971)

The escalation of the war, and resistance to the war, instigated a crisis for the New Left by 1968, as national leaders were murdered and cities burned in urban riots. Echoing this crisis and the shift to a more radical politics, Levertov's speech from this period analyzes the Vietnam War as part of a system of imperial oppression extending both outward into other countries and inward, into every American citizen. Her language now shifts from dissent to resistance, with revolutionary overtones, as she explicitly links the struggle of the Vietnamese with the struggle of U.S. blacks for self-determination and declares that in order for the peace movement to "become the revolutionary movement, [it] must work to educate people to the realization that the struggle of black people inside the U.S. is a struggle for self-determination parallel to those outside the U.S., and this will become a race war if we, white radicals, do not act toward revolution" (PW 121). Increasingly, Levertov's involvement in Berkeley with the radical movement against the war—and that movement's own increasing alienation from American society and adoption of a revolutionary rhetoric and perspective—effects fundamental changes in the identifications and representations of Levertov's war resistance poems.

The continuing war, and the limits of her antiwar poems, created a poetic crisis for Levertov, registered in Relearning the Alphabet (1970), To Stay Alive (1971), and Footprints (1972), which comprise Poems 1968–1972. If until the Vietnam War, Levertov's verse can be called, in Charles Altieri's term, a "poetics of presence," then the war itself compelled her to question the limits of such a poetics for these new circumstances. A poetics of presence—articulated by Williams in his dictum "No ideas but in things!"—represents the world through the local and the particular. The poetics of presence, accordingly, considers its world the tangible and immediate surrounds and through its consuming eye takes everything in. Levertov's poem, "O Taste and See," explicates this poetic in its very first line—"The world is / not with us enough" (Poems 1960–1967 125)—and continues to delight in everything around her, from fruit rinds to street signs. The world, in Levertov's poem, might include the human, but most of all it is populated by the natural.

The first poem of this new phase, "The Cold Spring," registers the shock of war and the crisis of poetics that it brings, in an ostensibly "natural" landscape. She asks, in the second section,

> What do I know?
>> Swing of the
>> birch catkins,
>> drift of
>> watergrass,
>> tufts of
>> green on the
>> trees . . .
> It's not enough. (*Poems 1968–1972* 6)

Levertov's sense of failure as a poet—that describing the natural world in its budding particulars "is not enough"—directly emerges out of her traumatic (if secondary) witness to the war, and implicitly calls into question a poetry bounded by the domestic sphere alone. The final lines bear out how fundamentally her identification, in its primal specularity with the Vietnamese victims of atrocity, has challenged the core of her identity:

> Reduced to an eye
> I forget what
>> I
> was.

> Asking the cold spring
> what if my poem is deathsongs. (*Poems 1968–1972* 10)

At the moment of traumatized witnessing, of identification with the abject victim, the poet's usually strong compass of self is lost. The "eye" of identification, in trauma, causes the poet to lose her "I." The process of identification as infection, as an invasive force which threatens the organism, overtakes the language of indigestion of the earlier poems and suggests the perils of identification to the coherent, composed self.

The crisis of poetics—how to represent a war that threatens to overtake the poet's imagination—only surfaces briefly in *Relearning the Alphabet*; it is not until *To Stay Alive*, entirely dedicated to overtly war resistance poems, that Levertov's crisis has registered visible changes in her poetry. In her preface, the poet explains that this book contains not only new poems but also the other major political poems from her two previous books. Her justification, she argues, is "esthetic — it assembles separated parts of a whole" (*Poems 1968–1972* 107). The "vicious police attack" in the People's Park in Berkeley in 1969, the pacifist civil disobedience in Times Square, the draft resisters, and even the self-immolators — all compel the poet to create a "document of some historical value, a record of one person's inner/outer experience in America during the '60s and the beginning of the '70s, an experience which is shared by so many and transcends the peculiar details of each life, though it can only be expressed in and through such details" (*Poems 1968–1972* 107). Attempting to create a document of war resistance that would be both poetic and historical, Levertov's project confronts the crisis of representation by turning her vision from the distant war to the more proximate activities of the resistance movement. In her embrace of a located poetry working between documentary and lyric, she works in the tradition not only of Rukeyser's "Book of the Dead" but also of Barbara Harlow's "resistance literature" — literature produced in national liberation movements that challenges the dominant political and cultural narratives. In this context, poetry becomes a resource, a repository of the past and a means to narrate an alternative history. Salvadoran poet Ernesto Cardenal's poetics of *exteriorismo* emphasizes the documentary role of poetry as "an account of the daily historical and historic details, events, and actors of the revolutionary struggle" (Harlow 73).

Yet, Levertov's *exteriorismo* is complicated by her *interiorismo*, the legacy of the post-Romantic lyric poem she inherited, which asserts a fundamental alienation from bourgeois society. Desiring to harmonize the post-Romantic lyric with New Left revolutionary politics, Levertov theorizes that poetry is "intrinsically revolutionary . . . but only . . . deeply and truly revolutionary . . . by being *in its very substance of sound and vision* an ecstasy and a giving of life" (*PW* 106). Levertov proposes that a revolutionary poetry can balance the romantic and the radical and exist in "an ecstasy and a giving of life." It would be easy to dismiss such a formulation as a literary-romantic appropriation of politics. But Levertov's articulation is not merely a poetic version of New Left politics; on the contrary, Levertov's language points to the fundamentally lyricized nature of New Left politics itself. According to Todd Gitlin, the New Left developed a politics based upon the primacy of personal relationships, Romantic expressivity, spontaneity, and pragmatic utopianism. These political values have roots in Thoreauvian anarchism, constituting an outright rejection of the Old Left's reliance on rationality, tradition, and connections to communism.[7] Levertov attempts to balance in "Staying Alive"—the main poem of *To Stay Alive*—what she struggled to balance in her daily life: an ongoing absolute commitment to poetry (and the lyric poem's investment in individual subjectivity) and the increasing demands of resistance activity.

"Staying Alive" collages first person lyrics, haiku, demonstration fliers, speeches, news accounts of draft resisters in jail, "concrete" poems, quotations from traditional poets such as Gerard Manley Hopkins and John Keats from newspaper stories, quotations from activists and nonviolent thinkers such as Gandhi and A. J. Muste, and letters to friends. Levertov's crisis of poetics caused her to valorize the poem as historical document written for and to resistance movements. The poet's identification with the antiwar activists capitalizes on the strengths of her poetics of presence—it turns her gaze toward her immediate surroundings, including her husband Mitchell Goodman's trial for draft resistance, her work with the antiwar movement to build People's Park, and her return to England, her birthplace.[8] Levertov's identification with the antiwar movement, and her equally intense disidentification with the "war-makers," causes the poet to forgo any notion of an imaginary, unified (and national) audience of poetry. Because the trauma of the Vietnam War exposed the fissures already present in the United States, Levertov's book becomes a symptom of such differences. Perhaps more problematically, the book refuses the notion of the poem as a Yeatsian "argument with ourselves"— that is, a poetics that questions its own authority claims. The book does not question the poet's relationship to radical activism, nor does it really question the activism itself, nor does it question the language of revolution. In her opening to "Staying Alive," she poses the alternatives as "Revolution or death . . . Revolution, of course. Death is Mayor Daley" (*Poems 1968–1972* 137). The language of revolution, itself an artifact of the time, might strike us today as either overly apocalyptic or naïve. Yet, particularly in the Berkeley scene, many activists believed that they were living through a revolutionary moment; Gitlin and others recall how that historical moment showed signs of a revolutionary situation.

Levertov's poetic attempts at articulating her vision of revolution differ, however, from the street fighting and terrorist actions that attracted the most alienated and destructive elements of the war resistance movement. In fact, "Staying Alive" is centrally preoccupied, as its title suggests, with trying to construct a life, a reason to live amid a larger culture of death—a culture that Levertov had ingested in "Life at War." Despite the fact that Vietnamese deaths go largely unreported in "Staying Alive," death permeates the poem, in the form of political self-immolations, Keats's and Hopkins's Romantic poetry, suicides, and her own near death by haphazardly running into traffic. Perhaps even more than in her previous antiwar poems, in "Staying Alive," we see the dangers of identification to the one who identifies. Fuss's invocation of identification as a traumatizing "death encounter, open to the very possibility of communing with the dead" (1) is nowhere more apparent than in "Staying Alive," where Levertov struggles against her desire to end her own life while horrors continue in Vietnam.

Levertov's probing of revolution resembles her previous poetic attempts to grapple with the mystical and ineffable; her images both of revolution and of divine presence (in the tradition of Williams) rely on the most quotidian, often natural, things of the world, and anticipate her later attempts to envision a nonviolent poetics:

> What is the revolution I'm driven
> to name, to live in? — that now roars,
> a toneless constant, now
> sings itself?
>
>   It's in the air: no air
>   to breathe without
>   scent of it,
>   pervasive:
>   odor of snow,
>   freshwater,
>   stink of dank
>   vegetation recomposing. (*Poems 1968–1972* 148)

Levertov's revolution manifests itself dialectically in the enjambed line: "it's in the air: no air / to breath without / scent of it." Here Levertov takes a cliché ("it's in the air") and literalizes it, making revolution as natural as air; at the same time, the lack of air ("no air") oppresses, threatens to take away one's life. The final image of the sentence evokes an event that the poem later documents: the Berkeley movement's creation of "People's Park," where activists came together to clear out an old parking lot where the university had intended to build a dorm and make it into a park. By altering "decomposing" into "recomposing," Levertov overturns our preconceived expectations and turns our attention to the dialectic between the destructive and creative aspects of revolution while avoiding the rhetoric typical of the discourse of revolution.

To be sure, "Staying Alive" is slack with lines that lack her typical succinctness and attention to the energy of poetic lines (rhythm, enjambment); however, some of the passages lacking poetic energy illuminate critical debates within the war resistance movement. For example, reflecting on the "saints of outrage" who immolated themselves in protest against the war—the Buddhist monks, Norman Morrison and Alice Herz—Levertov wonders

> Maybe they are crazy. I know I could never
> bring myself to injure my own flesh, deliberately.
> And there are other models of behavior
> to aspire to—A. J. Muste did not burn himself
> but worked through a long life to make from outrage
> islands of compassion others could build on. (*Poems 1968–1972* 135)

At the same time, she argues that these saints are more than necessary, they are "brands that flare to show us / the dark we are in, to keep us moving in it" (*Poems 1968–1972* 135–136). For Levertov, the protest of self-sacrifice literalized the way in which the war wounded not only "other people's children" (*Poems 1968–1972* 135–136) but also ourselves. Ultimately, while she rejects the death-oriented sacrificiality of these acts, she sees them as illuminating the darkness of the times and as an image to compel one to keep "moving," to reject despair. Whether or not one supported the extremity of protests taken by individuals and groups against the Vietnam War (and later, against what Paul Potter described as "the system") became a crucial issue that ended up tearing apart many of the fragile coalitions resisting the war. Levertov's lines offer a provisional space for such actions, even while suggesting that they should be seen not as nihilistic but rather as a call to further resistance— a reason for staying alive. In short, Levertov's poem, while not always doing its aesthetic work, labors to document the news and debates of war resistance communities.

Other pieces in the "Staying Alive" collage document war resistance activities and offer a window into the confluence of earnest antiwar activism and more playful countercultural values. For example, a flyer called "WHAT PEOPLE CAN DO" delineates some rules that activists should follow to build the resistance community in Berkeley. The list ranges from the practical and logistical ("The Free Church and Oxford Hall medical stations need medical supplies") to the more romantic ("Be your brothers' and sisters' keeper"). One item in particular demonstrates the odd harmony between radicals and hippies: "BRING YOUR KITE AND FLY IT.

Use nylon strings. Fly it when you are with a crowd. A helicopter cannot fly too near flying kites" (*Poems 1968–1972* 154). Using a kite to disrupt surveillance or police violence against crowds might never occur to post-hippie activists. Such advice was prescient, as President Reagan would later call in helicopters to pour tear gas on a peaceful demonstration in front of Sproul Hall.

Even though "Staying Alive" does its cultural work of documenting the resistance movement, it also points to the dangers of such a constriction of address. In the vehemence of its disidentification with the American government and the American military—what she called in her preface "the whole system of insane greed" (*Poems 1968–1972* 106)—the poem shows the anxiety at heart in her identifications, both with the antiwar movement and with the Vietnamese. Levertov's disidentification with the Mayor Daleys might also elide the ambivalence of her identifications with the revolution both in America and in Vietnam. These disidentifications might also enact a disavowal of an identification already made; they might, in a sense, work to hide Levertov's relative privilege in the "whole system of insane greed" of United States life.

THE POET AS WITNESS (1972–1975)

As the New Left and war resistance splintered into increasingly alienated and violent groups such as the Weather Underground, Levertov's resistance took an another level of peace commitment when in 1972, Levertov, along with poets Muriel Rukeyser and Jane Hart, traveled in a delegation to North Vietnam in order to witness firsthand the devastation of the war. The trip, depicted in her prose account, "Glimpses of Vietnamese Life," as well as in her poetry, unfreezes her traumatized vision of victimized Vietnamese bodies. While "Glimpses" does point to the poet's inability to get more than glimpses of a life she has imagined, it also provides a way to understand *The Freeing of the Dust*. Because Levertov finally was able to witness life in Vietnam, her ability to identify with the Vietnamese in their struggle for national sovereignty freed her from only representing the abject bodies of women and children wounded in bombings. In fact, the representations of Vietnamese vary widely, and for the first time in her poetry, Levertov began to depict crucial differences between herself and the Vietnamese she meets. In contrast to Fuss's identification as ingestion, or Silverman's incorporative identification, Levertov moved toward an identification that, in Silverman's words, "conform[s] to an externalizing rather than an internalizing logic—that we identify excorporatively rather than incorporatively, and thereby, respect . . . the otherness of the newly illuminated bodies" (*FD* 2).

However, if Levertov moved beyond her images of fragmented Vietnamese bodies, the idealizations of Vietnamese culture like those in "What Were They Like?" persisted. Not surprisingly, the poet noted that "the overwhelming impression" of her visit "was of a people who were not only unalienated from their society but who enthusiastically *identified* with it . . ." (*FD* 129). This sense of "identification with a difference" enabled Levertov, at last, to begin to make important distinctions between herself and the Vietnamese for whom she advocated. At the same time, what Levertov saw in Vietnam, then, might be a projection of what she herself had been lacking—a people who are not alienated from their society. The orchestration of the trip by the North Vietnamese government and the "Union of Women and the Committee for Solidarity with the American People," as recorded in "Glimpses," structured Levertov's gaze even as it overturned her earlier, apocalyptic fears of genocide. She wrote of her feeling of being a stranger to the place, embarrassed by her VIP vehicle, but noted that "there is no other way for us to see all that we are to see in a week, and we have come to accept it" (*FD* 131). Her other great fear, of natural destruction, was dispelled almost immediately by a land that "seemed endlessly green and impenetrable" (*FD* 129). These two impressions—that of a people steadily surviving and of a land which continues to live—are condensed in a single image and later replayed in the poem, "In Thai Binh (Peace) Province." The poet—after running out of film photographing "yet another child with its feet blown off"—walks outside, taken aback by the quiet of the land. Using her "dry burning eyes" now, she "photographs" the immediate world around her. This time, however, it is not America, but Vietnam:

> dark sails of the river boats,
> warm slant of afternoon light
> apricot on the brown, swift, wide river,
> village towers—church and pagoda—on the far shore,
> and a boy and a small bird both
> perched, relaxed, on a quietly grazing
> buffalo.   Peace within the
>   long war.
> It is that life, unhurried, sure, persistent,
> I must bring home when I try to bring
> the war home. (*FD* 35)

Although one might argue that Levertov represents a tourist's version of Vietnam, the "unhurried, sure, persistent" life must have been a profound relief to a poet who had envisioned Vietnam only in apocalyptic terms. The peace which Levertov evokes in this poem through the image of the boy on the buffalo, more grounded than the rhetorical peace that the poet wished for at the end of "Life at War," points toward an insistent concern of Levertov's—how to write a poetry of peace?

One of the insistent worries of war resistance literature has been that, despite a writer's intentions, even the most brutal representation of war can itself perpetuate war. As we have seen, many war resistance poets have thus chosen to resist war by writing toward a just and peaceful vision of social relations. In *The Life of Poetry* (1949), Rukeyser anticipates the limits of Levertov's Vietnam poetry in her analysis of 1930s poetry. Rukeyser argues that the "repugnance to the social poetry of the 1930s" was a result not only of reactionary politics but also of the "blood-savagery in it, ranging all the way from self-pity—naked or identified with one victim after another—to actual blood-lust and display of wounds . . . begging for attention and sympathy in the name of art that was supposed to produce action" (211). Because peace, Levertov would later write, "as a positive condition in our society" is so unknown to our experience, "it casts no images on the mind's screen" ("*PP*" 155). If identity is at least partially constituted by identifications and "peace" itself is not attached to images, then pacifist subjectivity is a contradictory project.

The peace of these poems, finally, happens in the renewed ability to differentiate between the experience of Vietnamese people and what she imagined of them. By the end of her trip, Levertov formulated a kind of productive difference which thaws the frozen, portentous identifications of the earlier poems. She noted crucial temperamental differences—"while I personally may be volatile, that is not what the Vietnamese are" (PW 139)—and sensed that "self-reproach can be a form of self-indulgence" (PW 145). But more important, she was aware of the failures of her and the movement's apocalyptic vision. In a telling moment, she writes that

> all that we have known about and have been trying to spread among
> other people seems unreal compared to seeing mothers at the bedsides of
> their half-destroyed children, or hearing the stories of women like these. I
> cling to the need for revolutionary optimism, I yearn for it; and we *see* it,
> we feel inspired by it—but we have a long struggle before us in order to

really share it. It seems to me such hope, faith, charity, can only emerge out of a suffering we have yet to experience. (*PW* 144)

She realized that, in a crucial way, she had not even begun to share in the struggle that the Vietnamese have endured and that her imagining has been unreal. When Levertov alludes to a "suffering that we have yet to experience," she makes a critical distinction between the suffering of secondary witness and the suffering of primary physical and psychic loss as a result of war's violence. In other words, Levertov saw that the war affected her differently than the Vietnamese that she meets; her imagination of the war was insufficient insofar as its inability to account for the human agency of the Vietnamese. Paradoxically, her inability to imagine Vietnamese agency made the imagined suffering almost unbearable. This distinction is meant in no way to underestimate the horrors of war on human beings; rather, it points to how the human imagination lacks an adequate vocabulary for pain.

Still, her empathy for the revolutionary struggle in Vietnam after her visit allows her to notice the differences between the experiences of American activists and Vietnamese revolutionaries. In "The Distance," the collective we engaging in acts of civil disobedience can "refuse the standard prison liverwurst sandwiches, / knowing we'll get decent food in a matter of hours" (*FD* 27). But even if the Vietnamese mourn, they become inspiring figures of struggle, with their "spirits / visible, crowns of fire-thorn / flicker over their heads" (*FD* 28). The poet's vision conflates Christ's crown of thorns with the pentacostal "tongues of fire," evoking the possibility that the sacrifices of the Vietnamese might evangelize, even baptize, the "infant feet" of American revolutionaries. That Levertov's poem ends with a question indicates a tentative and provisional solidarity. At the same time, the poet's use of Christian imagery to describe a largely Buddhist people points to the impossibility of representing these others beyond our limited imaginings of them.

Because of her renewed sense of "identification with a difference," or her excorporative identification, Levertov produced poems that have a renewed sense of balance toward the "war-makers" and a sense of self-irony toward her acts of civil disobedience. In "The Pilots," her position interviewing captured American pilots and later meeting one of their mothers, creates a competition of identifications. While she clearly identified more with the struggle of the Vietnamese, her meeting with "Mrs. Brown," who "has the same lovingkindness in her / that I saw in Vietnamese women" (*FD* 30) creates a deep conflict in the poet. The poem begins with the poet wishing, but unable, to excoriate the American bombers, and ends with her questioning her own identifications:

> Because they were prisoners,
> because they were polite and friendly and lonesome and homesick
> . . .
>
> if they did understand precisely
> what they were doing, and did it again, and would do it again,
>
> then I must learn to distrust
> my own preference for trusting people,
>
> And if it is proved to me
> that these men understood these acts,
>
> how shall I ever again
> be able to meet the eyes of Mrs. Brown? (FD 30–31)

Thrust into a face-to-face encounter with the other, Levertov's previous sense of disgust and rage at the bombers now finds itself foundering, unable to disidentify completely with the plight of the pilots and their mothers. Levertov's "Mrs. Brown" alludes to the essay by Virginia Woolf, "Mr. Bennett and Mrs. Brown," which explores aspects of life traditionally unexplored by male narratives. Mrs. Brown is the name Woolf ascribes to a woman she sits across from on a train, whose life the writer can only glean from her appearance and an overheard conversation. Imagining the particular suffering of Mrs. Brown, for Levertov, overcomes her desire for distance from Mrs. Brown's politics. The fundamental act of imagination reveals itself to be one of identification. At this moment—and more clearly, perhaps, than in any other poem—she realizes that the world cannot be unified by vision alone.

THE PERSIAN GULF WAR (1991–1992)

Some fifteen years later, during the Persian Gulf War, Levertov revisits the problems that haunted her Vietnam-era war resistance poems—whom to address, how to represent war (particularly in the absence of media coverage), and how to make present the victims of that war. Levertov's best Gulf War poems, in *Evening Train* (1992), provide new ways of visioning the effects of the war and the resistance to the official narrative of the war. Levertov's poems finally fulfill Cary Nelson's dictum that the best war poems in a television age foreground the very mediatization of the imagery of war. Four poems in particular—"Airshow Practice," "Protestors," "In News Report, September 1991: U.S. Buried Iraqi Soldiers Alive in Gulf War," and "In California during the Gulf War"—approach the problem of the war by rendering the Iraqis not as visible, suffering bodies but as an invisible or silenced presence. Levertov's mourning identification with the Iraqi dead, therefore, does not result in the poet's representing Iraqi suffering. But Levertov's refusal to write about the Gulf War and the suffering of Iraqis in traditional representational modes does not imply that Levertov has abandoned any simplistic poetic structuring of identification. Instead, these poems confront the problem of witnessing an "invisible" war by foregrounding the problem of media censorship and the ways in which identification itself is forestalled. In addition, these poems render American antiwar dissent in ways that do not merely enact an overheated disidentification with the "American people" but rather show the complicity of every American in the U.S. government's operations. Last, and perhaps most important, these poems locate the speaker as an American, in an American landscape, unable to imagine the war beyond. As a consequence, the landscape around her becomes haunted by the war's destruction.

In "Airshow Practice," for example, the poet's landscape turns into a kind of military grid, where even the lake and the nearby woods are immersed in the plane's exhaust. The poem, which begins in the tradition of nature poetry, evokes a scene already poisoned by "costly power:"

Sinister wreathing mist in midsummer sky
slowly disperses
as it descends
over the wooded hill, the lake, the bathing children:

streaks of exhaust left by Blue Angels. (*ET* 72)

Both the title and the first word of the poem, "sinister" provides a bit too much moralizing. Yet, in the description of the descending mist, the poem provokes two interrelated meanings. First, it comes closest to finding a language of Pure War. Pure War operates, not only by sheer force of power, as the poem shows, but through a kind of sinister dispersal, a self-erasure. Pure War is war precisely when it becomes so pervasive that it becomes invisible. Second, Levertov has begun to make visible the real connections between the natural and the political worlds, something that she has always struggled toward in her poetry. The sky into which the people look at the end of the poem is not the sky of Keats but a kind of television, that fantasy screen onto which we project our desires. The "Blue Angels"—the name itself signifies transcendence—become the point of identification that creates a false, monolithic community, a "multitude" that "gazes upward, craving / a violent awe, numb to all else" (ET 72).

Clearly, this poem does not solve the problem of Levertov's lyric discrimination (between herself and those others who are numb to violence). However, as in a poem such as "Protestors," Levertov articulates the way in which war resistance attempts to give voice to "the Iraqi people." The protestors attempted to make visible the bodies that mainstream U.S. media sources routinely excised from the narrative of the war.[9] The protestors, "living on the rim / of the raging cauldron (ET 74)" of America, can only witness the "disasters," but they still can speak. Echoing Hamlet's famous suicide soliloquy, Levertov suggests that the protest, the outcry against the war, is a matter of life and death: "The choice: to speak / or not to speak. / / We spoke" (ET 74). Because those who will bear the brunt of the attack—the Iraqi people—do not have the privilege to speak, the protestor acts as a kind of representative of the unspoken, the unrepresentable subaltern. In Gayatri Spivak's usage, the subaltern marks the site of exclusion in colonial subjectivity. She is the one who "cannot speak," who exists outside of the symbolic order; the Persian Gulf War and its media coverage, perhaps more successfully than in other wars, subsumed all Iraqis under the portrait of Saddam Hussein. Rather than simply depicting the whole people as inhuman, the official war narrative worked by a process of metonymy, substituting the part (Saddam) for the whole (22 million Iraqi people). However, Levertov's poem can only represent the Iraqi "silence" and cannot move any farther into listening; the will of the Iraqi people is what the protestors must, but cannot, speak for.

The work of resistance, as Levertov shows, involves not only confronting the willful censorship of the actual war but also making visible the logic that underscores that war by imitating the language of official sources. In "News Report, September 1991: U.S. Buried Iraqi Soldiers Alive in Gulf War," Levertov creates a found poem from a journalistic account of the U.S. mass burial of Iraqi soldiers, some of whom were still alive. By splicing this mediated representation, Levertov renders the traumatic effects of U.S. bombing. Repeating and juxtaposing the words of the U.S. military, the poet not only foregrounds the limited media access to the war (and hence, the impossibility of nonmilitary witness) but also underlines the war's connections to capitalism. Phrases like "carefully planned and / rehearsed" or "the tactic was designed" (ET 82) easily could have emerged from a corporate board meeting. The terrible limit of corporate thinking is captured in Colonel Moreno's assertion that the U.S. burial of Iraqis was justifiable because the possibility of American casualties while burying Iraqi bodies individually is not "cost-effective." In "Military Censorship and the Body Count in the Persian Gulf War," Margot Norris argues that the U.S. military censorship of journalistic media compounded an already widespread American Orientalism. This othering is "founded on a circular logic . . . we Westerners count our dead because we cherish human life; you Orientals hold human life cheap, therefore we may bury you uncounted in ditches (240)." The poem shows how the disparate number of American and Iraqi dead approached near genocidal proportions: "Not a single / American killed" followed by "Bodycount / impossible." But the juxtaposition at the heart of the poem argues the existence of a more complex relationship between Americans and Iraqis:

> "His force buried
> about six hundred
> and fifty
> in a thinner line
> of trenches."
> "People's arms
> sticking out."
> "Every American
> inside."
> "The juggernaut." (*ET* 82)

Levertov's placing a period after "inside" suddenly inverts the meaning of the sentence. The absolutely impenetrable safety of the Americans inside the juggernaut is reversed and "every American" is placed in the trenches next to the "arms," the synecdoche for the Iraqi soldiers. The poet's disturbing juxtaposition can be read in a number of interrelated ways. First, it implies that in burying the enemy alive, the American soldiers are actually digging their own grave. Second, and more important, it collapses the distinction between American military and civilians. The notion of unconscious complicity comes into clear focus here. It is not just the soldiers themselves who are buried but also "every American." Last, Levertov's move intimates that every American, in partaking of the war, experiences a commingling with the enemy. The effects of war, Levertov suggests, do not disappear, even if they are not consciously noticed; even more—the very passage of time does not erase the past.

Levertov counteracts the erasure of the past by the official narrative of the war, which promised that the Gulf War would heal the wounds of Vietnam, by suggesting that wars never really end. The trauma of a new war does not erase the first, thus "In California during the Gulf War" invokes the trope of regeneration, only to besiege it. The poem adopts the discourse of post-Romantic nature poetry, with a description of recent ecological damage to the California landscape, balanced by the appearance of rejuvenated blossoms:

> Among the blight-killed eucalypts, among
> trees and bushes rusted by California frosts,
> the yards and hillsides exhausted by five years of drought,
>
> certain airy blossoms punctually
> reappeared, and dense clusters of pale pink, dark pink—
> a delicate abundance (*ET* 84)

Ravaged by blight and drought, the land "consorted well with our bitterness and shame." The poet, however, invokes the poetic fallacy in a political way, suggesting that the suffering of the Iraqi people is not distant, but among us. She recognizes that though the ravaged land and the subsequent buds "lifted the sunken heart," they are not

> symbols of hope: they were flimsy
> as our resistance to the crimes committed
> —again, again, in our name: and yes, they return,
> year after year, and yes, briefly shone with serene joy
> over against the dark glare
> of evil days. (*ET* 84)

Levertov's use of the communal *our*, which she distinguishes as "some of us," recognizes both the community disgusted by the war and the larger community that is the nation. Her use of the pronoun "they" is equally multilayered. "They" seems to refer first to the buds, then to the resistance, then to the crimes of war themselves (in its colorful, almost floral bombings), and finally even to the dead. In a frightening way, the enemies "us" and "them" become conflated, tightly raveled together. The same pronoun collapsing occurs at the end of the poem:

> [The blossoms] *are*, and their presence
> is quietness ineffable—and the bombings *are*, were,
> no doubt will be; that quiet, that huge cacophony

simultaneous. No promise was being accorded, the blossoms
were not doves, there was no rainbow. And when it was claimed
the war had ended, it had not ended. (*ET* 84)

The pronouns of the poem—we, they, it—threaten to deconstruct the binaries
us/them, blossoms/bombs, natural/human, quietness/cacophony, peace/war, but
do not. The reader is left not with the healing and ease of natural rhythms but
rather with the anxiety of binaries that refuse to remain discrete; for Levertov, the
war can no longer be said to end. The trope of natural regeneration, of time as
meaningful repetition, is supplanted by the trope of trauma, where time is meaningless repetition, where history is doomed to repeat itself. The poem stands as a
stark invocation of a moment "during the Gulf War," as the title alludes, forcing
the reader to consider the limits of that historical moment, which increasingly
appears as part of a continuum of the havoc of war, a "cacophony /simultaneous"
with the seasons of nature.

If Levertov's Vietnam poems often expressed an increasing alienation with
American society at large, her best Gulf War poems attempt to overcome the
boundaries that separate peoples, delimit discourses, and ultimately make war
by combating the tendency to intransigence and excessive disidentification.
Though the recent collection of peace poems, *Making Peace* (2006), obfuscates the arc of her development as a war resister poet, it reaffirms the centrality of war resistance to her poetic life, and the need to imagine the scene of
war, to represent protest, and to envision peace. In light of military control of
media access to war, Margot Norris calls for an art that attempts to "recreate
a 'whole picture' . . . by weaving together what is known with what is known
not to be known" (228). Poetry is a site for "supplementing the 'truths' of war
not only by censorship but by phenomenal limitations of experience by human beings" (242). If the Gulf War has turned into "instant history" in the
mainstream media, Levertov's work constitutes a refusal of such disappearance. Her poems render a new meaning to Williams's famous lines about poetry and the news—that poetry indeed can be a site of the unspeakable, can
mark the disappearance of the real.

PART 3.

The Persian Gulf War

PROTEST AND THE POSTMODERN

FIGURE 3: *Cartoon from the time of the build-up to the Persian Gulf War. Reprinted by permission of Tom Tomorrow.*

The troops are quiet tonight, but it's not alright
because we know they're planning something...
We must keep our eyes open.

—FUGAZI, "KYEO" [KEEP YOUR EYES OPEN]

6. The Gump War

LYRIC RESISTANCE POETRY IN CRISIS

Catch if you can your country's moment, begin
where any calendar's ripped off: Appomattox
Wounded Knee, Los Alamos, Selma, the last airlift from Saigon
the ex-Army nurse hitch-hiking from the debriefing center; medal of spit on the
        veteran's shoulder.

        —ADRIENNE RICH, *An Atlas of the Difficult World*

There is no news-sourced documentation . . . of any incident of antiwar activists
spitting on veterans. Yet during the Gulf War . . . [some] veterans testified to
having been spat upon. How are we to make sense of an image so compelling
that people believe it happened to them, when that image does not appear to be
supported by empirical evidence?

        —JERRY LEMBCKE, *The Spitting Image: Myth,*
        Memory, and the Legacy of Vietnam

    In *Forrest Gump*, the Oscar-winning Hollywood film of 1994, the
cognitively disabled but magical protagonist is invited to Washington DC after having saved a handful of his platoon during a surprise attack in Vietnam.
Some antiwar protestors, in full countercultural regalia, assume that the by-
stander Gump is one of the veterans slated to speak against the war, and they
thrust him in front of a massive protest on the steps of the Lincoln Memorial.
Unaware of the political implications of the situation, Gump begins to speak
about the war; however, at the very moment he opens his mouth, an angry
member of the military brass pulls the plug on the amplifiers. We, the audience, simply see Gump's mouth moving. Gump continues to speak, not
knowing that his words do not carry beyond his own mouth.
    In a movie that dissolves postwar American history and identity into a
pop cultural romp through the images and songs of the Boomer Years, it is
at the precise moment when American identity and nationalism revealed
all of its divisions and antagonisms—during the Vietnam War—that the
movie must pass over into silence. If Gump gives a speech in defense of the

war, the audience will recognize Gump's innocence as the genocidal idealism and naïvete of Graham Greene's Quiet American; if he gives a speech against the war, he dispels the aura of national unity that the parade of songs and iconic images have built throughout the entire film. The undelivered message, lost in a momentary rupture of technology, is lost for good because of a sudden reunion between Gump and his girlfriend, Ginny. The political is once again privatized. The silence, then, creates a momentary discomfort but ultimately allows the audience to suspend considering the war further, or questioning, for example, how the film represents Vietnam as a place in which only American soldiers exist (the Vietnamese remain essentially untranslatable and unseen voices, with the exception of some distantly viewed cone-hatted peasants bent in rice paddies), and which Americans actively plan to convert into another America. In an astonishing moment of transparency, Gump's friend, an African American shrimper named Bubba, fantasizes about Vietnamese shrimp "once we take this place over."[1]

The movie proposes a fantasy construct whereby the politically and culturally disengaged ultimately succeed, and those who get involved in political or cultural movements for change will pay the price. Robyn Wiegman has noted how the film's revisionism stems from the way it replays "in haphazard and incoherent ways images of racial trauma and social dissent that we can't yet forget—the physical violence that attended desegregation, the street protests of the '60s, the bloodbath of the Vietnam War" (124). Gump's silence at the podium, then, marks the way in which the war remains an unspeakable trauma, something that "we can't yet forget" but still can't quite remember. Further, the movie privileges Gump—who unquestioningly obeys authority— over his politically active girlfriend, Ginny, who, in Slavoj Zizek's words, "is symbolically punished for her thirst for knowledge: at the end of the film, she dies of AIDS" (IR 201), while Gump becomes a millionaire. For Slavoj Zizek, "*Gump is ideology at its purest*—the ultimate lesson of the film is: don't even try to understand; obey, and you shall succeed!" (italics his 200–201).

We could also read Forrest Gump's silent speech not simply as a suspension of judgment on the Vietnam War but as a metaphor for the Persian Gulf War. Despite the pretense of live coverage, was there ever a war more censored, more controlled by the Pentagon? Offered up as an "instant history" that effaced the histories of colonialism and empire in the Middle East, media coverage covered up far more than it revealed. There is little doubt now that mass media sources from CNN to the local news acted principally as an extension of the military effort; this media saturation has led critics like Jed Rasula to suggest that the only proper way to resist the war was to refuse to watch television (376).[2] The silencing or skewing of dissent by mass media prevented the nation from engaging in a dialogue about the legitimacy of the war. In addition, the orchestrated public relations campaign by the Pentagon, combined with limiting media access to the war, ensured that the version of the war that Americans would receive would be officially sanctioned and promoted.

At the same time, the silence of Gump speaks more broadly, as well, to the intense nationalistic pressure driving mass cultural production, and with it, the intersubjective realm of the social symbolic. That pressure of nationalism, so evident in the writings of the Second World War CO poets, abated slightly during the heady half-decade from 1968 to 1973, when poets published work that continues to unsettle critics for its excesses. Not surprisingly, given the degree of media censorship during the Persian Gulf War, war resistance poets often found themselves trying to respond adequately to the new conditions of postmodernity. At their worst, the Gulf War poets expressed the isolation of Second World War conscientious objector poets but without the sense of conviction, and the alienation of Vietnam War poets but without the sense of revolutionary zeal; in this sense, these poets succumbed to the tendency in the lyric to escape to a transcendental subjectivity, isolated from others, bereft of a sense of audience or history.

The predominant conditions of postmodernity, evident in the war's execution and mass representation, complicated the gestures and significations of war resistance poetry.[3] That postmodernism is so quickly reducible to a style worthy of commodification, or a way of thinking that replicates, rather than confronts, imperial ideology, points to one of the principal qualities of postmodernity as condition—the triumph of capitalism to commodify and coopt oppositional strategies. In particular, the rise of the image-production and information industries in its various forms—television, film, the Internet—has led to a cultural situation in which the very notions of news and "history" are thrown into crisis. If "news" is fundamentally an ephemeral market commodity, ever transforming itself into a better and fresher product, what happens to history? History itself, as posited by Forrest Gump, becomes yet another product. Fredric Jameson's five constitutive features of the postmodern—a new depthlessness (simulacrum), a "consequent weakening of historicity," "a whole new type of emotional ground tone" (related to the euphoria of the sublime), an inescapable relationship to the new technology, and the notion of "built space" (6)—sound like the crib notes to the Pentagon's plans on how to sell the Persian Gulf War.

The Persian Gulf War, then, was a Gump War, offering a fantasy regression back into the Second World War, when dissent was marginalized and media coverage censored and cleaned of corpses, while bringing us futuristic "missile-eye" views of targets being bombed, to legitimate what was, arguably, part of a larger U.S. imperial project. The TV Gulf War was always a Hollywood production—part melodrama, part action film.[4] For Saudi financier Adnan Khassoghi, the war was "like going to a movie: we paid our money, we went to the theater, we laughed, we cried, the movie ended, and an hour later we had forgotten about it" (qtd. in Masland 2F). The relative absence of postwar coverage ensured Gumpish mass amnesia.[5]

In the postmodern media spectacle of the war, the bodies of the dead actually disappeared. Thanks to censorship and the fascination with the new technology: "the technological regress of the video image within the televised military briefing, watching screens upon screens, the view of a camera's eye . . . [the viewer had] a perception of war at an impossibly mediated and media-imbricated remove that reduces the human victim to the implied presence inside miniaturized and flattened dots of abstracted and stylized targets (Margot Norris 233).

The disappearance of the physical body occurred not simply because of Defense Department policy but also because, in conditions of postmodernity, the body itself, so marked and re-marked by technology, capitalism, and ideology, ceases to be. Arthur and Marilouise Kroker, in "Theses on the Disappearing Body in the Hyper-Modern Condition," anticipated the disappearance of the corpse during the Gulf War in their argument that the body itself, in a hyper-modern age, "has achieved a purely *rhetorical* existence: its reality is that of refuse expelled as surplus-matter no longer necessary for the autonomous functioning of the technoscape" (Kroker and Kroker 21). Though the technoscape may not have required actual bodies for its "autonomous functioning," the screen images could not screen out the effects of war; *Wag the Dog*'s popularity suggests the disappearance of the proof and signifier of war—the dead—which led to confusion over whether a war actually took place; the war itself, in retrospect, took on the tenor of hoax that Baudrillard had already ascribed to it, and the movie plays upon the *ex post facto* suspicion that the government may have duped the public.

The crisis of resistance—that is, how to forge a position of oppositionality against a war that seemed to render resistance futile—appeared most visibly in the impasse between Jean Baudrillard's postmodern analysis of the war (aptly demonstrated in the title of his provocative book, *The Gulf War Did Not Take Place*) and Christopher Norris's Chomsky-inflected critique (no less provocative in the directness of its attack: *Uncritical Theory: Post-modernism, Intellectuals, and the Gulf War*).[6] Neither articulates a completely convincing reading of the war, and each, in light of the counter-theory, feels two-dimensional. The presumed irreconcilability of these paradigms requires an analysis flexible enough to value the productive paranoia of Baudrillard and hyperrationality of Norris/Chomsky (hereafter referred to as the Chomskyan mode). The Baudrillardian mode, on the one hand, impels us to: (1) question not only mass media coverage but information itself, insofar as it becomes indistinguishable from propaganda in times of war, particularly in what Baudrillard calls "the profound immorality of images"; (2) recognize the way in which war itself has become virtualized, simulacral, and based upon the logic of deterrence; (3) describe the war as a Western civilian experiences it, where the media and military use of optical technology merge to a single aim; and (4) pursue a risky rhetorical strategy that mimics the dominant narrative in order to subvert it. The Chomskyan mode, on the other hand, provides us a model that helps to: (1) deconstruct U.S. media coverage of the war by producing an historical narrative of U.S. foreign policy that emphasizes its complicity in the situation it aims to solve by war and by producing an alternative narrative of war resistance, both at the center of empire and in the Third World; (2) investigate the effects of war on the ground in Iraq (not to mention in the United States, where thousands of veterans suffer from Gulf War Syndrome); and (3) suspend the (postmodern?) illusion that just because something is not covered by the U.S. press does not mean that it's not real. Yet, both critical paradigms also fail to articulate fully their own positionality, their own subjective history, relying instead on either articulating the simulacra or narrating of U.S. state terrorism.

The intractability of this debate between Baudrillard and Norris—itself symptomatic of the conditions of postmodernism—played itself out in the poetry world when, at the quadrennial poetry conference held at Orono in 2000, Amiri Baraka confronted Barrett Watten during Watten's presentation on Language poetry and its relationship to the radical political movements of the 1960s. For Baraka, Watten's framing of Language poetry as the inheritor of radical politics belied its institutional and formal elitism—not to mention its whiteness—and thus ignored the very people on whose behalf it purportedly was attempting to struggle. One of Baraka's nicer insults was that Watten was engaging in "struggle free intellectualism" (qtd. in Prevallet). The impasse that resulted in a subsequent session to work out this debate, as Kristen Prevallet notes, was "an absolute breach" of communication, and later attempts to continue the dialogue ended without much further discussion.[7]

Oddly enough, the debate about postmodernism between Baudrillard and Norris and the debate about the 1960s between Watten and Baraka—who, at least on the level of poetics, aim for the same radical political ends—parallel the differing aesthetic aims of performance poetry and language poetry, respectively, the two poetries that Paul Hoover heralds as ascendant in his anthology of postmodern poetry. Though the analogy is by no means foolproof, it does suggest that we ought to pursue multiple strategies for illuminating (and writing) war resistance poetry. Norris's stance, informed by the Chomsky-based analysis of U.S. mass media, necessitates a poetry consonant with Hoover's "performance poetry" or Mark Van Wienen's "partisan poetry": a documentary, factually based, polemical, topical, and empathic (identificatory) poetry that participates in a larger community of resistance.[8] As Prevallet puts it, a poetry whose goal is not to "alienate but to educate; to inform and mobilize readers to stand up and fight the imperial powers that work to keep them silent."

But what does it mean to privilege the documentary over the imaginative, particularly during a war where the factual and the fictional blurred so completely? What does one do, for example, with Adrienne Rich's "Atlas of the Difficult World," in which the radical poet repeats the myth of the "spat-upon Vietnam veteran"? According to Jerry Lembcke, the absence of documentation of spat-upon veterans did not deter countless pre–Gulf War media accounts of Vietnam vets getting dissed by protesters; these accounts helped justify the war and quash dissent under the notion that supporting the troops required backing the war. (Perhaps, in light of Gulf War Syndrome, supporting the troops might have required not having them fight at all.) On the one hand, we might read the image of the "medal of spit on the veteran's shoulder" as Rich's critique of the failures of the antiwar movement during and after the Vietnam era; "Atlas" explicitly criticizes the demonstrators who failed to link the fight for peace with the fight for social justice, who failed to act against apartheid and injustices at home and only marched when the bombs were already doomed to fall. On the other hand, Rich's lines ironically participate in the revisionism that erases the work of veterans who opposed the Vietnam War. The "documentariness" of partisan poetry, therefore, privileges factual referentiality in a way that is intentionally and explicitly oppositional to the dominant narrative, but in doing so it always risks its own unraveling in the face of new narratives and new "facts."

Thus, Baudrillard's stance, in contrast to Norris's, would call for an entirely different kind of poetry, one commensurate with the conditions of postmodernity— in particular, an avant-garde poetry that responds to the realities of media spectacle, propaganda, and the exhaustion of oppositional modes of subjectivity. Baudrillard's theoretical intervention exposes the limitations of resistance/partisan poetry, particularly in terms of the postmodern context in which these poetries are produced. The language poets and the post-avant poets and critics have articulated an avant-garde project that resists both the commodified and privatized lyric and the rhetorically oppositional "political" poem, offering an alternative past and future for war resistance poetry as resistance through form itself.[9]

Yet both directions of war resistance poetry deserve investigation; the latter, for its formal and theoretical critique of what Jed Rasula has termed the "subjectivity racket" of contemporary American poetry, and for its project of radical poetry in a postmodern age; the former for its working to stretch the lyric tradition into a tool for social change. Though poets did not play as crucial a role in war resistance during the Persian Gulf War as they did in past wars, they did participate in both political and poetic ways in resistance and actively worked through the conditions that marginalized them as poets and war resisters. Since no study has examined Gulf War poetry, and since activist poetry is by definition ephemeral and often contextual, this investigation highlights some exemplary moments; though these poems are not always aesthetically rich, they demonstrate ongoing poetic war resistance. Postmodern conditions call for a critical strategy that values poetry not only in terms of its formal or experimental interventions but also in terms of its material history of production and circulation in war resistance movements—that is, based on its cultural use. Norris's critique, like Jameson's notion of postmodernism as both style and social context, invites a consideration of poetry that resists the dominant narrative both in itself and in its use in activist contexts. Though poets engaged in local activism through poems and symbolic actions in less widespread ways than during the Vietnam War, a number of important interventions did take place: in readings and demonstrations, in journals and newspapers, and in anthologies.

The Ephemeral Poetry of Signs, Readings, and News

Despite the swift entry into war and its overall brevity, poets and activists organized readings and participated in demonstrations, just as they had during the protracted Vietnam conflict. However, because of the Gulf War's relative shortness and because of the lack of resources to counteract the censorship of information, the archive of Gulf War activist writings does not have the breadth of that of the Vietnam War. Still, the rapid response suggests how the peace movement itself had become institutionalized, with its own structures in place to inform, educate, and mobilize against war. The occasional poetry of demonstration signs at an antiwar rally in Los Angeles, published by the *Nation* magazine, manifests a stew of issues and range of tones (from the angry to the comical) but nevertheless addresses the particularity of the conflict and the peace movement's struggle to overcome stereotypes of pacifism and the Left. Clearly, the audience for such occasional poetry, unlike the intended audience of academic poetry, is the public in the most general sense: readers and listeners and passersby, or those who might catch a glimpse on television or in newspapers. Given the inherent spatial limits of the placard—the message must be short, memorable, and visible to others, including photographers—these activist poets used binary aphorisms and rhyming couplets to embody their resistance. Even without seeing the signs, we can imagine line breaks: "EDUCATE / DON'T DETONATE," "RICH PEOPLE'S OIL / POOR PEOPLE'S BLOOD," "WISE POLICY / NOT SMART BOMBS," "SAVE THE REPUBLIC / STOP THE EMPIRE," or "ANTI-WAR / NOT ANTI-AMERICAN" (from "Signs of Dissent"). "EDUCATE / DON'T DETONATE" could be read as "educate others, don't detonate them," as well as "educate thyself, don't detonate thyself!" In other words, the exhortation to get educated could prevent one from getting detonated later on; this seems all too real in light of the class inequities in our professional army, with the middle class going to college and the working class to the military. Beyond the messages, the sheer multiplicity of statements and the handmade appeal of the signs suggest the creativity and independence of the sign maker, the poet-artist who stands with and stands by her words.

Even as we recover the poetry of activism, we cannot forget the way in which many traditional movement strategies—mass demonstrations, marches, and speeches—were often misrepresented, sidelined, or ignored. Not only did the mass media pull the plug on dissenting arguments once the war began, but it trivialized street demonstrations by undercounting and stereotyping participants, showing favoritism for rightist demonstrators, and marginalizing coverage to the back pages. Though mass media coverage sometimes operated from a disturbingly commodified nationalism, the bad coverage speaks also to the limitations of demonstration as a mode of articulating dissent. On one hand, the collective occupation of public space has been a traditional strategy for dissenters, particularly when other modes of information transmission are blocked. On the other hand, the media's structural biases—in Parenti's coinage, favoring "personality over issue, event over content, official positions over popular grievances, the atypical over the systemic" (191)—suggest that street demonstrations play into the hands of mass media. The chanting of slogans, the colorful costumes, libidinal displays of physical freedom, and acts of violence or destruction often dominate the demonstration, and even replace the constructive praxis of a movement itself.[10]

Perhaps war resistance—and political activism more generally—has reached an impasse; after the Vietnam War, spectacles engineered by dissenting movements might appear to the disengaged viewer as empty gestures. The simulacral experience—in which one finds oneself imitating an already existing image of reality—extended even to protesters. A friend involved in the antiwar movement recalled how he felt during a takeover of a university building as if he were in a simulacra of a protest—it was as if he and those around him were trying to emulate the images of Vietnam-era protest that they had seen only in movies. When demonstrations vie for national television coverage at the expense of creating a culture of resistance, the movement becomes virtual at its core. However, poetry and other arts have shown the ability to manifest and embody that spirit and that movement in ways that locate agency in local community movements, even if they appear drained of meaning to a national consumer.

Local readings and art exhibitions attempted to articulate connections with a longer tradition of war resistance, despite the difficulty of claiming such a tradition in a cultural climate that demonized the Vietnam War dissent as antipatriotic. On January 21, 1991, at the Poetry Project in New York, Bruce Andrews (with George Cartwright, Michael Lytle, and Evan Gallagher) improvised "word constellations" which he later transcribed, in his typically diachronic collagist work, where the war occasionally became visible as "forcefed . . . syllables / suck . . . a scud—Top Gun tessitura; move into a new Kuwaiti neighborhood / / & I'm not prepared to say! / Pouncy, uptight, but calm—only the concussions are known / (pushy whisper) / A tabletop theater strapped to their ejection seats" (24). In such a wordspray, Andrews captures the Gulf War coverage's information overload, as television broadcasts of the war became a paralyzing forcefeeding. To take another example, an impromptu local organization Poets and Artists Against War, from Eau Claire, Wisconsin, created a pamphlet of poems for peace and participated in an open exhibition entitled Art against War, March 3 to 7, 1991. In the catalogue essay for the exhibition, Michael Peterson notes the impossibility of creating any unified statement behind the exhibit; he hopes that the exhibit strives for what Michel Foucault called "a plurality of resistances" (unpaginated). While aware of the limitations of art as resistance, Peterson still asserts the importance of art to producing what he calls a "peace culture." Such local acts of resistance provide an essential cultural foundation out of which national political action may take place.

Despite the relative quietism of journals and magazines on addressing the war through poetry—due to the snail's pace of journal publication, the relative lack of political engagement in MFA programs, and the disappearance of poetry in mass publications—at least one notable exception deserves mention (and the lone British poem in this American survey), for its swift emergence: Tony Harrison's *Guardian*-commissioned poems "Initial Illumination" and "A Cold Coming," appearing in the *Guardian* on March 5 and March 18, respectively, which became the first significant literary war resistance. Bloodaxe Books promptly published the poems in book form, displaying on the cover the grotesque photograph of "the charred head of an Iraqi soldier [as it] leans through the windscreen of his burned-out vehicle, February 28. He died when a convoy of Iraqi vehicles retreating from Kuwait City was attacked by Allied Forces" (inside cover). Taken by Kenneth Jarecke, the photo became the subject of Harrison's "A Cold Coming," told from the point of view of a poet interviewing this dead soldier. Written in heroic couplets, a form whose self-consciously artificial and poetic rhymes in Harrison's hands have a parodic quality constitutive of Jameson's postmodernism, the poem creates an absurdly comic "exclusive interview" between poet and dead soldier. Like many poems subsequently written about the Gulf War, this poem desires to uncover the hidden horror of the war while simultaneously questioning its ability to articulate the truth behind the terrible charred image; as the dead Iraqi states, "isn't your sort of poet's task / to find words for this frightening mask?" (9).

Throughout the poem, Harrison forcefully reasserts the human cost of the war. While the poet begins to despair, the Iraqi asks the poet not to look away from him:

> an armature half-patched with clay,
>
> an icon framed, a looking glass
> for devotees of kicking ass,
>
> a mirror that returns the gaze
> of victors on their victory days
>
> and in the end stares out the watcher
> who ducks behind the headline: GOTCHA! (13)

Harrison's characterization of the Iraqi in the Iraqi's voice emphasizes the odd identification between the poet and the corpse, and the way in which the charred body becomes a kind of admonishing gaze upon those who see war simply as "kicking ass," a phrase used by President Bush at the time. Even if the headline from a newspaper read "GOTCHA!," that half-disintegrated face "stares out the watcher" (16). Indeed, perhaps the vehement reaction by the public against the media's showing images of death late in the war, such as the photograph meditated upon by Harrison, points to the strange desire to repress the contemporary economy of war—that of inflicting bodily harm. The poem ends with the poet rewinding the tape of his interview, then pressing play: "and I heard the charred man say: [blank page]" (16). Here, appropriately, the poem ends. The silence of the corpse in the photo, here reproduced as wordlessness on a blank page, becomes an unrecordable cry, an unimaginable grief.

Harrison's use of rhymes self-consciously points to the artifice of his conceit, as if to point out the mediatized nature of the war itself. Further, his poetic obsessions with sex and technology merge with one of the primary narratives of the Gulf War—that of the triumph of American military technology and the triumphalism that surrounded discussions of that technology. Even if the absence of historicizing of the conflict detracts from the poem, its metaphors transmute the images of battle into questions about the suffering behind victory, and thus render the poem as an instant memorial against the hegemonic version of a clean war.[11]

The Anthology as Site of Resistance

The anthology, the most compact and concentrated source for antiwar poetry produced during and after the Gulf War, offers a more comprehensive archive of war resistance poems, despite the fact that their prior contexts (as occasional poems or as poems for antiwar readings) have been effaced. Though the anthology exists as a cemetery for poems shorn from their original contexts in antiwar communities—thus prohibiting the reader from making connections between the local and the national, the cultural and the political—it also can be an important site to instigate those connections between writers themselves. Yet the poetry anthologies responding to the Persian Gulf War tend to replicate the problems of lyric poetry—elision of poems' historical context and lack of political oppositionality in favor of a bourgeois antipathy toward the mass representation of war—even if they also provide a site for gathering and sustaining war resistance beyond the event itself. The major American poetry anthologies to emerge from the Gulf War—*Journal of the Gulf War: Poetry from Home* (1991), *Rooster Crows at Light from the Bombing* (1991), *After the Storm* (1992), and *War after War* (1992)—mark a continuity to war resistance during the Vietnam War and throughout the Cold War. Further, these collections negotiate the problem of audience in relation to the reading public of the U.S. in fundamentally different ways, representing a continuum of address from the most moderate to the most radical, and exemplify the problematics of war resistance poetry during the Gulf War.[12]

Journal of the Gulf War: Poetry from Home renders all too painfully the isolation experienced by war resistance poets, and the contradictory foreword demonstrates the demoralization of poets and activists alike. The cover of the book reproduces Lawrence Ferlinghetti's angry painting, "Unfinished Flag of the United States"—which depicts a map of the world slashed by emphatically heavy strips of blood-red, thus dramatizing the damage of U.S. projection of its own power over Iraq and the rest of the world—yet John Penner's contorted foreword insists that this poetry anthology will not take sides, for as he puts it, "as neither side [pro- or antiwar] can be characterized as representing a *movement*, that struggle [between militarist and antiwar ideologies] remains no more than a philosophical cold war" (Logue et al. Foreword). Penner's careless comment belies the work of activists and coalitions who fought U.S. involvement since the first deployments of troops in August 1990. Rather than taking sides, he evokes the language of conscience even while he disavows the possibility of collective resistance when he calls for Americans to come to terms with this battle "within ourselves." The "ourselves" is significant, insofar as Penner attempts to speak to the broader national community; it summons the Yeatsian "quarrel with ourselves" as well as the notion that the lyric poem must somehow embody, represent, or locate itself in a nationally representative voice.

The liberal position that dissent in America must be confined to the cage of the solitary conscience manifests itself in the alienated tone of *Journal of the Gulf War*. The poems are frequently haunted with self-pity and self-condemnation, manifesting the lyric's inherent limitations as an isolationist, escapist, and bourgeois form antagonistic to collective resistance. Mira Ingram's poem, "POWs," goes as far as describing the Americans at home as imprisoned: "We are isolated / In our cells of despair / Pondering in our minds / What will never be discussed" (21). While such paralysis afflicted many Americans, the absence of active response recalls Peter Sloterdijk's critique of the bourgeois subject, whose beliefs and actions remain fundamentally split. In *The Sublime Object of*

Ideology Slavoj Zizek comments on *A Critique of Cynical Reason*, illuminating the failure of cynicism to surmount its "enlightened false consciousness"; for Zizek, belief is radically exterior. In the most literal way, we believe what we do; our belief is the sentence of our actions.

The anthology does provide poems resisting the bloodless military terms of war, the sexual politics behind the rhetoric of the war, the perceived ineffectuality of poetry in the face of state violence, the illogic of the bombing, the environmental devastation of war, and the need to confront the Persian Gulf War in its particular historical moment. Even as "A Poem for the Human Voice" asserts, "you can't stop wars with poems" (34), the poems assert a hope for, as Bruce Isaacson writes, a "poem / [that] can perform a daring midnight raid" (29). With the exception of Allen Ginsberg's "Hūm Bom"—a dada attack on cheerleader punditry composed of three sections written in 1971, 1984, and 1991—only one other poem, "Beyond Vietnam," displays any degree of historical consciousness about war resistance. Recalling memories of growing up to the televised images of Vietnam and the pleasing images of flower children, the poet Gwynne Garfinkle recounts an exchange with her father in which she says she "can live without politics." To which the father says: "I hope not" (15). At stake in the exchange is the definition of the political. The father's notion of politics absolves the citizen viewer from an active responsibility for the actions of government, while the daughter's notion mainly resists the feeling of being "stuck inside history." As she looks back in the midst of this strange conflict, she

> tried to piece together
> recent history.
> Nothing prepared me for this.
> Not novels set in the sixties
> Dylan or Denise Levertov
> Vietnam documentaries
> or Hollywood movies
> Phil Ochs singing
> "I Ain't Marching Anymore"
> or Martin Luther King speeches
> Grenada or Panama (15)

The poet, while empowered and aware of the inspiration of the resistance to the Vietnam War, finds herself unprepared for this new war, strategically engineered to stifle protest and manufacture a state of mass enjoyment of the conflict. Indeed, as should be clear by now, the Persian Gulf War was quite different from the Vietnam War; the tradition of war resistance poetry is not a finished endeavor but a constant struggle to write a poetics commensurate to the new conditions of conflict. In the end, the poems from the *Journal* mainly point to the insufficiency of the lyric poetics of individual expressivity.

In contrast to the ambiguous self-positioning of the *Journal*, *Rooster Crows at Light from the Bombing*, a collection of poetry and essays, stakes out a vociferously antiwar position. Many of the essays, written by poets such as Wendell Berry and Robert Bly, cover ground that the poems are unable to traverse. Bly's poem "For These States," for example, degenerates into metaphorical gestures at the "thin-lipped king" who waves the troops on to their death. Anthony Signorelli's "New York Honors Troops," on the other hand, explodes with rage at the celebrators: "Despicable! / The whole country / pretends its men are heroes . . . America! / Have you no shame? Have you no grief? / I spit in the face of your celebration"(29). Rivaling the anti-Vietnam poems in anger and alienation, this poem's rage marks it as an occasional utterance; however, it suffers in its context as an anthologized poem. The poem's imagined or summoned audience appears to be an audience of one. If the poem had examined the speaker's (writer's) relation to the celebrations—whether he silently succumbed to the celebrations or whether the poem was an actual address to passersby (which would have been a daunting act indeed)—we might be able to forgive its alienated proclamation of rage.

Though many of the poems in *Rooster Crows* speak from afar when they condemn official rhetoric and call for a remembrance of the dead, Coleman Barks's "Becoming Milton" is a throwback to earlier antiwar poems, marking the cost of war on soldiers; he recounts a conversation with an airport driver whose soldier son Tom recently returned from the Persian Gulf. Reminiscent of the war stories from Vietnam, the poem explores the psychological toll of war on a soldier who has "screaming flashbacks, can't talk about it / anymore" (60–61). The son's job, to clear the bunkers, involved throwing grenades into "those holes they hid in" and exposed him to "freshly killed guys, / some sixty, some fourteen, real thin. / They were just too scared to move" (60–61). The father explains understatedly, how his son

> feels pretty bad about it, truthfully,
> all this yellow ribbon celebrating.
> It wasn't a war really. I mean, he says
> it was just piles and piles of their bodies. (60–61)

The son's determination in carpentry to fit boards smoothly almost appears as a kind of repetition compulsion of the war itself; if the boards aren't fitting properly, the father relates, "he'll tear the whole thing out if it's not right / and start over (61)"—in an odd echo of Curtis LeMay's threat during the Vietnam War to "bomb them back to the Stone Age!" The graphic violence that the son has had to endure and perpetuate has not gone away. Like some of the best war resistance poetry, the graphic exploration of violence locates war in multiple sites, not simply at the scene of battle but carried around in the bodies of veterans and in the culture at large.

After the Storm, the most accomplished poetry anthology to emerge from the Gulf War, collects the work of the best known war resister poets in the United States. Editors Jay Meek and Frank Reeve compiled the anthology by soliciting poems that had already been written in response to the Gulf War; although they took some poems written on demand, they conceived of the anthology as a site to gather, not elicit, war poems. Basing their anthology on the model established by *Where Is Vietnam?* (1967), Meek and Reeve "invited 100 American poets to contribute poems in response to the war. . . . Robert Bly, Allen Ginsberg, Donald Hall, and William Stafford, have poems in both anthologies, and I think it's curious on the whole to compare the tenor of poems in the two collections" (Meek letter, December 3, 1999). However, Meek and Reeve experienced long delays in finding a publisher for the anthology. Since Meek and Reeve sought to produce an anthology that would contribute to the public discussion of the war, they wanted their book to come out before the war disappeared from media or public awareness, yet neither university nor small presses could provide poetry as instant activism. Robert Merrill, editor of Maisonneuve Press, who finally accepted the project, introduces the anthology of "poet activists" as "an antidote to the simulations offered by governments and mass media—our official national imagination" (back cover), listing the extent of human and infrastructure damage as a result of the bombing. Merrill evokes a tradition of poets "who have been among the most courageous in calling to consciousness what the powers proscribe" and who call us to "imagine the Persian Gulf War, not in the horror of its presence, but through the multi-refracting prism of our national ignorance and silence in order to go through it and come out on the other side. These poets grasp for ways of imagining what was unpresentable" (back cover). If the struggle for war resister poets was to represent the unpresentable in past wars, the Gulf War provided the least visible, but most televised, of conflicts.

Like the *Journal of the Gulf War*, editors Meek and Reeve call for a "heroic . . . exercise of civility in the midst of war and its atrocities" (4) and stake a claim for a poetry that speaks out and thus poses "an inward danger to the heart" (4). So even though the poets articulate a critique of the conflict, they, like Penner, see poetry as a conscientizing tool rather than as a part of resistance itself. Have these editors failed to see the possibilities of alternative structures or communities as answers to the grim unrealities of national complicity, or has the anthology as a cultural production exerted a disciplinary pressure on their rhetoric? The disturbing conundrum of war resistance in the United States is that any potentially revolutionary act is so rapidly coopted and commodified that resistance sometimes seems futile.

Though *After the Storm* includes poems that could be categorized as historical, agitprop, symbolical, domestic-natural, and language-based, the most successful poems challenge or even violate the expectations they set up. They are poems, in some sense, at war with the limitations of the lyric. That these poems can be so easily categorized reflects their limitedness as aesthetic objects, but not necessarily their lack of utility as news or as didactic tools. Poems which invoke or rely upon historical examples of wars develop a narrative continuity between the present conflict and previous ones. These poems often expose the false promises of the American government to end all wars and the failure of our historical memory to recall the conditions which bring about war after war. For example, Donald Hall's "The Coalition" invokes the pressure of war upon democratic culture—"maps of Sparta replace maps of Athens"—and the historical and transcultural continuity of military logic: "If Lord Gilgamesh should remain unreasonable, we will coalesce to / incinerate retreating Uruki soldiers, furthering the project / of Pharoah Death, Imperator Death, Shogun Death, President Death" (42). Referring to the classic poem, *The Epic of Gilgamesh*, and its benighted Sumerian hero Gilgamesh (who hailed from the location of present-day Iraq), Hall draws us back into both political and poetic history as a way to understand the present conflict.

Jayne Cortez's "Global Inequalities" stands out as one of the few poems of the anthology that hearken back to Vietnam-era war resistance poetry's critique of empire and the excesses of exploitative capitalism. Emerging from the Black Arts tradition of linking radical critique with performance poetry, Cortez's poem confronts the gap between the corporate oil industry elite and the suffering and famines in Third World countries, often where that oil is drilled:

Chairperson of the board
is not digging for roots
   in the shadows
There's no dying of hunger-stare
   in the eyes of
   Chief executive officer of petroleum
Somebody else is sinking into
   spring freeze of the soil
Somebody else is evaporating in
   dry wind of the famine (22–23)

Although this poem does not advance much beyond the agitprop tradition of self-assured neoimperialist critique—that the politics of empire have displaced labor exploitation from the United States to the "undeveloped" nations through transnational corporations—what it reminds us is that sheer geographical and cultural distance renders oppression almost unthinkable for most Americans; it is, as Cortez suggests, "somebody else" who suffers from decisions made at the center of the empire. Further, it foregrounds the argument made by the war resistance movement at the time in the slogan "no blood for oil"—that the geopolitics of oil control had more to do with the U.S. involvement in the Gulf War than the ethical imperative to protect Kuwait from the depredations of a madman dictator. It also suggests, in its odd opening, that political correctness—the P.C. doxa which would add "chairperson" to our lexicon to acknowledge the inclusion of women in the executive ranks of corporate culture—has not altered fundamentally the exploitative relations between corporations and the Global South.

In contrast to the historical or agitprop poems, the poems that use symbolic allegory or surrealism move through indirection. Unhindered by the overt realism of the political allegorists, these poems delve into the psychological underpinnings of warfare. Philip Dacey's "The Neighbors" takes its imaginary setting from a quotation appearing in the *Christian Science Monitor*: "Ask yourself who you would prefer as a neighbor—Saddam Hussein or George Bush" (24). The poet imagines the brief hellos shared with his imaginary neighbors, calmly taking care of their yard work and occasionally sharing greetings on the street. The poet assures us, "they're good neighbors," then describes what is hidden under the grass:

Only occasionally
a small hand pushes up

from the ground their lots enclose,
breaking the level green,
the fingers uncurling
toward the light
and moving with an appearance
of great expressiveness,
and then only briefly
before a small engine starts up
and low blades
whirr quietly, restoring
the uninterrupted expanse
of the neighborhood
we take such pride and pleasure in
on summer evenings
like this one. (24–25)

In a scene reminiscent of David Lynch's *Blue Velvet,* the dead buried in the lawns of the poet's neighbors "only occasionally" resurface and then are mowed down again. The poem points to the void that the mass media version of the war only circled around—the hundreds of thousands of deaths that, in the symbolism of the poem, permeate even the American suburban landscape.

Poems using autobiographical lyric conventions to frame the experience of the war often explore the strange relation of the personal and political mediated through a lyric self. Perhaps more than the other types of war resistance poem, they embody Terrence Des Pres's call for a poetry that creates "potent figures that anyone's imagination might kindle to and take hold of" (26). As in Vietnam War resistance poetry, these poems work to bring the war back home—even into the bedroom—where people witnessed the real-time coverage of the conflict. Jonathan Holden's poem in *After the Storm* thus begins: "And didn't our love seem almost a political act, / to turn away from the footage of F-15s" (47). Carol Muske's "To the Muse," for example, takes place on a pleasure boat anchored next to an aircraft carrier; a drunk female reveler's exhibitionism becomes a meditation on the role of poetry in a man's violent world. Every time she thinks of the carrier, now in the Gulf, she sees that girl, "as if / / the two are linked: the bare-breasted dancer / and a war about to be fought over oil" (82). In lyric poetry, at least for the space of this poem, Muske longs for the language magic to "reinvent war" (83), as she addresses her muse, this girl, "O passionate / agitatrix, swearing to you this time I can make it right" (83). Muske's poem offers the vexation of a speaker trying to make sense of how not only her own society but her own language-creations somehow partake in the logic of war—another example of how lyric poetry can offer simultaneously an image of subjectivity-in-conflict and a dramatization of resistance.

Poetry which foregrounds the battle over language addresses the war through questioning the very structures of poems themselves. Written in exaggerated couplets, Reginald Gibbons's "Poetry after the Recent War" asks many of the questions implicit in recent critiques of the politics of form, while the dominant narrative continues to defame language itself:

> in the recent war, before the soldiers were sent into
>   combat, they were ordered to dig fifty thousand graves in
>   the sand.
> After news of that, should I elaborate a simile? . . .
>
> "Like shooting fish in a barrel," "like a turkey shoot,"
>   "like a video arcade," "like roaches when you turn on the
>   the light," four pilots said to television reporters after
>   climbing out of their planes.
> Should I ponder the master tropes of metaphor and metonymy? (33–34)

That Gibbons's poem questions the form and structures of poems only on a rhetorical level, but does not enact its critique by rejecting rhetorical gestures or traditional forms, demonstrates a typical weakness of the lyric approach. Though the poem ends without resolution, the poet seems to reaffirm the need for poetry that struggles against war, poetry that could strike through "the crazed frenzy of climactic explosions" of the televised Gulf War.

The final war resistance anthology focused on the Gulf War, War after War (1992) integrates political and cultural analysis with contemporary poetry and art in ways that hearken back to the "for use" tradition of earlier Vietnam War anthologies; for example, the full-page agitprop art pieces—some of which are remarkably provocative—appear designed to be photocopied for leaflets or broadsides. Perhaps because this anthology came out a year after the war was over, and in contrast to the embattled tone of other anthologies, the overall tone of the anthology is marked by a militant defeatism. Nancy Peters begins her introduction in strident language: "The Gulf War, a contemptible and totally obscene episode in the history of American imperialism, was remarkable for its savagery, its brevity, and for the hypocrisy and lies of its staging" (i). While War after War succeeds in proposing an anti-imperialist critique of the war, setting it in the context of U.S. foreign policy in the wider Middle East, its tone seems too often shrill and veers into a circular address. While such an address to war resistance might be necessary—to solidify its constituents' commitment—how many people not yet converted to this narrative would persist in reading past the first line of the introduction?

Situated among political essays and dynamic agitprop art, however, the poetry need not make the same arguments more easily made in prose. The poems chosen for this anthology, in contrast to the other anthologies, come almost exclusively from the performance poetry tradition, not the mainstream lyric tradition. The tone of the poems often follows the tone of the introduction and essay; despite the good reasons why this war made war resisters alienated, strident, and leaden, one might hope for poetry better than Karen Finley's "The War at Home," which ends: "We are hated / We are doomed / AMERICA GET A LIFE. / GET A NEW POLICY" (89). If only we could get a new poetry as well. More nuanced is Wanda Coleman's "Notes of a Cultural Terrorist," which casts the speaker-poet as a soldier in the devastated landscape of urban America. For Coleman, the war abroad virtually ensures the bombed-out ghettoscapes: "after the war the war begins the war goes on / / i am a soldier. look at my boots / soles worn for seeking work" (111). Echoing Langston Hughes's "A Dream Deferred," the poem references the 1991 riots in Los Angeles and alludes to the ongoing war of urban poverty. Finally, gesturing to the broader chorus of voices beyond her own, Coleman's work moves between first person lyrics and parenthetical prose paragraphs which give voice to a rioter, a sick person in the ER, a group of women in a bar, and a kid arrested in the gang war. The collaging pries open the cramped confines of the monologic lyric into the multiplicity of voices who are casualties of a war behind the lines, a war whose effects were both buried in the sand and right in front of us.

Book-Length Poems on the Gulf War

Since 1991, a few book-length collections emerged, all from small presses, dealing with the Gulf War: *Mother of Battles* (1991) by Michael Hulse, *Ribbons: The Gulf War* (1991) by William Heyen, *Persian Gulf Poems* (1992) by J. T. Hollis, *Desert Storm: A Brief History* (1993) by Lenard Moore, and *Bad History* (1998) by Barrett Watten. Only Heyen's and Watten's deserve serious treatment, because the other three are frustratingly ahistorical, ultimately more committed to a deeply constraining poetic form than to any real engagement with the particular contours of the conflict.[13]

Heyen's *Ribbons: The Gulf War*, a diaristic account, traces the speaker's days from January 14, 1991—"hours before deadline in the Persian Gulf" (13)—to the first days of March, when the war ended. That Heyen has chosen to focus so rigorously on the days of the conflict enables him to explore the hyperkinetic, at times hyperreal, consciousness of day-to-day living in time of war and to dispel the myth that the homefront is somehow simply distant from the scene of battle; in fact, Heyen's long poem confronts the pervasive war at the homefront, in everything from the frenetic casino culture in Las Vegas to the suburban conformity of Brockport Village. Overall, Heyen's poem spans personal, literary, and national histories, and explores a number of poetic strategies and tones as he confronts and resists the war and its transmission.

The poem begins, in the nights before the war, at a craps table in Las Vegas, where the poet confronts his own complicity in the culture of excessive consumption. After a day of gaming, the poet

. . . dreamt of soldiers
with slots for brains: they're young,

& smile, & their foreheads revolve with reels
of roses & pterodactyls.
They're there

in the Gulf, my president says, for me, that petroleum-
based vial of shampoo showing up each day
by magic in my room (13)

In his dream, the soldiers get condensed into a slot machine. The "slot" echoes in at least two ways. It homophonically implies that the innocent soldier is a blank slate upon which the state can write. At the same time, the soldier, by merging with the slot machine, becomes an extension of the economic apparatus at its most libidinal. Perhaps the soldier is not simply fighting for the nation, or for the interests of the upper class, but for capital itself.

In the second section, "The Reich," Heyen returns to his first experience of war, during the Vietnam era, and discusses how his resistance to U.S. involvement led him to write about the Holocaust in his collection *The Swastika*

Poems. Though Heyen admits his early writings did not match his active political opposition to the war, the poet is most vexed by the feeling of complicity. Even as the Vietnam War ended, the poet

> was moving toward the Third Reich by then
> by reason of family & reading & ambiguous dreams
> in which I ran from Nazis, but with them,
> slept in haystacks, but knifed them,
> torched a synagogue, but died with Torah in my arms. (15)

Haunted by the sense that he is somehow also the enemy, the speaker only occasionally allows himself the distance of oppositionality or irony. Overall, Heyen's sequence of poems explores a broad gamut of tones and postures — sardonic comedy and rage, euphoria and despair, meditations on the past and nightmares about the future.

Heyen's thirty-eighth section in the sequence, "The Truth," published first in *After the Storm,* finally moves the poem from commentary about the war to action, exploring the effects of planting a black bow and ribbons on his rooftop, to counter the orange and yellow ribbons that dominated the landscape around his house:

> Up there, I saw how it divides the winter sky
> with its alphabet of one emotional letter, a vowel. . . .
> At first, no one noticed, but then a car turned around.
> Later, a police cruiser slowed down, & then another.
> A reporter stopped for that infamous photo that appeared in *Time*
> & the first of a hundred interviews I declined,
> & the neighbors gathered. My phone kept ringing off the wall,
> people yelling "bastard," & "traitor," & "get it the hell down,
> or else." . . . Eventually, my best friend came to my door
> & asked me why. I explained, "I can't explain." Others followed,
> & insisted. "No comment" I said. "I don't want trouble,"
> I said. "Read Hawthorne's 'The Minister's Black Veil.'" (52)

The subsequent harassment by neighbors, police, reporters, and even friends merely adds meaning to the poet's act done because he was "half bored / & half nuts with war." Like Reverend Hooper's black veil in the Hawthorne story, the black ribbon undergoes the "terrible transformation . . . into symbol." The poem recounts a small act of resistance — itself "merely" symbolic — which troubles the surrounding community far more than the poet expected; the weight of cultural symbols remains strong, the poem implies, and symbols can be used to wear down the inherently unstable hegemonic use of other symbols. Not surprisingly, the harsh reaction and threats from neighbors indicated how subversive even a simple act could be. Part of the subversiveness of the black ribbon, it turns out, was in the symbol's illegibility; because no one knew exactly what the symbol meant, it could not be explained away, as many antiwar slogans could.

Working through the occasional mode, Heyen composes the only fully realized full-length collection devoted to the Gulf War, published while the conflict was still in the news. Oscillating between complicity and resistance, between grief and protest, and between witness and resistance, *Ribbons* offers a compelling lyric history of the war, from the standpoint of one distant from the battle but no less a witness to its mediatized representation. In the end, it testifies to the value of such occasional, daily acts of writing as a mode of witnessing to one's own inevitably implicated subjectivity when the nation is at war. That this poetry documents resistance, and itself becomes an act of resistance, ensures its place in the canon of war resistance poetry.

Thus, the Persian Gulf War forced poets to confront the limits of lyric responses as such; when they failed to account for how its mediated representation on television altered fundamentally the American civilian experience of war, they tended either to rely on outworn models of poetic protest or to retreat to representing their own paralyzed subjectivity, privileged yet myopically distant from the carnage. Still, the level of poetic response, however ephemeral, however quixotic, speaks to the persistance and vigilance of a poetic culture unwilling simply to wallow in self-pity. In the next two chapters, I show how two poets, June Jordan and Barrett Watten, embodied ascendant modes of poetries (performance and language-school) flexible enough to challenge the new conditions of postmodern warfare.

7. June Jordan's Righteous Certainty

POETIC ADDRESS IN RESISTANCE POETRY

Despite the fact that racial minorities, immigrants, and working people bear a disproportionate burden in times of war, with higher degrees of participation and casualties than their white counterparts, and despite the fact that the trajectory of war resistance has moved parallel to, and often in symbiosis with, the Civil Rights struggle, many accounts of war resistance suffer from a lack of representation of minority voices. Yet the peace movement has never been reducible to simply a white movement. African Americans have contributed crucially to the peace movement—at least since the Second World War, when Bayard Rustin became a conscientious objector who would later organize the 1963 March on Washington—and they have challenged the peace movement to confront the homefront as a site of war and to see how that homefront conflict is connected to the national liberation struggles of the postcolonial world.

In *Race against Empire*, Penny Von Eschen recounts the incident during the Second World War of an anti-imperialist Calypso song, "Rum and Coca-Cola" penned by Trinidadian musician Lord Invader, becoming the third-best selling record of the 1940s for the Andrews Sisters—without credit given to the original composer. The song describes the ways in which the arrival of American troops to the island creates a market for prostitution and leads to dramatic social upheaval for the local population: "Since the Yankees came to Trinidad / They have the young girls going mad, / The young girls say they treat them nice, / And they give them a better price" (qtd. in Von Eschen 37). For the Trinidadians—as for many other peoples in the Global South—the Second World War and the influx of U.S. soldiers occasionally led to a tumultuous social crisis in terms of genders and generations. Sung by the Andrews Sisters in the United States, the song's meanings threatened to turn from biting social protest to a white society's fascination with the sexual power of "the Yankee dollar" (37). Yet, for its black listeners—and for the readers of the newspaper story in the Chicago *Defender* by Romona Lowe—it must have echoed the master-slave narratives of the American South and the subsequent cooptation of "race music" for white listeners. Finally, that the African American press saw fit to expose this story suggests—as Von Eschen does throughout her book—that African Americans saw their own situation mirrored in the oppression and national liberation movements of colonized peoples throughout the world.

During the Vietnam War, coming on the heels of the Civil Rights movement and the burgeoning Black Power movement that would follow, African American poets took the forefront in theorizing, envisioning, and creating a Black Nationalist imaginary. The Black Arts movement, headed by Amiri Baraka, Larry Neal, Sonia Sanchez, and others, through sheer force of rhetoric and commitment, captured the imagination of the older generation of black poets such as Gwendolyn Brooks (and, more recently, a younger generation of rapper-poets such as Chuck D of Public Enemy and Michael Franti of Disposable Heroes of Hipoprisy and Spearhead). I have previously shown how African American intellectuals and poets connected their struggle with the struggle of Vietnamese people. As the Black Panther Party and the Black Arts movement espoused supporting Vietnamese resistance to what they saw as U.S. colonialism, so too did African American poets write poems against the war or in support of the Vietnamese people. In "Vietnam #4," for instance, Clarence Major drives home how the inequities in U.S. casualties in Vietnam replicate the inequities at home:

a cat said
on the corner

how come so many
of us niggers

are dying over there
in that white
man's war

they say more of us
are dying

than them peckerwoods
& it just
    don't make sense

unless it's true
that the honkeys

are trying to kill us out
with the same stone

they killing them other cats
with

you know, he said
two birds with one stone (Goodman 175)

That black GIs were dying at higher rates than white GIs doesn't lead to a condemnation of the war itself, but rather to the way in which, for Major, the overseas war is a projection of the war at home. The concerns of Black Nationalist
poets thus resided much more strongly in creating what Larry Neal in his essay
"The Cultural Front" (1965) calls "arriving at an understanding of the Afro-
American . . . through his culture." In other words, the real action for African
American poetry at the time—and indeed, the real war, for black people—was
happening in American cities, not just in some jungle in Vietnam.

June Jordan emerged from the crucible of Black Nationalism in the early
1970s into a consciousness that embraced a progressive vision that was feminist, internationalist, and against imperial war. If at first she focused on
African American issues—in her words, "the people I was writing for and on
behalf of and hoping to reach . . . were black people" (CW 139)—then later
she increasingly focused in both poems and prose on linking the struggle of
African Americans to those of the Third World, especially in areas of colonization and state oppression: South Africa, Central America, Palestine, and
Lebanon.[1] Indeed, June Jordan's war resistance poetry—articulating its protest
against American neocolonial militarism and its solidarity with the peoples of
the Middle East bearing the brunt of U.S. bombing and U.S. policies—sutures
the struggles of black Americans to the struggle against war.

In this chapter, I explore how Jordan's poetry—in particular, her poems
that protest war, where the question of audience is particularly vexed—work
through the problematics of poetic address. Far from simplistic rhetoric, Jordan's poetry imagines—even creates—a rhetorical situation that alternately
hails and repels its audience(s). Even though her poetry occasionally lapses
into self-congratulatory righteousness and absolutism, Jordan's stance of
"righteous certainty" is itself a necessary performance of self-empowerment

on behalf of the disenfranchised selves that Jordan identifies with and champions—in particular, the people of color both at home and abroad victimized by American power. Her poetry, an extension and elaboration of her politics, challenges the accepted conventions both of the dominant verse culture—which never really accepted Black Nationalist poetry as legitimate—and of the Black Nationalist and feminist poetics that initially influenced her. A brief examination of the question of poetic address—so important in Jordan's poetry as rhetorical act—illuminates how Jordan's poetry both bypasses the limits of nationalist poetics and presents new questions regarding the nature of poetry and of war resistance.

The radical politics of the late 1960s that spurred on oppositional cultural aesthetic programs encouraged poetry directed to its own "nations"—whether defined in racial, gender, or political terms (as we have seen in Levertov's narrowing poetic address to the New Left). Phillip Brian Harper has argued that Black Arts poetry relied upon an address that actually worked to separate, rather than galvanize, African Americans into those who were part of the program and those who were "Uncle Toms." Harper argues that though the Black Arts aesthetic proposes an antiwhite oppositionality, "the drama of interracial strife that this rhetoric represents also serves to further another objective of Black Arts poetry—the establishment of *intra*racial distinctions that themselves serve to solidify the meaning of the Black Aesthetic" (240). Harper uses Benveniste's theory of "peculiar relation that obtains between the second-person pronoun and the first-person (singular) pronoun, emphasizing that 'you' is necessarily designated by 'I' and cannot be thought outside a situation set up by starting with 'I'" (249). The use of the second person pronoun, a deictic, for Harper, "precludes the construction of an effective black nationalist *collectivity*" (italics his 250). The oppositional logic inherent in the I/you dichotomy plays out as a fundamental opposition within black subjectivity (250). Underlying Harper's argument is the notion—and one that has been worked over throughout African American literary history—that the Black Arts poems addressed to African Americans have another addressee besides simply African Americans. At the same time, as Michael Davidson notes, "this shifting pronominal usage . . . is made unstable by the fact that the 'I' is constructed around hierarchically ordered gender divisions" (*GLU* 131); this 'I' in Black Arts poems such as Amiri Baraka's "SOS" is implied to be a (black) man talking to other (black) men (*pace* Wordsworth).

In response to the patriarchal culture that not only suffused mainstream American culture but even permeated the radical subcultures as well, feminist poets such as Adrienne Rich, Susan Griffin, Marge Piercy, and Judy

Grahn emerged to critique patriarchy and attempt to build their own nation. The prevailing feminist formulation, hijacking Wordsworth's notion of the poet as "a man speaking to men" (Montefiore 399), called for a poetry of "women speaking to each other" (Montefiore 11). Yet, as Jan Montefiore has argued, radical feminist poetics inherited an "unrecognized romanticism" that privileges the feminist poet's ability to speak representatively about woman's experience. The feminist right to speak representatively did not go unchallenged, as women of color exposed how such (white female) representative speaking elided other women's voices, just as (white) male representative speaking had. In light of her experiences in Black Nationalism and in feminist liberation, June Jordan's poetry—indeed, all her writing—has negotiated the problematics of (poetic) address by tending toward a transnational poetics of resistance. Like K. Anthony Appiah's idea of a postcolonial novel that rejects both "the Western imperium . . . [and] the nationalist project of the . . . bourgeoisie" (435), Jordan's poetry, despite its origins in the United States, asserts and summons a community *not bounded by nationality* that must resist imperial oppression. The notion of resistance is so central to Jordan's poetry and her activism that it displaces revolutionary politics for a resistance to the flagrant abuse of power. In an essay, "Notes toward a Model of Resistance," Jordan recounts her experience of two rapes, traumas about which she has frequently written in the past. She laments that she

> had been unable to find within myself
> the righteous certainty
> that resistance
> requires
> the righteous certainty that would explode my paralysis
> and bring me to an "over my dead
> body"
> determination
> to stop
> his violence
> stop
> his violation of everything that I am. (AA 149)

Jordan performs or exercises "righteous certainty" in ways that most American poets, weaned on an aesthetic of ambiguity and disinterestedness, might find unnerving. But Jordan's righteous certainty is not the occasionally masculinist and exclusivist ideology of Black Nationalist poetics—

where assertions of black male power could shut out female and nonblack contributions to the struggle for justice—even though her stance shares a nationalist will to power.[2] In the poem above, righteous certainty as a performative stance enables the poet to "explode [her] paralysis"—that sense of utter lack of physical control as a result of rape. As Jordan situates herself among the voiceless and the powerless, her writing becomes at once an (self) exhortation to the voiceless and a cry of outrage against those who silence voices with their force; in other words, righteous certainty is not a proclamation of a fundamentalism that proposes to know the truth for everyone. Rather, it is a performance of self-worth in the face of physical and psychological brutalization.

There is perhaps no better articulation of how racial oppression complicates the Yeatsian dogma of poem as "self-argument" and its distance from rhetoric than Audre Lorde's "Power." Written in response to the not guilty verdict of a police officer who killed a ten-year-old boy (in which a single black woman of the jury "was convinced" by the eleven white men), Lorde casts the stakes of poetry in starkly violent terms:

> The difference between poetry and rhetoric
> is being
> ready to kill
> yourself
> instead of your children (qtd. in Rich WIFT 68)

For Lorde, the difference is not a matter of argument but of absolute consequences, death and life. In Lorde's recalibration of Yeats's distinction between poetry and rhetoric, poetry is a kind of self-murder, insofar as it calls one to be ready to sacrifice the self for the sake of the future. The line breaks here exacerbate the tension between violence against another and against oneself—and suggest that these violences are intimately connected. Further, the lines suggest a kind of Sophie's choice—either you will die, or your children will. Lorde's desire to overcome her own self-protection—just as she wished the single black juror had, to stand up for the sacredness of that murdered child—requires her to access her own destructive impulses and, in her words, "to use / the difference between poetry and rhetoric" (qtd. in Rich WIFT 69) to be able to live without hating all white people.

Like Audre Lorde's, then, Jordan's poetry works through the dialectic between truth telling and community building. On the one hand, Jordan defines poetry as "a political action undertaken for the sake of information, the faith, the exorcism, and the lyrical invention that telling the truth makes possible. Poetry is a means of taking control of the language of your life" (*Muller* 3). On the other hand, Jordan also sees poetry writing as a viable way of building the self and the beloved community: "this inward and outward attunement [of poetry] seems to me a most reasonable basis for the political beginning of a beloved community: a democratic state in which the people can trust the names they have invented for themselves, and for each other" (*Muller* 8). Explicitly, a tension exists between the righteous certainty of the self and building community. In her formulation, the names that people invent for themselves may not be the names that others give them. It may be true as well, though, that righteous certainty is indeed a stance toward those outside the community, toward the state and its repressive apparatuses. The line between a poetry of self-creation and a poetry of community building is precisely where Jordan's poetry constantly labors, both hailing and seeking, both inquiring and exhorting.

It is in her poetry dealing with violence and war that we can mark the movement of Jordan's poetry between an exhortation to the brutalized self and a protest for the weak against the abuse of power. An early autobiographical poem, influenced by Elizabeth Bishop's coming-of-age poem "In the Waiting Room," Jordan's "War and Memory" explicitly connects the abusive violence of her father to a system of racial domination that manifests itself both "at home" and abroad in physical violence. In contrast, though, to Bishop's quietly turbulent meditation in the waiting room, Jordan finds herself in a home that resembles a war zone. Her father Granville regularly brandishes literal and emotional knives at his wife, while June the child tries to find ways of intervening on behalf of her mother:

> I'd match him fast
> for madness . . .
> I would race about for weaponry
> another chair a knife
> a flowered glass
> the radio
> "You stop it, Daddy! Stop It!:
> brandishing my arsenal
> my mother
> silently
> beside the point. (*DD* 464–465)

It is only through her own weapons that she can defend herself and her mother, who remains "beside the point"—that is, she is both without agency to influence the monological argument of the father and literally threatened by the "point" of the knife.

Her identification with her mother and, implicitly, her disidentification with her father and his violence, emerges over how each "reads" war—whether we should read war as ultimately about the victims or the victimizers. When the family looks at pictures from the *National Geographic*—another echo of Bishop's poem—during the Second World War, the mother interprets the photographs (and implicitly, the war) to be "about the Jews," while the father argues that the war is about "the Nazis" (*DD* 466). The mother's identification with Jewish girls and women forced to "march through snow until they die" makes Jordan wonder

> if my family was a war
> going on
> and if
> there would soon be blood
> someplace in the house
> and where
> the blood of my family would come from (*DD* 466–467)

The national wars—the Second World War, the Korean War, the Vietnam War, the War on Poverty—emerge against that sense of "war" as something that pervades daily life. Jordan recalls, as a child, phoning the government to tattle on her parents' consumption of Victory resources or her father's abuse of her mother, but the state never intervened in either case.

Given Jordan's background, it is not surprising that she might approach war resistance and the struggle for peace in a way that foregrounds her own identity as a warrior for justice. Toward the end of "War and Memory," Jordan asserts "peace never meant a thing to me" and "I / thought I was a warrior growing up" (*DD* 469–470). Her personal militancy, along with her growing race and gender awareness through involvement in Black Nationalism and feminism, led her to develop an anti-imperialist solidarity with Third World movements for liberation in countries like Cuba, Palestine, and South Africa. Jordan's contextual pacifism, therefore, is hardly absolutist. In one essay, she recalls how "South Africa was how I came to understand that I am not against war. But war means that you fight. I know my life depends on making this fight my own" (*OC* 17–18). Mary K. DeShazer has shown how writers such as Jordan, Audre Lorde, and Maxine Hong Kingston have all used the imagery of woman warriors in order to interrogate their own oppression and articulate their own means of liberation. True to the spirit of the woman warrior, who needs to summon the "righteous certainty" that the society has refused her, Jordan ends the poem with a litany of actions that steel her against the degradations of war:

> And from the freedom days
> that blazed outside my mind
> I fell in love
> I fell in love with Black men White
> men Black
> women White women
> and I
> dared myself to say The Palestinians . . .
> and I wrote everything I knew how to write against apartheid
> and I
> thought I was a warrior growing up
> and I
> buried my father with all of the ceremony all of the music I could piece
>   together
> and I
> lust for justice
> and I
> make that quest arthritic/pigeon-toed/however
> and I
> invent the mother of the courage I require not to quit. (*DD* 470)

Jordan's litany, buoyed by the repetitions of the phrase "and I," becomes a kind of self-making, in which the speaker figuratively gives birth to herself in the final line. To invent one's mother is to reinvent the past in order to live a different present. In this line, Jordan also alludes to the central character in Bertolt Brecht's *Mother Courage and Her Children*, a woman who is battered by war, losing all three of her children over the course of the play. The invention of a "mother of the courage" is precisely what Jordan refers to as "righteous certainty"—when her burdens become almost too heavy to bear, she needs to invent herself a certainty in order "not to quit."

Jordan's other war resistance poetry not only adopts the conventions of the autobiographical lyric to situate itself but also occasionally satirizes those conventions; war resistance poetry, after all, has a long tradition of subverting mainstream language and texts for agitprop purposes. "War Verse," for example, mimics the opening line of Robert Frost's "Mending Wall" in order to rethink both the logic of war and the rhetoric of poetry:

> Something there is that sure must love a plane
> No matter how many you kill with what kind of
> bombs or how much blood you manage to spill
> you never will hear the cries of pain
>
> Something there is that sure must love a plane
> The pilots are never crazy or mean
> and bombing a hospital's quick and it's clean
> and how could you call such previous insane?
>
> Something there is that sure must love a plane! (*DD* 385–386)

Jordan thus takes Frost's line—"Something there is that doesn't love a wall"—from a poem that appears to advocate that neighbors question the boundaries that they place between one another—and uses it to her own sardonic ends. Jordan's poem hails the literate reader and invites her not only to question Americans' mystical attraction to air power but also to rethink the politics of the Frost poem. Though Frost may have been politically conservative, "Mending Wall" unsettlingly dramatizes the dialectic between the conservative injunction for hard boundaries and the liberal longing for openness. In the original poem, the something that doesn't love the wall is nature itself—the frost working its way in the stone wall; here, that which doesn't love boundaries is the plane. In Jordan's reworking, we are forced to consider the politics of space in warfare—how warfare's conduct fundamentally concerns the violation of the spatial integrity of other states, and inevitably, the physical wholeness of the bodies that occupy those spaces.

Poetry for the People and the Persian Gulf War

Jordan herself became a kind of Mother Courage to her students as well; in the late 1980s, Jordan began to experiment with combining the study and the writing of poetry in her Women's Studies and African American Studies classes, founding a project known as Poetry for the People. Jordan recounts that bringing together poetry reading and writing was part of her belief that "the creation of poems [is] a foundation for true community: a fearless democratic society" (Muller 3). The Poetry for the People project became a crucible for Jordan's activism against the impending Gulf War, which led to a teach-in on the Persian Gulf crisis: "Faculty colleagues of many disciplines, and student activists of several ideologies, and of every color and ethnicity and sexual persuasion fixed their energies to create a powerful day that was decently documented by local television, radio, and press. Ours was . . . the first such "Teach-In" in the U.S.A." (Muller 7).

During and after the war, she engaged in activism, attending numerous antiwar rallies (including one called Poets and Politicians against the War), and published articles in the *Progressive*, including "A Big-Time Coward," which criticizes the waste of government funds on warfare. Listening to a recording of her at the Poets and Politicians against the War on the Democracy Now! website, one can hear the power and authority of Jordan's voice as she asserts her pride in "the increasing numbers of African American conscientious objectors" (AA 15), the number of black congressmen who voiced their opposition to the war, and the overall skepticism of African Americans to support the war. At the end of the piece, she directly addresses the president, as war resisters like Lowell and others before have done, in words and through their actions, allying herself with the "weak": "But all of us who are weak, we watch you. And we learn from your hatred. And we do not forget. And we are many Mr. President. We are most of the people on this godforsaken planet" (AA 15). One might argue that Jordan moved from writing on behalf of African Americans to writing on behalf of the weak; that "the weak," in Jordan's coinage, tend to be people of color is doubtless, though Jordan had no problem with confronting people, regardless of race, who abused their power.

During the early 1990s, Jordan and her students gathered and published their work, under the title "Poetry in a Time of War," and included a selection in *June Jordan's Poetry for the People: A Revolutionary Blueprint*. The diversity of the poems reflects Jordan's sense of war as something that is not simply a conflict between states; her wider understanding of warfare reflects women's experience of violence. Leslie Shown's "What I Mean" argues against the notion that the U.S. entered the war because of an ethical injunction to stop rapes by Iraqi soldiers of Kuwaiti women:

> there's nothin
> an Iraqi soldier might do to a Kuwaiti woman
> that an American soldier wouldn't do to an Iraqi woman
> that the Contras didn't do to a Sandanista woman

that there's nothin
an Iraqi soldier might do to a Kuwaiti woman
that an American man hasn't done to an American woman
somewhere in my neighborhood
in the last twenty-four hours. (Muller 200)

Shown's piece does more than expose the illusion of a foreign policy based on moral principles; it casts American life itself as a condition of warfare against women, where women live in the knowledge of physical violence. Jordan wrote explicitly about the connection between rape and war; in *Passion* (1980), poems about rape like "Case in Point" and "Rape Is Not a Poem" move directly into critiques of imperialism like "A Poem about Vieques, Puerto Rico," where the militarized colony of Vieques becomes the site of U.S. target practice and of sexual rape. Similarly, in *Kissing God Goodbye* (1997), Jordan's viciously sardonic "Bosnia Bosnia" suggests that the lack of oil in Bosnia had something to do with the U.S. government's inaction when Muslim women were being raped and brutalized: "too bad / there is no oil / between her legs" (*DD* 542).

Jordan confronted warmakers and the imperial racism that justified the Gulf War through her own poetry, as well, in "The Bombing of Baghdad" (1997), which uses a variety of poetic and rhetorical devices alternately to summon and repel her audience. Far from being a simplistic agitprop piece, the poem at its best moments complicates our notion of audience by foregrounding the implied national "we" that has undergirded much American poetry. "The Bombing of Baghdad" is built, first and foremost, on anaphoric catalogue—a repetition of an initial phrase that becomes a kind of chant. Chant is a crucial element in both late twentieth-century poetry (particularly the Beats) and African American cultural forms. Kim Whitehead has written about how Jordan's poetry comes out of the "nontextual, communal, performance-based" traditions like blues, gospel, spiritual, jazz, and Black English (93). Jordan's war resistance poetry is a community-building action, which "builds a sense of an integrated and deeply rooted political project that nevertheless recognizes, respects, and even relies on difference" (86).

Motivated by a specific event, and performed for and directed toward a particular audience, "The Bombing of Baghdad" uses chant both to invoke the relentlessness of the 42-day bombing campaign as well as to catalogue the human catastrophe that led from the destruction. Alternating between elegy, protest, and alternative wire service, the poem hurtles directly from the title into the thick of battle:

> began and did not terminate for 42 days
> and 42 nights relentless minute after minute
> more than 100,000 times
> we bombed Iraq we bombed Baghdad
> we bombed Basra/we bombed military
> installations we bombed the National Museum
> we bombed schools we bombed air raid
> shelters we bombed water we bombed
> electricity we bombed hospitals we
> bombed streets we bombed highways
> we bombed everything that moved/we
> bombed Baghdad
> a city of 5.5 million human beings (*DD* 535–536).

Jordan's catalogue reports to us the bombing targets, alluding to the extent to which civilians and civilian life bore the brunt of the war; in other words, this poem acts as a kind of uncensored news story. In addition, Jordan's use of the word "we" is dual—it refers to the national community, but it also refers to the war resistance community, which by virtue of national passport and taxes (and even by watching CNN) ultimately shares complicity in the destruction. Jordan's cagey use of the pronoun "we" constitutes a refusal to make the distinctions between protestors and patriots, and acts as a kind of provocation to both. Here, as in Stafford's poems and Levertov's early antiwar poetry, there is no rejection of the national collective, but rather a concerted attempt to include herself in that we. In terms of its community-building function, at this point the poem acts as an admonishment to the community—whether imagined nationally or ideologically—and to herself.

In succeeding sections of the poem, Jordan introduces two other elements to the bombing narrative: (1) a personal lyric, one of physical love; and (2) a historical narrative that recounts the death of Crazy Horse and the exploits of Custer. Though the personal lyric shows us the primacy and endurance of physical love—"The bombing of Baghdad / did not obliterate the distance or the time / between my body and the breath / of my beloved" (536)—it also relates how the war did not manifest itself physically for American civilians. The historical narrative, which dominates the poem from sections III to VI, makes an explicit connection between the "guts and gore of manifest white destiny" of Custer and U.S. Western expansion and the bombing of Iraq, and shifts the poem into one of outright, even traitorous, opposition. Jordan compares Crazy Horse's singing and "the moaning in the Arab world" and asserts defiantly "I am cheering for the arrows / and the braves" (537)—those whose weapons are anachronistic and who are doomed. Perhaps such a gesture is possible only in retrospect, given the fact that the genocidal inequality between the U.S. and its foes (whether Native American or Iraqi) was only clear after the devastation was complete. (It would be instructive to know how and when Jordan composed and read this poem to audiences, though I have not been able to track down the poem's early reception.) The (belated) identification with the "braves"/Iraqis, in any case, does not stem from a naïve attachment to Iraqi nationalism, but rather comes out of a solidarity with the weak—those who are silenced, victimized, and erased from history.

Does Jordan's identification with those who are weak or voiceless cause her to collapse the real differences in the histories of Native Americans and Iraqis, thereby weakening the poem's historical analysis? Undoubtedly, Jordan elides numerous distinctions between these two events and opens herself to criticism that the poem is either treasonous or based on faulty comparison. At the same time, Jordan's analogy suggests an historical analysis of imperial racism and thereby makes connections that are not immediately obvious to most Americans. Jordan is not the first to argue that the U.S. imperial adventures appear to be a kind of repetition compulsion of the clearing of the West and the genocide of Native Americans. The poem therefore invites, perhaps even summons and creates, an audience familiar with or marked by the histories of African Americans, Native Americans, and Arab Americans (not to mention those non-American peoples who might read or hear the poem) allied through common experience of imperial racism.

As she summons this multicultural, multiracial audience, like the Black Arts poetry that Harper analyzes, Jordan makes a provocative exclusion, against those who exclude others from their definition of humanity:

> All who believed some must die
> they were already dead
> And all who believe only they possess
> human being and therefore human rights
> they no longer stood among the possibly humane . . .
> And all who believed that waging war is anything
>   besides terrorist activity in the first
>   place and in the last . . .

And all who believed that holocaust means something
   that only happens to white people (*DD* 537–538)

Here, Jordan attacks the myth of American exceptionalism—that notion that
the United States somehow is qualitatively different from other nations and
not subject to the same problems or critiques. In particular, Jordan homes in
on the way in which the United States has either failed to acknowledge, or occasionally even abetted genocide, particularly in the Third World. This is the
language of righteous certainty, where Jordan's political vision clears away—
perhaps too assiduously—the ambiguous self-critique of the first part of the
poem. In contrast, perhaps, to the poems that exclude others on the basis of
race (and here one might include a range of poems from segregationist to
Black Nationalist poems), Jordan's poem excludes on the basis of belief, or
ideology. In other words, Jordan makes a strategic choice that she cannot address certain people; they, in her words "were already dead" (537). Such a
strategy is exhortative, since, as opposed to the categories of identity like race
and ethnicity, belief is malleable and subject to change. The poem, then, invites the reader to identify with the living; even if one resists the
Manicheanism of these lines, they have a moral force that compels the lis-
tener to be on the side of the living.
   In its final stanzas, the poem becomes both elegy and apology, turning to
address the "victims of the bombing." The community of the poem opens out
again, desiring to reach beyond all national bounds:

And in the aftermath of carnage
perpetrated in my name
how should I dare to offer you my hand
how shall I negotiate the implications
   of my shame? (538)

Jordan's rhetorical gesture to the victims of U.S. policy, repeated in an earlier
poem "Apologies to All the People in Lebanon" (1989) proposes an alternative
to the Yeatsian "quarrel with ourselves" even as it emerges out of a similar
sense of conflictedness, paralysis, and complicity.
   In the poem, "Apologies to All the People in Lebanon," Jordan addresses
the entire poem to, as she notes in her epigraph, "the 600,000 Palestinian
men, women, and children who lived in Lebanon from 1948–1983" (381). The
poem ends:

Yes, I did know it was the money I earned as a poet that
paid
for the bombs and the planes and the tanks
that they used to massacre your family

But I am not an evil person
The people of my country aren't so bad

You can't expect but so much
from those of us who have to pay taxes and watch
American tv

You see my point;

I'm sorry.
I really am sorry. (DD 382)

Here, even as she addresses the other, the poem turns the accusation against herself, but in a way that suggests first a resistance to that sense of guilt and then an acquiescence to it. In both poems, Jordan's linguistic gesture, finally, is one of peace—the offering of the hand, the language of "negotiation." The peace proposed is elegiac, a "song of the living / who must sing against the dying" (DD 538), but an elegy of solidarity of futurity, rather than one of solipsism and melancholia for the past.

Can a poem literally reach outside of its national bounds, or is Jordan's addressing of Iraqi and Lebanese civilians merely an empty gesture? Unlike the poetry valorized by and written for the New Criticism, Jordan's poetry constantly breaches the boundaries of—and requires us to move past—the page. Jordan's poems ask to be read aloud, in disparate contexts, and not remain an urn to be admired behind the safety of museum glass. Throughout her life, she traveled to places like Lebanon, Nicaragua, and other war-torn countries to witness to—and provide support for—people living through the devastation of civil wars that her country occasionally sanctioned or even covertly supported. One imagines that she may actually have had the opportunity to read poems like these to hardly imaginary audiences in Nicaragua or Lebanon, who would hear her attempt to offer her hand despite her government's actions. Unlike the urn poetry of the New Criticism, this is a poetry that foregrounds itself as a provocation, as something to be argued with, rather than as an object to admire or venerate.

These poems ask that we struggle with and against them—with their outrageous acts of solidarity with others, against their occasionally swift denunciations of nuanced self-questioning. Further, the poems themselves ask for similar actions of the reader and provide themselves as scripts for future movements against war and on behalf of the silenced and the brutalized. Jordan's lifetime work interweaving her political and poetic visions offers a model that inspires and admonishes those of us engaged in the tricky balancing act of art and activism. Finally, her work challenges the peace movement to abandon simplistic notions of peace, with its keen vision of how structural and actual violence can permeate nearly all spaces of human life.

8. Barrett Watten's Bad History

COUNTER-EPIC OF THE GULF WAR

The debate between Baudrillard and Norris (and Chomsky) outlined in chapter 6 renders all too clearly that the Gulf War caused a crisis for intellectuals and artists alike, struggling in the shifting sands of the new warfare to find their ground; the war's televisual representation—i.e., missile-eye camera perspectives, obfuscatory debriefing sessions, the blitzkrieg speed, and the general absence of physical evidence of conflict (the dead themselves)—nullified the kinds of lyric responses upon which war resister poets traditionally relied. Perhaps because of its avoidance of lyric immediacy and imagery, Barrett Watten's *Bad History* (1998) wrestles with the war in a way that is almost commensurate with the logic of what Paul Virilio calls "Pure War": that state of preparedness for war that constitutes the real war. At its best moments, *Bad History* articulates a poetic strategy that mediates the theoretical deadlock between Baudrillardian postmodernism and Chomskyan rationalism. By embracing a Baudrillardian strategy of immersing oneself in the spectacle, without fatuously reveling in it, while at the same time offering for a source-heavy, Chomskyan poetic critique of the war that does not extract itself from its own subjective position, Watten's *Bad History* effects a resistance that moves beyond smug, self-congratulatory rhetoric. By invoking, and then countering, a poetic form that itself has glorified wars—the epic—in a poetry adequate to the conditions of postmodernity, *Bad History* stands out as the most fully realized poetic engagement of the Persian Gulf War.[1]

At the same time, to say that the only way to read *Bad History* is as a poem *about* the Gulf War would be overzealous. Of the thirty prose pieces comprising the book, only the first seven—the first 27 pages of a 128-page poem (part A of parts A–F), with 21 pages of endnotes—centrally concern the event of the war. The range of subject matter—from readings of office buildings to meditations on William Carlos Williams, from reflection on being named his mother's executor to mulling over the ongoing shifts in area codes and the subject positions of screen savers—belies any reading of this poem as a "Gulf War" poem. Yet, that *Bad History* is framed by the language of the art review (the poem entitled "The 1980s") and the language of a financial prospectus (the poem entitled "The 1990s") evokes the conditions of postmodernity in which a war like the Gulf War takes place. *Bad History*, in short, is not simply about the Gulf War; however, by its attempt to lay bare the problematics of narration, of subjectivizing the history of the 1980s and 1990s, it actively resists the representation of that war as star-spangled tracers and ticker tape parades.

Because of its obsessional relation to narration and history making, *Bad History* evokes most particularly the tradition of twentieth–century epic initiated by Ezra Pound's *Cantos*, itself a counter to the tradition of epics narrating the birth of a nation through the heroism of warfare. *Bad History* counters its own epic tendencies in three basic ways. First, it problematizes the history-making procedure of epic through enacting a "poetics of interference" and by stretching an account of the Gulf War beyond the forty-plus-day television event known as "Operation Desert Storm." Second, it articulates a subjectivity vacillating between complicity and resistance, creating a text at war with its own positionality. Third, even though it forgoes the rhetorical oppositionality of antiwar verse, it nonetheless resists through form. Using hypotactic sentences, footers, columnar style, and hefty appendix of secondary sources, it challenges the formal and ideological limits of mainstream lyric poetry through a language-based "poetry for use."

The Poetics of Interference and the Epic Poem

How to frame a poem attempting to cover a subject as virtualized as the Persian Gulf War? The photograph on the cover of *Bad History*, "Decoy #1" by Michal Rovner, introduces some of the essential problems of any history of the Gulf War (see http://www3.iath.virginia.edu/pmc/issue.503/13.3metres.html). It is itself an enactment of Bad History. Slightly off center on the cover, the photo depicts a gray, indistinct figure also set slightly off center in the photograph, holding both arms above his or her head. Nothing else is visible, and even the ground is indistinct from the sky, creating the impression that the figure could be suspended *in utero*. The grainy grays of the photo render it, indeed, somewhere between a uterine photograph and the televisual images released from the Pentagon, which were replete with target markers and "missile-eye" views of the buildings, bridges, and vehicles to be destroyed. Lacking all contexts, our reading of the image is blocked. We do not even know, for example, if the figure is American or Iraqi; is the gesture one of victory or surrender? We do not know, as well, whether the figure faces us or someone else outside of the picture. We do not know when or where the picture was taken, or even if it is a photograph at all. It seems equally possible that it appeared as a cave sketch of sun worship. But even if it contains the possibility of being an image of either Iraqi or American—and this is most crucial—because the image blocks particularity and is void of affect, it also blocks identification.

Rovner's work anticipates the poetics of interference central to *Bad History*. In a review of Rovner's exhibition, Watten noted how the artist's premise was that "where unthinkable events are concerned, interference is as much a form of knowledge as clarity" ("Michal Rovner" 14). In contrast to the tradition of war photojournalism, where the photograph articulates in its fine detail not only the scene of war but also the position of the journalist-witness, and hence the imagined audience at the homefront, Rovner's images, according to Watten, "obstruct and render virtually abstract the faces of war . . . through the limits of the media, and in Rovner's self-conscious imitation of the gaps in transmission through techniques of reprocessing and reframing, what is depicted is a new relation of knowledge to events. . . . This knowledge is open-ended, a permanent threat" (14). In other words, Rovner reproduces the war in such a way that it lacks decisiveness, it lacks a narrative, it lacks the fine grain of the hero's face. Yet, because Rovner's images enact the technology of information transmission, in all its gaps, they are themselves historical records of the Gulf War, insofar as the war was one of information transmission and obstruction, where the war's first hero, in the words of a CNN video, was "the Patriot missile."

Watten, along with others in the language poetry movement emerging in the early 1970s, have similarly worked to articulate a poetry resistant to commodification, absorption, and manipulation, countering the image-economy which is the engine of mainstream lyric poetry. I will forgo a full examination of language poetry's history, innovations, and principal agents, since it is not the central focus of this project to show how Watten is a Language poet, but rather a poet who, by virtue of his experimental approach to language, offers a sophisticated critique of past war resistance poetry and a new direction for its future. Further, such an analysis is probably increasingly unnecessary—given the current critical attention on the movement (or, in Ron Silliman's term, the "moment")—and perhaps impossible, given its heterogeneity. However, a brief glance at some of the contours of language poetry might suggest the way in which Watten's experimental tactics emerge precisely from the realization of lyric poetry's failure as social action during the Vietnam War. According to Bob Perelman's witty definition, Language writing was "a range of writing that was (sometimes) nonreferential, (occasionally) polysyn-tactic, (at times) programmatic in construction, (often) politically committed, (in places) theoretically inclined, and that enacted a critique of the literary I (in some cases)" (*MP* 21).

Perelman's parenthetical amendments suggests the degree to which the writ-ers who found each other in the early 1970s shared a multiplicity of poetic tac-tics rather than a single poetic strategy—even though this multiplicity of tactics suggests something unique about the movement. Frequently, those tactics had aims that struck at poetry as a discourse that offered illusions of transparency: transparency of subjectivity (the lyric self), transparency of language (common language made pure), and transparency of image (the image as window onto the real). For example, in their 1988 essay, "Aesthetic Tendency and the Politics of Poetry: A Manifesto," Watten and four other language poets offer two propos-als: (1) to dissociate the "marginal isolated individualism" (Silliman et al. 264) of the narrative persona so valued in contemporary poetry and (2) to write a "contaminated" rather than a "pure" language (269).[2]

These proposals for a new poetry, from a certain angle, address the way in which some lyric war resistance poetry assumed a position of pristine distance from which one could compose transparent images of U.S. war atrocities on Vietnamese civilians, without regard for the ways in which American poets were implicated in the war by their position of distant privilege. In the end, this poetry undergirded the illusion that a pure lyric language could resist an-other pure language without consequences—in particular, the bureaucratic language of the Department of Defense, with its technocratic terms such as "body counts," "collateral damage," and "friendly fire."

Watten's poetry prior to *Bad History* pursued a rigorously abstract, theoretical, self-distancing strategy that might be considered the absolute negation of the lyric; at times, it is difficult to tell the difference between Watten's theoretical writing and his poetry. The only difference is often the publication context—that is, to state one of Watten's poetic concerns, *a frame* that tells us "this is a poem." In a poem alluding to Pound's *ABC of Reading*, Watten's "The XYZ of Reading" (1988) waxes theoretical about the danger of the lyric as substitute for political action (an implicit attack on the work of Levertov and Carolyn Forché) and anticipates *Bad History*:

> Romantic negativity, the avoidance of any conditions that compromise
> the subject leading to the subject's lyrical denial of itself, is too easily
> symptomatic. It's easy enough to feel victimized by the daily news, for

example, and that may be what is intended. Lyrical horror is our "participation in democracy" at the level of violence of compulsory voting in El Salvador. Taken as an assertion, then, such lyricism no longer works even as a form of bondage between writers. (*Frame* 153)

Watten's language here aggressively provokes the question: how is this a poem? There are none of the poetic devices that one might encounter in a traditional poem; it reads more like a poetic statement or manifesto rather than a poem. What we have, at its most stripped down, is the movement of a mind troubled by poetry of witness, insofar as it appears a symptom rather than a symbolic action. For Watten, poets today can no longer retain any illusions that writing lyric poetry is a kind of (or replacement for) participatory democracy, as writers like Levertov had felt during the Vietnam War. What Watten pursues is a kind of poetry that might move against expressions of lyrical horror—which, itself, often become aestheticizations of violence for the purpose of bourgeois consumption—and instead locates itself in a consciousness constantly worrying over its own epistemological limits.

By countering the lyric's tendency to rely on image (not only on the cover but throughout the book), *Bad History* revises the televisual history of the Gulf War. Later, I demonstrate how Watten filters the images of war through a disembodied voice that hyperconsciously details the overdetermined nature of those images. However, here let it suffice that this poem resists by resisting the illusion of transparency. But Watten does not simply replace the official media representation of the war with a Chomskyan alternative history or a Forché-influenced lyric poetry of witness. In his evasion of the image-economy and lineation of lyric poetry, Watten's poem uses the sentence as his principal formal device. Heralded by Todorov as "an appropriate form . . . for a thematics of duality, contrast, and opposition," the prose poem has an extensive tradition as counter-poetry (qtd. in Monroe 19). But unlike mainstream narrative prose poetry, the New Sentence, in the hands of experimental poets like Ron Silliman or Watten, has an unsettlingly nonnarrative and cross-discursive thrust. Watten's combining and deforming multiple and often disparate discourses moves beyond the Orwellian critique of political language outlined in his "Politics and the English Language," in which Orwell maintains a faith in transparent, common-man language. In *Bad History*, we encounter a poetic subjectivity that cuts diagonally through art criticism, journalism, romantic lyric, dream language, and financial prospectus. The sentences stretch, harry, and perhaps even subvert the discourses they invoke. Poetry is not a kind of language divorced from these various discourses but rather, to paraphrase Jerome McGann, a complicating procedure toward and within those discourses (McGann "Contemporary Poetry" online). The poet becomes, at least for the span of certain sections, a dissenting journalist.[3]

Watten, therefore, moves beyond the space-time miniaturization of the lyric (in its private individual moment) into larger, more expansive cross-dimensional spaces, and over longer stretches of time, through a strategic invocation of the epic. This is admittedly a strange subgenre for Watten to choose, since the epic poem emerged as the form of nationalism *par excellence*, the story of a people's triumph by battles; even more so because televisual coverage of the Persian Gulf War resembled an epic where generals and technological weaponry were equal characters. However, with Pound's *Cantos* arose a new kind of epic, in opposition both to the lyric poem that had risen into dominance by the early twentieth century and the old epic, which required a more unified and univocal society. In Michael Andre Bernstein's formulation, Pound's "modern verse epic" might still court the strategy of articulating a national (or Western) culture, but it does so "in a society no longer unified by a single, generally accepted code of values . . . justifying its argument by the direct appeal of the author's own experiences and emotions" (79). Pound's *Cantos* opened the way for modernist experimentation in poems that would collage different texts, voices, and narratives into explorations of national (and even international) subjectivity, opening the field for a new American poetry.

Bad History's blurb suggests that the poem both invokes the Poundian epic—a poem "including history"—and yet also counters it—"In . . . *Bad History*, history includes the poem," by questioning the notion of the text that can somehow exist outside of history while it attempts to record history. Watten's "epic," therefore, is fundamentally at odds with the formal characteristics of epic but not with the project of epic making, of narrating a subjective (and even national) history. The opening caveat in the book's acknowledgments page, that "*Bad History* is a work of literature and makes no claim to factual accuracy" reverses the docudramatic co-optation of reality for literature, even while in practice *Bad History* rigorously harries any stable notion of history and factual accuracy. Further, the epigraph, from Mark Cousins's "The Practice of History Investigation" alludes to Watten's cagey approach to history, one equally as interested in the problem of trauma and representation as in censorship and representation: "The evident irritation expressed with a concept of event which does not measure up to its canons of evidence, the shock expressed at a practice whose interpretations refer to events which 'historically' may not have happened. . . . Imagine a practice of interpretation which prefers secondary sources, and unreliable witnesses!" (qtd. in Watten *BH* vii).

First, we see that Cousins is interested in the "irritation" and "shock" expressed by people (most likely historians) who are confronted with a countermethod that questions the very bases upon which "objective historiography" has relied. Second, we should note the distinction between the event and the evidence of the event, and the blurring of fiction and history. Finally, in a war where media coverage rendered impossible even the fantasy of secondary witness (that is, mediated witnessing), *Bad History* foregrounds the difficulty of American civilians to reconstruct what actually happened; any reconstructed narrative must rely, as Ramsey Clark attempts in *The Fire This Time: U.S. War Crimes in the Gulf*, on secondary witnesses and shaky sources. But if we are to take the quote as somehow representative of Watten's poem, then the preference for secondary sources represents a provocation, since this preference does not imply the availability of only secondary sources.

The Gulf War—itself an event to which most of us were secondary or even tertiary witnesses, if we witnessed it at all—is the ground from which *Bad History* emerges. For Watten the event of the Gulf War cannot speak for itself alone. Perhaps because of the incredibly brief span of the war, in marked contrast to the Vietnam War, Watten's text draws backward and propels forward, beginning in the 1980s and ending in the late 1990s. The war isn't just the war, but the social historical conditions that yielded its brief, deadly blooms. Part A, "The 1980s," begins with something not immediately concerned with the Gulf War: Philip Johnson's "postmodern office building." His art-critical musings, rather than simply avoiding history and the war, actually *look awry* at both history and war. By suspending an immediate discussion of the war and by focusing on a particular building that signifies the cultural historical (postmodern) spirit of the 1980s, Watten's move intimates that any discussion of the war must reach backward into the past, rather than at the particulars of the war's beginning. The office building becomes a mnemonic for the 1980s; even more, it suggests the way in which structures of monumentality signify a certain way of remembering. The book begins:

> Philip Johnson's postmodern office building at 580 California. The
> combination of facing motifs shows a simultaneous fascination with
> ironic control and the disavowal of any consequences. Cynically
> juxtaposing corporate-induced localism with functional office grids, the
> artificer has reduced all construction to a memorial bas-relief. Each view

is a little tomb, complete with signature crosslike prison bars. These bay windows must be our final release! (1)

His description indicates how the architecture itself foregrounds "ironic control" and "disavowal of any consequences" (1), two aspects that marked the position of the television viewer of the Gulf War. In this sense, then, the building anticipates the war—or perhaps even creates the conditions where such a war could be possible. In addition, each window view—"a little tomb, complete with signature crosslike prison bars" (1)—suggests the television screen merging with the crosshairs of a weapon sight. Moreover, the building seems to enact a kind of faux sublime transcendence—"these bay windows must be our final release!" (1)—and becomes instant memoir, just as the Gulf War became instant history. Echoing Baudrillard, each pedestal on the rooftop is a "blank marker for an event that might have been but never took place" (2). The building, in the end, suggests a widespread cultural situation in which events themselves could be mediatized out of existence.

A Homer Who Sees He Doesn't See

Bad History is a counter-epic in another sense, insofar as epics also have traditionally been the founding stories of nations, mythologizing its inner conflicts and external wars from the perspective of an impersonal communal voice. Because the media representation rendered the Gulf War—at least for the American viewer at home—an antiseptic affair, a Hollywood fantasy rewrite of Vietnam, Watten's counter-epic refuses the nationalist narrative and becomes itself a bad history. That is, it is a naughty history, an antinationalist history that shows bad form, that subjectivizes another history. But contrary to a simplistic rendering of Chomskyan oppositionality, Watten's self-positioning is a rejection of the antiwar argument (and, implicitly, Jamesonian positivism) that there is good and bad history, and that bad history is the one promulgated by mass media and administration lackeys, whereas good history is one that accounts for leftist critiques of U.S. power.

Bad History, therefore, is an epic of worried subjectivity, attempting to resist even while knowing its own complicities and limits—all the while refusing to bracket the moment at which the text is being produced. True to Cary Nelson's articulation of history as a palimpsest of past and present, the writing of *Bad History* itself is an event essential to understanding *Bad History*. In other words, as Watten wrote in a letter, "I'm living what I'm writing, not writing about what I experienced" (email November 22, 1999).[4] *Bad History* thereby rejects the tradition of war resistance verse that relies on a poetry of witness. It should not be surprising in Watten's poetry, insofar as the Language poetry movement reached back into another poetry tradition, that his antiwar influences also evoke another war resistance poetry tradition—the tradition of Pound, Duncan, and Ginsberg—one that "engages the irrational" and "rejects any form of symbolization for a more processual, and temporal account, one that does not simply leave the poet on the higher ground" (email November 22, 1999). His whole project, in fact, can be read as a reaction to Levertov; a witness in Berkeley to Levertov's participation in the People's Park demonstrations, Watten recalls "Denise Levertov on the steps of Sproul Hall, acting out her fantasies of revolution, just before the chain link fence of People's Park was stormed (Berkeley, 1969)" (email November 22, 1999).

Informed by his numerous reviews of art exhibitions in the early 1990s, Watten's *Bad History* struggles against three prevailing artistic pitfalls that emerge in the art of that period: first, oppositional art frequently responded just to the event itself, not to the conditions that made that event possible; second, oppositional art "preached to the converted," embracing its own marginality in such a way that closed down its possible audience; and third, oppositional art tended to foreground identity politics in such a way that limited exploration of its own epistemological limits. In his article "No More War! '*An Unwanted Animal at the Garden Party of Democracy*' at Southern Exposure Gallery," Watten meditates on the problem of oppositional strategies in light of the state of readiness that Virilio had theorized some years before: "Artists concerned with oppositional strategies [during this new war] must therefore take into account that there is a well-developed 'state of readiness' for what could be a protracted struggle for the social control of meaning—a struggle in which art may well have a role. We are not starting at ground zero; the War has been with us for some time" (1). Given the state of "preparedness" of the Pentagon for the Gulf War, the art that simply responds to the event itself might fail to be oppositional at all. The war itself would simply be the conclusion of a long argument; to attack it is to miss its body.

Oppositional strategies must deal not only with the cultural-political problem of preparedness but also with generic demands from within its chosen field— whether art or literature—in particular, the high modernist notion that intentionally oppositional art is destined for failure. In ruminating over *An Unwanted Animal* and other agitprop art exhibitions during the Gulf War, Watten suggests that intentionally oppositional art that embraces marginality might actually be a strategy of self-protectiveness and could lead to a dangerously circular mode of address; that is, despite its politics and poetics of collectivity, the exhibition nonetheless succeeds only in demonstrating its oppositionality rather than communicating in some way with its audience.

Watten argues that, beyond the more obviously rhetorical modes of oppositionality, art can be, in Zukofsky's formulation, "thinking with things as they exist": "as complicated as 'things' must now be for us—including all the negations of formal exclusion and media displacement—such a formulation gives a value to intention and art that avoids the circularity of both 'representing the unrepresented' and 'preaching to the converted.' . . . It is 'aesthetic tendency' (*Social Text* 19/20)—a poetics that de-emphasizes identity in favor of an encounter with language, a politics of collective identifications" (19).

Two of the most successful Bay Area art projects, for Watten, demonstrate the broad range of possibility for an oppositional art that "thinks with things as they exist." The first, the Chomskyan "Break the Media Blockade" placards in Sproul Plaza, broadcast news summaries of the war from other countries on large placards, much like the Chinese students did on Tiananmen Square. The other, a more personalized project, involved the production and distribution of pins with the word "Iraqi" written on them. Daniel Davidson's "Iraqi pin project," which invited people to wear these pins identifying them with "Iraqi" people, was able "to initiate a process in which identity could be tested and redefined in terms of particular identifications. . . . [T]o understand the dimensions of Davidson's work demands not an esthetic judgment—the typical problem for the critic faced with political art—but a cultural history, an account of what was done and what resulted" (19). So while the placards offered an inclusivist revision of what "we" knew, the pins offered a way to reopen that cramped sense of the "we" in the first place. For Watten, "a politics of particular identifications, rather than of general identity, offers a way out of this plotted circularity [of audience], by not aligning simply with 'us/them'" of nationalist discourse (18).

In contrast, for example, to Levertov's "Staying Alive," her poem invoking a romantic collective identity of the Berkeley resistance movement during the Vietnam War, Watten's *Bad History* is saturated with a sense of subjective isolation. Perhaps only in this way, Levertov's and Watten's poems are similar in that they most closely articulate the particular epistemological and political limits of war resistance during their respective historical moments and demonstrate the tremendous differences between Vietnam and the Persian Gulf War. So even as *Bad History* refuses the traditional subjective position of the nationalist epic poet, it also is inflected by the successes and failures of oppositional art from the period; rather than simply relying on a self-protective oppositionality, it becomes a subjective history swinging between complicity and resistance. The resistance of *Bad History* bridles against its own limitations, situated at the homefront, distant from the scene and effects of the war.

After part A's postmodern office building, section I, called "Bad History," initiates the emergence of this resistant/complicit I, puzzling over the language of wars' beginnings and endings:

> A bad event happened to me, but its having occurred became even more complicated in my thinking about it. Even if this event had happened only to me, it was only recently made available for retrospection; it had to be proved as taking place in every other event. Take the War, for example; I no longer know for certain which war is meant . . . . It is always "the era between two wars." So there was a very long war before a period of time in which that war had just been over for a very long time — even though it took its place as immediately preceding that time. Then a very short war called that very long time to question . . . . All those times even now seem to guarantee each other, as part of an assertion of the reality of the first and only war. (5–6)

This is a disembodied, indeterminate, distracted voice, worrying over the problem of language and temporality. The I is like a voice in an echo chamber, reverberating until estranged into a flattened affect, as if amnesiac: "a bad event happened to me, but its having occurred became even more complicated in my thinking about it" (5). But rather than sounding like Fredric Jameson's postmodern subject, whose affect in the end represents a fundamental loss of historicity, Watten's speaker pursues relentlessly his own flattened sense of time. It is as if the lyric subject as such had been traumatized by the event, which, though distinct, "had to be proved as taking place in every other event" (5). The War, too, becomes a floating signifier, not attached to any specific war but somehow including all the permutations of war — the Second World War, the Korean War, the Vietnam War, the Gulf War, the Cold War. The Cold War — "always on the verge of ending" — lingers over all the wars. This sense of an ongoing perpetual war echoes Virilio's notion of Pure War, in which the Cold War superpowers engage in a war marked by the constant preparation for war; what Watten's speaker gropes for is a name for that war's perpetuity, the war without end.

The subject's disbelief in the War, necessitated perhaps by the psychic inability to remain in a state of constant crisis, paradoxically leads to a feeling of responsibility for its existence. This stance creates a demonstrably different tone from a war resistance poetry reliant upon the clarity of oppositionality. When the war ended, "it was a relief—I always doubted the extent to which the poet could just by writing think he could keep it going, even for the space of a lyric poem" (8). Watten's line reverses the formulation that the war resistance poet writes poems about the war in order to end the war; what this line suggests, rather, is that the lyric poet writes about the war in order to make it real for that writing self distant from the conflict. Paradoxically, Watten's lines suggest that the lyric poet who seeks to resist the war through means of imagery does so in order to convince herself of the reality of the war, but ends up initiating a vicious circle of traumatized representation, as in Levertov's identificatory poems during the Vietnam War.

The Cold War, its small and distant wars, and the possibility of its leading to nuclear Armageddon, forced people into a condition of disbelief, who "willed ourselves into a kind of suspension" (7). Watten's echo of Coleridge's famous formulation from *Biographia Literaria* regarding the reader's necessary openness toward his "supernatural" poems in *Lyrical Ballads* suggests the way in which fictional and historical narratives function by the same logic. Watten also references how Robert Creeley's poem "The Tiger" invokes a "reassuring but freakish monstrosity that would rivet us in our seat, as in a Stephen King movie" (8). At both moments, Watten pursues a Baudrillardian line of analysis that applies both to the Cold War and the Gulf War. The Cold War was the war that lacked overt signs of warfare, and hence could be disbelieved; the Gulf War, experienced by the distant television spectator as a virtual media event, could be believed only insofar as one was willing to enter into its fictionalized televisual representation, with Hussein as its Godzilla to be destroyed.

Watten's notion of disbelief, incidentally, spans both the willing consumer of the Gulf War as heroic epic and the (Chomskyan) dissenter who sees this representation as frankly "unbelievable." In other words, by focusing on the problem of disbeliefs, Watten's poem addresses the dilemmas of being an American civilian at the center of empire, distant from the conflict, without choosing the more comfortable, but ultimately less productive, oppositional mode. In order to believe in the Gulf War, the viewer needed to suspend the disbelief that wars have human consequences, which always principally requires a faith in technological mastery. In this war, perhaps more than any previous war, technology itself took its place as a key character in the postmodern epic. Here, again, Watten avoids the extreme oppositional mode, trying to retrace the thoughts of a speaker who is haunted by the seeming reality of the virtualized televisual conflict:

> each new war being the culmination of our old belief in the supersession of a new technology. . . . Only later did we find out that the success rate for Patriot missiles was only 6 percent. How can we be so thoroughly trained to disbelieve the evidence of our senses? Didn't I see an incoming missile come down through the sky from the vantage point of a TV crew in Dharan, Saudi Arabia . . . while the cameraman tracked the outgoing Patriot to an explosion that was visible proof of its success? (9)

The speaker expresses puzzlement at how the information regarding the Patriot's success rate violates his sense of the images he "witnessed."

This puzzlement is contrasted with a glee of a certain poet who failed to think about the consequences of all of this virtualization: "the poet didn't want to think about that ground [which would be destroyed by the Patriots and Scuds], so pleased he was with the spectacle of a disbelief that called into question any criterion for an historical event" (10). It is unclear who this poet is; this character experiences pleasure in the totality of the spectacle of a disbelief. If this line read "pleased . . . with the spectacle," we might say that Watten is critiquing Baudrillard's euphoria over spectacles themselves. But the line reads: "the spectacle of a disbelief," which makes it seem equally possible that it refers to some Chomskyan dissenter who is resisting the spectacle as well. The poet could be Watten himself as well, engaging in self-critique. In the end, naming names matters less than acknowledging how the speaker is disturbed at how the poet's pleasure in his stance toward the event seems to distance him further from the brute reality of the bombs.

This section concludes by tracking the circulation that Watten's ruminative repetitions of words and phrases have enacted. The "bad event," obscured by false witnesses and faulty technologies, still remains at a distance. However, its very repetition through representation—particularly in the form of these Patriot missiles hitting their targets—finally instigates the speaker to language: "it was the continuous, circling treadmill of its displacement for a very long time, brought to a single image—obscured, interfered with, reprocessed at a third remove over remote-control channels of communicative links—that got me here to say this" (10). The speaker's voice itself, then, becomes an analogue for the virtualization of the Gulf War; only through such a poetics of interference, Watten's poem suggests, might we become conscious of the obscuring workings of interference itself.

Watten's poem does not rest in its own fascination with the interfered virtualized images, as an eviscerated Baudrillardian analysis might, and instead pursues the consequences of the "ground." However, in contrast to a Chomskyan analysis, Watten's juxtaposes dissident witness accounts of the effects of the bombing to a narrative of vexed American subjectivity. Part III, "Iraqi," suggests the gulf between the American civilian and the Iraqis (and those other Arab and non-Arab civilians caught in the "cross fire") who bore the brunt of the bombing. His definition—"Iraqi: various scenarios for wearers of a mark of distinction and/or shame" (15)—that begins the section opens the poem into a consideration of how identification with the other is always complicated by the ease with which we can disown that identification. Watten retells the story, told in Ramsay Clark's *War Crimes*, recounted by a Jordanian woman whose husband had been strafed by machine gun fire from American planes; the husband, driving his cab to Amman, becomes an example of "the consequences of appearing Iraqi at a particular moment in time" (*BH* 15). Juxtaposed to this story is the (American) speaker's account of wearing a pin from the Iraqi pin project that identified him as "Iraqi": "Guys would loom out of the crowd, saying, 'Hey, an Iraqi!'" (16). The speaker becomes so conscious of his pin that he "always remember[s] to take my pin off for official meetings at work" (16). While the Jordanian man's misidentification as Iraqi leads to his death, the American maintains distance from his adopted identity for "official meetings at work." So even though the pin communicates a willingness to stand with Iraqis, it also problematizes that relationship and forces its wearer to acknowledge the gulf between his experience and that of the Iraqis. Finally, this section foregrounds the way in which even the story of atrocity comes secondhand, from secondary witnesses and distant sources.

Because the war was not simply the event of war, but the years of cultural and military preparation for the war, what better place to begin than children's toys? Section IV, called "Museum of War," meditates on how the constant preparation for war requires young warriors to be prepared, as well as how the constant preparation for war leads to the inevitable sacrifice of children. This Museum of War does not exist in actuality; rather, it is a virtual museum of Watten's imagining, one which perhaps corresponds with the Museum of Childhood and the Imperial War Museum (both in London). Taking his son Asa to the Museum of Childhood, Watten describes an artist's diorama where "each display is designed to be the perfect miniature of a moment of loss" (17). The diorama both resembles a child's toy and invokes the bombing of the Amiriyah shelter during the Gulf War, where "at least 300 children and parents were incinerated in a structure we knew had been built for civilians; now they must reelect the entire PTA!" (18–19). The absurd non sequitor "PTA" brings us to the insurmountable gap between our experience of raising children and the horror of the Amiriyah bombing. The imagined diorama makes us wonder whether representations of war are always already domesticated by our limited vision of what war is.

Layered into this section's description of these two museums is the profusion of statistics and numbers. The employment of statistics invokes the military's (and mass media's) fascination with weaponry specs and lingo—"Imagine the 'daisy cutter' effect of a 7.5 ton superbomb manually pushed from an open end of a C-130 cargo plane—shock waves ripple out in all directions, leveling all structures 500 meters on either side" (19)—and the way in which the naming of weapons seems to take the place of visualizing their effects. Watten's imagined dioramas in the Museum of War return us to the more disturbing conundrum evoked by Levertov's poetic struggle; can one both represent the war and still resist it? Is the process of representation a kind of repetition, a reenactment of the trauma? Watten suggests that representational art as such might always fail to be oppositional: "Here an on-line editor objects that imitation of war in rapid displacement of incommensurate remarks is not an argument against war—it could likewise be a form of participation" (19). Still, Watten suggests that, for example, evoking the devastation of the Highway of Death so as to re-member it, to make it present and erase the censored blank spaces, is both necessary and perhaps impossible. Watten cannot "remember a flatbed truck containing nine bodies, their hair and clothes burned off, skin incinerated by heat so intense it melted the windshield" (20). Would it have made a difference if such images appeared in mass media? We will not know. What we can know is that, in light of the Gulf War's fantasy representation, poetry and art became two places where war was returned to the realm of the traumatic and perhaps unrepresentable real.

In section V, "Intellectuals," like Coleman's "Notes of a Cultural Terrorist," Watten yokes together Marxism and Romantic lyric in a piece on the 1991 Los Angeles riots. Donald Pease has argued that the Rodney King beating, the innocent verdict of the white California police officers, and the resulting rioting "activated an alternative memory" (576) that dispelled the illusion of internal consensus against an external enemy manufactured during the Gulf War. The riots interrupted "U.S. spectators' previous identification with the surveillance apparatus of the New World Order . . . [and] reversed the effects of U.S. disavowal of neocolonialist brutality in the Gulf" (561). The King verdict and riots laid bare the unsettling divisiveness within the United States around race and class. What burns Watten, however, is the distance between the intellectual, in his ever higher highwire morality act, and the reality on the ground:

> Who will save us? Intellectuals—split off from the mass of revolutionary clouds returning from a daily fog bank? The fog moves back to reveal smoky haze rising over burnt-out districts of Los Angeles, o intellectuals, you who speak as if there were no one to hear you! But this smoky haze has spoken again, as we knew it would. . . . O intellectuals, wheeling back and forth in a conscious morality play—a balancing act of self-undoing moral tightropes, not falling into the waiting gasps of the crowd but spinning always higher, dangerously out of reach, while the crowds below realign your center of gravity for you! (23–24)

The ironic call—"who will save us?"—mimics the intellectual's (and one might also add, the lyric poet's) desire to rescue the masses from the most powerful even as it mimics a more bourgeois voice, wondering who will protect him from the advancing destruction of the crowd. In the second voice, the answer is tautological—the police, whose violence set off the violence of the rioters, will save us. The intellectual, by contrast, cut off from the discontents that led to the conflagration, can only perfect his own hermetic moralism.

The tautological (and fraternal) order of police is also, not surprisingly, a mirror to the larger tautology of Pure War. In section VI, "Against All," Watten spins out, in Steinian fashion, a traumatized repetition of battles:

> Always already, all wars are ready. But this is the war of all against all. The war has begun again, the war to renew all wars. Everywhere is war. Echoes answer war already—echoes always answering war. "War is not the answer." We need to escalate! (25)

In this thickly intertextual passage, Watten deftly weaves theoretical, philosophical, and pop cultural references into a Steinian attack on war: a war of words. Using the Althusserian formulation, "always already," which designates the illusion that ideological constructs are natural and eternal, Watten suggests that wars, rather than promising to end war, seem only to ensure future wars. The "war of all against all" refers back to Hobbes's philosophical pessimism, and rubs against Marvin Gaye's plaintive protest song "What's Goin' On," which itself adopts one of the antiwar slogans of the 1960s—"war is not the answer." But Watten's poem reverses Gaye's plea: "Father, father, we don't need to escalate." Gaye's plea is one that has not only domestic implications (Gaye was later murdered by his father) but also racial ones; Gaye's song is as much about the tumult in U.S. ghettos and the state response as it is about Vietnam. The Gulf War, which begins the book, therefore, cedes to the race/class war of the L.A. riots, to Waco, and beyond, to global financial war. If what follows in *Bad History* moves further outward from the Gulf War, one might argue that it moves further inward into the Gulf War as well—the Gulf War as symptom of a cultural-historical situation. However, such a reading might obscure the fact that the permutations of war in *Bad History* are ultimately subordinate to the problems of national and personal history.

De-Forming the Epic

Bad History counters the televisual representation of the Gulf War as a heroic epic not only through its foregrounding of the interfered image, its manifestation of a vexed complicit/resistant subjectivity, but also through its form. In particular, *Bad History* employs the generic conventions of both newspapers and scholarly texts, with its central newspaper-like column, running footers, and endnotes. The running footer of dates to the text and the columnar print style invoke newspaper format. However, instead of quoting and then critiquing the mass media representation of the war, Watten's text does not try to create an exact relationship between the dates and the text. The dates, in fact, do not speak for themselves, nor do they take control of the text. Here, Watten acknowledges in his notes his indebtedness to the work of Iranian-born Seyed Alavi. Alavi's artistic reworkings of newspapers— principally, the removing of the dates—enacts a vexing counterpoint. For Watten, Alavi's work counterposes two versions of time—the unfolding artistic process of subjectivity and the ongoing pressures of the dominant culture to consume that process. Unlike the typical manipulation of headlines for political ends, Alavi's work resists the overdetermined language of official history.

Similarly, Watten's use of historical dates invokes a Chomskyan concern for drawing out an historical counternarrative. The text's dates begin with January 16, 1991, and skip ahead and back to other dates: March 1, 1991, January 28, 1990, April 19, 1993, and end finally with December 27, 1993. January 16, of course, marks the beginning of the bombing, but what about the other dates?[5] How should we read the connections between the footer date and the text itself? Watten, in contrast to the Chomskyan mode, leaves these investigations to the reader; part of the reader's work, perhaps, is not only to figure out the significances of those dates but also to take part in the construction of the history of the poem. One finds, for example, that March 1, 1991, marks the day after the official ending of the conflict (even though the war continued long after that date and continues, in different permutations, to this date). Yet January 28, 1990, is not immediately clear. However, Watten has revealed that the date also marked the death of his mother, and that her birthday was April 19, the day that would later be remembered nationally for the Waco conflagration and then a year later the Oklahoma City bombing, committed by Gulf War veteran Timothy McVeigh. Watten's use of this date of personal significance suggests, therefore, the limits of the outworn notion that Language poetry requires active construction by the reader. By introducing something from his own biography not knowable within the text, yet somehow essential to the text's meaning, Watten shows that he cannot escape the biographical contours of his own subjectivity, however objectivized.

Finally Watten's dates, particularly the evocation of the official beginning and ending of the war, also enable us to question the primacy of those dates as markers of conflict. When did the Persian Gulf War begin? If we look at three different chronological tables—(1) PBS *Frontline*'s Gulf War website, (2) *Seeing through the Media: The Persian Gulf War* (1994), and (3) *Beyond the Storm* (1991)—we note the degree to which the event of the war depends upon what led to the war. From the official history provided by *Frontline*, the first date provided is August 2, 1990, when Iraq invades Kuwait. But the second source presents an introductory caveat, noting "in order to understand the historical meaning of the Persian Gulf War, we need to go as far back as World War II and the British reconfiguration of the territorial boundaries of the nations of the Middle East" (307). Instead, it begins with July 17, 1990, when "Saddam Hussein accuses the U.S. and the Gulf states of conspiring to cut oil prices" (307) and then notes the infamous exchange between Saddam Hussein and April Glaspie on July 25. The third source, *Beyond the Storm*, provides an even lengthier historical trajectory, beginning in 1869, when "Suez Canal and powered river transport open up Mesopotamia to international trade" (356). It goes on to detail Western oil investment and military intervention and covert operations in Iraq beginning in 1912, and provides a thorough account of the politics of the Middle East. Obviously, from these three examples, how we discuss the war as an historical event can vary significantly, depending on how one frames the events that lead up to war. When wars begin and end is fatally unclear—and perhaps less important, in light of Pure War, than foregrounding the limits of any framing of them.

Thus, framing itself becomes a self-conscious act, with political meanings. In the material construction of the pages of *Bad History*, the text is impinged by margins that are almost as large as the text. The white space, the unspoken, lingers on either side of the hypotactic sentences. It is as if we were reading the only column of a newspaper to which we do not have complete access, which we cannot completely read. In contrast to the slim margins of an industry-standard book, the extensive margins create an eerie effect, the feeling of something missing. It also gives the active reader much room for marginalia, to make connections with the text. Although it would be easy to overinterpret such a formal gesture, it nonetheless points to Watten's obsession with frames—his desire to counter the domination of authorial presence, and his humility in the face of what he does not, or cannot know.

The extensive annotations at the back of the book provide a useful archival function, in the mode of a Chomskyan dissenter; at the same time, they show Watten's indebtedness to a whole range of texts and knowledges—from high literary theory to human rights texts, from chance encounters to unavoidable fate. In contrast to Chomskyan analysis, however, these texts do not provide the ultimate truth, but rather create a tangle of narratives from which we must wrestle our own bad histories.

Our lives, *Bad History* suggests, are no single story, but overlapping ones: "life cannot be lived as 'one story' but as stories that overlap, from one to the next, with no final form to hold them together" (74). They overlap with each other's and with the grand narratives of nations and empires, in ways that are often obscured and often unknown to us. History is enacted in a financial prospectus, no less so than in the newspaper or on a calendar, the date marking the death of a mother and, at the same time, the date of the Waco atrocity and the Oklahoma City bombing. The poetry of war resistance constantly foregrounds the inescapability of such connections, where the war is made visible in the weft of daily lives—not just glowing on TV screens but as absent-presences in a phone tax, an investment in a stock portfolio, a cut-rate price for a tank of gas.

Bad History's limitation as a poem of war resistance lies, perhaps, in how it abandons the investigation of what remains outside its ken and instead focuses on the limitation of its perceptual frame, in all its primordial negativity. For example, continued investigation of the ongoing narratives of the Gulf

War in Iraq and in U.S. veterans, or further dialogue with activists and war resisters in the United States, may have enabled the text to function as an agent of further texts and events. But such limitations are built into what it means to be a subject, much less a resister. That Watten's poem resists the tendency to bow quickly for the emperor's laurel should not surprise; however, that it scrupulously avoids the congratulations from the like-minded and already converted ensures its value not only as poetry but also for a culture of war resistance.

PART 4.

Coda

FIGURE 4: *Untitled, from* Phantasies of a Prisoner *by Lowell Naeve*

Proliferations

The other half, Awe with its ersatz religious capital letter, we can resist.
The weapons are huge and thoughtless, but they don't deserve a shred of awe.
A small victory, but it's one weapon destroyed, the one they always use first.

—BOB PERELMAN, "Against Shock and Awe"

The Poetry of Grief and the Poetry of Conspiracy
after September 11, 2001

Though there have been single acts far more devastating than what happened on September 11th—the dropping of nuclear bombs on Hiroshima and
Nagasaki come to mind—the September 11 terror acts were different, even
unique. These attacks were the first domestic scenes of warfare that the
United States had seen since the Civil War (excluding Pearl Harbor, as
Hawaii was not officially part of the Union at that time). Second, it was principally an attack on civilians during peacetime. Third, it was carried out
through the use of technology (hijacked airplanes) and made more devastating by the targets' inhuman size (the massive and massively symbolic World
Trade Center towers, and the Pentagon). Fourth, though it was witnessed by
some in "real time," the event emerged as a national trauma in its ceaseless
repetition on television. On television, the initial stunned speechlessness was
rapidly replaced by rumors, speculation, flags, and logos: "America under Attack," "America at War," and "America Strikes Back"—the last weirdly echoing the movie *The Empire Strikes Back*.

The trauma of September 11 was a momentary rupture in the national
imaginary. In stark contrast to what might be termed the schizophrenic representation of the Persian Gulf War, the representation of the terrorist attacks momentarily opened a gap in the national self-definition, as the word

"empire" now became visible as part of the discourse. As early as the September 14, 2001, issue of *Time* magazine (devoted entirely to the attacks), Nancy Gibbs's article entitled "If You Want to Humble an Empire" renders visible in a mainstream magazine the self-identity of U.S. with empire, even if it employs the word "empire" without explanation. On October 15, just a month after the attacks, Max Boot contributed "The Case for an American Empire" in the *Weekly Standard*. The use of this term in much of the mainstream discussion did not imply a reconsideration of the imperial adventures during and after the Cold War that arguably fostered the attacks on the World Trade Center and the Pentagon on that dark day.[1] Rather, the U.S. administration officials implicitly embraced the new thinking, coining War on Terror as war in which nations would be either with us or against us in the search for Operation Infinite Justice. The War on Terror, then, became the latest brand name for Pure War—both in its furthering of the national security state at home and in its policy of preemptive strikes on "states that sponsor terrorism." In other words, the terms of critique employed by the Left—"empire" and "Pure War"—now became visible and justifiable in light of the terrorist attacks. Rather than seeing the attacks as "blowback," the CIA's own term for the consequences of U.S. meddling in the affairs of other nations, the national media tended to repeat ad nauseum the Bush administration's narrative that the September 11 terrorism was the initiating act in a war that would justify the very actions that might lead to further blowbacks.

September 11, 2001, also occasioned a tremendous outpouring of poetry, though this poetry largely remained confined to elegiac effusions. Aided by the new technologies of the Internet (e-mail, electronic mailing lists, Web sites, and later, blogs), people chose poetry as the occasional mode for the outpouring of their grief. By February 2002, everyday people submitted over 25,000 poems to a popular amateur poetry site, poems.com, in response to September 11. (And three years later, the number had more than doubled.) Auden's "September 1st, 1939," one of the poems he himself expurgated from his *Collected Poems*, became a principal shared text among e-mailers. Later, *September 11, 2001: American Writers Respond*—a collection of poetry and reflections by poets and writers edited by William Heyen—became a top seller and offered immediate but not uncomplicated responses to the attacks.

One stark and most public example of war resistance poetry that emerged from September 11 was Amiri Baraka's scandal-making and somewhat messy "Somebody Blew Up America." The scandal surrounded not only Baraka's use in the poem of an Internet myth that 4,000 Israelis vacated the World Trade towers prior to their destruction, but also his subsequent defense of the poem's veracity as an argumentative utterance (not principally as a poem) and the fact that he was the poet laureate of New Jersey. Written and performed a year after the attacks, the poem is a splenetic (though occasionally funny) anti-imperialist rant, cataloguing the history of crimes of Western empires and of the Anglo-American empire in particular. Piotr Gwiazda has shown how the reception of the poem in U.S. media, and the subsequent discussions of the poem both by media and by poets, demonstrates the abyss between American poetry and the public's understanding of what poems do; however, Gwiazda avoids the fact that Baraka's defense of the poem replicates precisely the same argument of the outraged public, only from the opposite side of the political spectrum. In other words, rather than arguing that the poem is the dramatized utterance of a suppressed but valuable point of view, Baraka asserts his absolute identification with the poem's rhetoric.

The poem is, I would argue, smarter than the poet's argument on its behalf. Gwiazda notes Baraka's "weakness for conspiracy theories" (467), yet the poem, in my reading, enacts the intoxification of conspiracy theorizing itself. Conspiracy theory emerges as a kind of spastic groping after fact and reason precisely when events do not make sense; it comes out of the fantasy of governmental power and out of Manichean binaries of absolute evil and absolute good. While the poem's catalogue of crimes committed by this efficacious empire is mostly irrefutable (with the glaring exception of the notion that Israelis and American administration officials knew in advance about the attacks), the desire to place all the blame on a singular, though unnamed "Somebody" dramatizes the temptation and weakness of a totalizing critique of empire. The ending of the poem clinches this reading:

Like an Owl who know the devil
All night, all day if you listen, Like an Owl
Exploding in fire. We hear the questions rise
In terrible flame like the whistle of a crazy dog
    Like the acid vomit of the fire of Hell
   Who and Who and WHO (+) who who
Whoooo and WhooooooOOOOOOooooOooo!
    (http://www.amiribaraka.com/blew.html)

In its concatenation of "Who's," the poem concludes with a comic-gothic, loony-bird quality that suggests the libidinal excess that conspiracy theorizing brings with it. Baraka's poem thus suggests the dangers of the slippery thinking of conspiracy theories, even as it courts the same conspiracy theorizing in the process. Finally, it suggests that, while the documentary impulse—and its information gathering and dissemination procedure—is an essential aspect of war resistance poetry, information itself in the Internet Age is extremely vulnerable to manipulation, and poets need to take care in how they handle it, lest their handiwork become weakened by its misuse.

The Reemergence of War Resistance Poetry

While September 11, 2001, marked a return of poetry to the mainstream cultural life of America, it also fundamentally challenged the peace movement to consider the limits of pacifism as a political strategy. The flagrant aggression of the Iraq War, a preemptive war conducted against a tinpot dictator who represented—it turns out—no real threat to the region or to the United States, provided a much clearer occasion for mass war resistance. Poets have taken a central place in this movement, extending the tradition of a vital war resistance poetry begun in the twentieth century. While the results may reflect the limits of occasional activist verse, autobiographical lyric, and experimental poetry, they also demonstrate the possibilities of a new rapprochement between poetry and war resistance culture.

In a surprisingly brief span in 2003, when the Iraq War ("Operation Iraqi Freedom") began, four anthologies—100 *Poets against the War*, *Poets against the War, enough*, and *101 Poems against War*—were published, the first two in record time. The first, edited by Todd Swift and published in book form by Salt, claims to "hold . . . the record for the fastest poetry anthology ever assembled and disseminated" (back cover)—first planned on January 20, 2003, and published as an e-book on January 27 and as a paperback on March 3, 2003. The second, edited by Sam Hamill and published by Nation Books, emerged from Hamill's solicitation by email of antiwar poems from "Friends and Fellow Poets" after refusing an invitation, as Robert Lowell had in 1965, to a White House symposium on "Poetry and the American Voice." Hamill received over 13,000 poems, which were posted on the website poetsagainstthewar.org, read on February 12 at over 200 readings nationwide, and later entered into the congressional record, since the White House poetry event had been cancelled. The third anthology, *enough*, edited by Rick London and Leslie Scalapino emerged as a response to the Afghanistan War from the experimental writing community and offered an alternate vision of war resistance poetry. The fourth anthology, *101 Poems against War*, published by Faber and Faber, suggested the way in which major publishers saw in this burgeoning movement a marketing niche.[2]

These anthologies require a fuller investigation than this coda will allow, but let me focus principally on Hamill's *Poets against the War*, the best known of the collections, and suggest some characteristics of war resistance poetry and its use of the anthology as a mode of dissemination. First, we note the increasing relevance of the Internet as a mode of poetry (and war resistance) solicitation, gathering, and dissemination. Email communication and website posting enabled a rapid mobilization of thousands of poets to contribute to the movement. Second, the speed with which the anthologies themselves emerged suggests a new relevance for what was commonly conceived as a moribund genre for activist ends, always dragging its recollections from tranquility. Third, the sheer volume of poets contributing poems ensured a built-in audience, not only of poets but also of those who saw in the poetry a tool for antiwar activism. Fourth, the anthologies became events-in-themselves, a documentary of its own documentation, a pulse of the moment, a movement within a movement, which spurred on events under the umbrella Poets against the War.

These characteristics, these possibilities of and for the new antiwar anthology, are not without pitfalls. While the Internet and email proved to expedite the whole anthology-making process and expose the message to a broad number of people, those technologies also proved to be limited. The *Poets against the War* anthology and movement tended to rely (perhaps inescapably) on Copper Canyon authors with whom Hamill worked; about 22 of 160 poems chosen were by Copper Canyon authors. While this reliance upon one's own stable of horses is by no means unusual, it underscores that the process of selection—and the time crunch to get work in print—invariably privileged well-known and familiar voices and poetry affiliations. The poems of *Poets against the War* largely work within the autobiographical lyric mode in ways that should, at this point in our study, be fully recognizable: poems that juxtapose domestic (American) life with what is happening overseas, poems that address the president, poems that summon the ghosts of past wars (particularly Vietnam), and poems that imagine some mode of resistance. Many, of course, fail to convince; of the 160 poems, probably 20 will resonate beyond the span of the war and the life of the anthology. Bruce Bawer, in the *Hudson Review*, railed against the type of poem as "presenting the news of war as an unpleasant intrusion upon an (American) life lived in harmony with nature and characterized by a taken-for-granted feeling of safety and tranquility" ("Plague"). Such a critique suggests not only the limitations of the autobiographical lyric mode for the "instant anthology" but also the ways in which such lyrics (descended from Yeats and Lowell) rely upon a kind of privileged distance from conflict—and too frequently wallow in impotent sensitivity. Still, it bears mention that, for the lyric poet, writing about an event that has not yet taken place (and when it does, would be a highly mediatized event) would present serious obstacles; with nothing to reflect on, and little to witness, the noncombatant lyric poet has recourse only to a kind of guilt-suffused documentation of one's own distance from the scene of war. This problem of the lyric poet explains, in part, the dizzying array of poems reflecting on not only the Iraq War but also the ghost of wars past and present: the collection's final poem describes what the speaker would tell a Palestinian girl suicide bomber, to convince her that life is worth living. Such a disparate collection of poems begins to force the question about *which war* the poets were writing.

However, one noticeable shift in the poetry of the Iraq War from this collection regards the return to traditional forms; if the (professional) poetry of the Vietnam War was largely free verse, the poetry of the Iraq War also marks the renaissance of poetry's old wineskins: sonnets, sestinas, even a pantoum, though these forms occasionally are broken open, as an acknowledgment of their limits. In "Guernica Pantoum," for example, Paula Tatarunis uses the incantatory repetitions of the pantoum to perform an ekphrastic autopsy of the famous antiwar painting by Picasso memorializing the death and destruction of Guernica during the Spanish Civil War by fascist forces. *Guernica* itself had recently been the subject of controversy when, in February 2003 just prior to the war, Colin Powell delivered his (now discredited) speech on the danger of Iraq's weapons of mass destruction programs, and the United Nations covered up its huge reproduction of the painting that hung on the walls of the U.N. Security Council building. Though the poem does not mention the incident, it hangs in the context of our reading, since the poem essentially witnesses to what the administration could not face up to: the inevitable horror of death. Not only is the poem "seeing" what is blocked from our sight, but the painting in the poem "looks back" at us, the viewer:

> Of the eighteen eyes in Guernica, sixteen are open.
> Of its nine mouths, eight gape and cry.
> There is a bull, a bird, a horse, one child broken,
> One mother grieving; elsewhere, others fall, flee, watch, die. (Hamill 225)

The poem's stately approach to the form—in stark contrast to the chaos of Picasso's surreal modernism in the painting—manifests that Duncanian principle of the war resistance poem as "altar." Not only do the second and fourth lines recur in the succeeding stanzas (as the first and third lines), but the lines also rhyme; here, Tatarunis's sculptural approach freezes the chaotic painting into a new focus. Counting the eyes and mouths and noticing what they are doing, renders a care for the bodies represented in a way that the military—despite its legal and moral energies devoted to avoiding civilian deaths—simply cannot do. Are the sixteen open eyes, we wonder (the painting not in front of us), the eyes of the living or the eyes of the dead, and what are they asking of us? The "elsewhere" of the painting—itself representing the elsewhere of the war—comes home, inevitably echoing the recent attacks of September 11 and anticipating similar scenes of falling, fleeing, watching, and dying.

Like the anthologies of the Vietnam War, the PAW project was conceived to enable poets to lend their words to protest against the war; its website (poetsagainstthewar.org) archives over 20,000 poems, maintains a regular newsletter, links to poetry readings and activist events and information about how to create more readings, and links to media archives. It even documents its own history. After Sam Hamill's public refusal to attend the White House symposium, "Poetry and the American Voice," hosted by First Lady Laura Bush, he

> asked about 50 fellow poets to "reconstitute a Poets Against the War
> movement like the one organized to speak out against the war in
> Vietnam . . . to speak up for the conscience of our country and lend your
> names to our petition against this war" by submitting poems of protest
> that he would send to the White House. When 1,500 poets responded
> within four days, this web site was created as a means of handling the
> enormous, unexpected response. (www.poetsagainstthewar.org)

Further, the PAW phenomenon inspired a documentary called *Voices in Wartime,* and a book of interviews and poems by the same name. What remains less well defined is how the PAW project is connected to *political* activism. The occasionally self-congratulatory tone of the PAW project leads one to question: should an antiwar poetry anthology just instigate more poetry readings? Yet, despite this apparent disconnect between poetic activism and the larger political movements against war, PAW does return poetry to the fray by reconnecting poets not only to each other but also to the poetic tradition of war resistance.

In contrast to the national attention accorded to the PAW anthology and movement is the solid work of O Books founder and editor, experimental poet Leslie Scalapino, whose three anthologies (*enough, War and Peace,* and

War and Peace 2) represent multiple strands of experimental writing (from Jackson Mac Low and Anne Waldman to Judith Goldman and Rodrigo Toscano, among many others) and draw out many of the problematics of Barrett Watten's *Bad History*: the problematic of the image and representation, the problematic of resistance by way of contaminated language, and the problematic of war both as event and as cultural condition (see chapter 8). Scalapino's *The Front Matter, Dead Souls* (1996) also emerged from meditating on the Gulf War; it is a highly disjunctive "motional" and documentary collage that resists attempts to nail down its meanings—and in this way, it is precisely the opposite of the prepackaged media coverage of the Gulf War. Including art, lecture, and poetry, these anthologies attempt to work through, often in exploratory and procedural poetics, a relationship to language that both represents language's contamination and proposes a form which enables resistance to the unmaking language of/for war. This is not a poetry for the uninitiated, despite the avant-garde's arguments to the contrary; some head-scratching poems miss the mark by being either too opaque or too stentorian. However, the anthologies' sophisticated attempts at making a language commensurate to the anarchic unmaking of war deserve further attention—not least because this project in itself has sustained a resistance community of poets.

When Will We End the Poetry War?

In the summer of 2005, Kent Johnson's chapbook *Lyric Poetry after Auschwitz* created what the poetry world immoderately calls a firestorm; the debates that followed clearly echoed the ghosts of past debates about the proper relationship between poetry and war resistance—between Lowell and Naeve, the Fine Arts Group and the War Resisters League, Stafford and "George," Duncan and Levertov, Baudrillard and Norris, Watten and Baraka. The book unquestionably acts as a provocation; after all, the title glosses Adorno's famous dictum about the impossibility of poetry after the Holocaust, and the front cover reproduces the contours of the infamous Abu Ghraib photograph showing Lynndie England holding a prostrate man by a leash, framed by cupids flying about, arrows loosed. The imagery conflates the Auschwitz and Abu Ghraib prisons and sets in motion a series of further provocations— not only regarding the seriousness of the Abu Ghraib scandal and the ongoing nastiness of the Iraq War but about poetry's role in light of such war crimes. This work protests against the Iraq War, but it is also, as the subtitle suggests, a "submission" to the war. It is also a protest against, and submission to, poetry itself, in echoing a second meaning of submission. It is poetry with the bow pointed into its mouth, a crying in as much as a crying out.

Insofar as the poetry of war resistance has been inflected by the Yeatsian lyric, staging the argument with the self in a way that enacts a democratic dialogism, Johnson's project follows suit. Though on his blog, Joshua Corey calls this book "addressed, suffocatingly, to himself," the conflagration of responses over the Internet—such as Jim Behrle's cartoons representing defenders of Johnson as literal shit eaters—suggests otherwise. The controversy, in part, stems from Kent Johnson's name-dropping of the New York School coterie in his poem, "The New York School (or: I Grew Ever More Intense)." The poem juxtaposes passages, the first of which describes New York School poets emerging from the speaker's toiletries, with which the speaker then ecstatically and pornographically cleanses himself; the second of which includes quoted (and probably fictional) passages of first person witnesses of atrocities (WWII, Japan, Rwanda).[3] Take, for example, the first two stanzas, which establish the dialogic pattern maintained throughout:

> I turned over the bottle of shampoo, and Frank O'Hara came out. I rubbed him all into my head, letting the foam rise, knowing I was just warming myself up, excited by the excess of what was to come. Soon, I began to make noisy climax sounds. The scent of oranges and oil paint from a general store in the outlaw town of Shishido (with all of its exotic wares) filled the stormy air.
>
> I couldn't help it, I thought of this: *"One day, a fortnight or so after my mother's death in Shishido, I was up in the hills playing with some friends. Suddenly one of them said, 'Look, the baby's hands are all swollen.' I touched the baby, which was still strapped to my back, and screamed—it was stone cold. My friends began to panic and jump up and down, shouting 'It's dead, it's dead.'"* (23)

The poem's yoking of daily hygiene rituals to New York School poets (here, Frank O'Hara, with a nod to his poem, "Why I Am Not a Painter"), juxtaposed against scenes of violent war-related death enacts a critique of poetry blithely unconcerned with its own material privilege. Further, the poem extends the avant-garde critique of a transparent poetry of witness but in a way that suggests the rhetorical necessity of testimony itself.

The poem thus links the poetry wars—where experimental poets and mainstream poets are seen as bitter enemies in a feud over the soul of poetry—with

the nation's conflicts. This poem suggests that, for Johnson, the almost univer-
sally beloved New York School poetry most embodies our own Americanness—
its nerve, its vivacity, its bawdy humor, its celebratory evocations of commercial
and popular culture—and offers little in the way of direct resistance to or confrontation of the exploitative relationships with the Global South that undergird
the American way of life. No doubt there is something to say for Ashbery's defense of escapism as a mode of resistance, or O'Hara's poetics of ecstasy, or
Koch's poetics of parody. What Johnson suggests and what the poem implies is
that it is not enough. This poem, despite its obvious self-lacerating (or maybe
because of it), succeeds, ironically, by employing the very strategies of the New
York School poets that it seems to critique—the vicious humor, the playful surrealism, the verve of naming names and shout-outs to friends—all pillars of
New York School poetry. The poem "The New York School" further acts as an
incitement to and a provocation of formalism itself (whether of the Language
School or New Formalist varieties), with its page-long explication of its invention of the so-called "Mandrake" form: "the following poem represents the first
instance of a new poetic form. . . . Finally, any 'Mandrake' must be led off by
some kind of brief introduction" (22). The obviousness and uselessness of this
poetics must be read as an attack on the self-importance of an avant-garde too
wrapped up in its own self-creations to respond to something directly.

Overall, the poems viciously point the finger inward. In particular, in
"Baghdad Exceeds Its Object" and "Lyric Poetry after Auschwitz: or, 'Get the
Hood Back On,'" American personae address Iraqi citizens (in the former
poem) and prisoners of war (in the latter), and in a crescendo of pornotrop-
ing, turn the screws—literally and figuratively—on Iraqi bodies. In the tradition of war resistance poetry's "bringing the war home," these poems invite us
to interpolate ourselves into the positions of the Charles Graners and Lynndie
Englands—*our* troops, after all:

Welcome, Kamil, I'm an American girl, nineteen, pregnant, my Dad is
an alcoholic, but my Mother is in recovery, with her own Daycare, and
I'll be taking over it after the Army, I've always wanted to have my own
business, and I'm going to expand beyond just one location, I'm not
thinking small. And since I believe it is always important to say what one
means and not beat around the bush, I want you to know something. I'm
going to hold a pistol to your head and tell you to jack-off, while you
recite the Koran as fast as you can, you heathen, Hell-bound fuck, and
then I'm going to look at the camera with a cigarette dangling from my
sultry, teenage lips, giving the thumbs up. (36)

Ironically, Johnson's poetry of excess falters when it veers into pure prose and away from the embodied dialogism exhibited in "The New York School." Though I share Johnson's frustration with Charles Bernstein's attack on mainstream antiwar poetry—in which Bernstein's celebration of the politics of form seemed like a salvo in the poetry wars rather than one on behalf of war resistance—Johnson's concluding piece "Enough" feels like a bludgeon compared with the sharpened two-sided blade of the poem "The New York School." Johnson's critique of the avant-garde, however, suggests the limits of a resistance based primarily on form, and at the level of the text, without engaging the third-dimension of spatiotemporal symbolic action. Still, it bears mentioning that many prominently self-identified avant-garde poets have worked hard to oppose the war not only through writing poetry and doing readings but also by publishing in newspapers (Bob Perelman's "Against Shock and Awe" and Charles Bernstein's "War Stories" were both published in the *Philadelphia Inquirer* in 2003), producing books (Leslie Scalapino's O Books has produced three poetry anthologies in the wake of the terror wars), and using blogs and other Internet sites for organizing (Ron Silliman's blog, among many others, features political entries as well as the regular reviews and analyses of poetry books). Ironically, one might say that the Language poetry legacy to war resistance is not simply the recognition that form is political, but that local affiliations and tightly knit communities of mutually supporting poets and writers who control the means of their production have the ability to effect cultural and institutional change. In this particular way, the Language poetry phenomenon shares with the peace movement its origination in local affiliation, small nodes of collectivities spread throughout a largely undiscerning and sometimes hostile cultural landscape.

The Useable Pasts and Multiple Futures of War Resistance Poetry

Antiwar poetry, which exists so frequently as a *response* to war—that is, almost as a parasite upon war as an event that requires belated symbolization and representation—can seem a retroactive and even futile undertaking. A vital war resistance poetry must move beyond both simplistic ephemeral agitprop and the lyric's belated and bourgeois subjectivity and draw from the multiple living traditions of oppositional and resistance poetry—from the lyric tradition, from the African American resistance tradition, from experimental writing, and from postcolonial resistance. Though each new war demands writing-through in new ways, to respond to the particular conditions of the conflict, war resistance poetry necessarily has useable resources in its multiple pasts, even as it recognizes their limits for the present. We can draw on, even as we can note the limits of: (1) the traditional lyric war protest poem, as practiced by the First World War soldier-poets, who relied principally on a poetry of the physical eye, combined with the high rhetoric of an individual lyric self dissenting against the machinations of bureaucracy; (2) the conscientious objector poetry of the Second World War CO poets, whose writing witnessed to and embodied the complex resistance to a total war; (3) the Vietnam War–era poetry of witness (whether from imagined identification or actual physical witness) and radical anti-imperialist revolutionary poetry; and (4) the poetry of the Iraq wars, which attempts to take into account the new conditions of a mediatized conflict—whether cleared of corpses (as in the Gulf War) or in a time when alternative Internet media propaganda renders more complex notions of witness and truth telling (as during the Iraq War). In the words of Muriel Rukeyser, "to be against war is not enough, it is hardly a beginning" (*LP* 213).

This study has shown the ways in which the poets themselves have, by virtue of their struggle to represent and enact war resistance, become models for resistance—both to war and to the heady fantasies of revolutionary resistance. In their self-questioning, in their urge to synchronize the beats of their language with the rhythms of peace movements, in their attempts to image and imagine the distant imperial wars, in their struggle for information and for understanding the syntax of war, in their worried or outraged utterances, in their desire to address their fellow citizens, these poets embody through words and deeds—through words as deeds, and deeds as words—a moral witness against the depredations of war. Even if the lyric poem may render visible the political unconscious of imperial privilege, the best lyric poems have always been maps that render empire visible and consciously draw tight the strands that connect American subjectivities to the rest of the world. Even if the audience-based rhetorical poetries of social movements, such as the 1930s radical proletarian poetries or the Black Arts poetries of the 1960s, may occasionally disappoint in their binaristic and propaganda-laden invectives, the best performance poems actively hail, respond to, and cocreate a community of resisters. Even if experimental poetries can alienate so absolutely in their disjunctive style, the best experimental poems court their reader in ways that can help create critical distance from the rhetorical tactics that bully citizens into distrusting their own deeply held knowledge about the ugliness of war.

Poetry has never been simply a handmaiden to the peace movement, nor is war resistance simply an occasion for poetry; but poetry offers to the peace movement a relationship to language that questions its own assumptions and extends its own possibilities, imagining alternate futures and new narratives beyond the religious, political, and philosophical foundations that undergird it. Take, if you will, Michael Magee's "Political Song, Confused Voicing," written in the wake of September 11, 2001, and a vital counterpoint to Amiri Baraka's "Somebody Blew Up America." It is a suitable ending to this consideration of the multiple strategies of poetic resistance, as it threads the traditions of political lyric, African American performance poetry, and experimental language play into a meditation on the politics of grievance. The poem blisters with energetic and absurdist wordplay:

> you tongued my battleship!
> you bonged my tattle-tale!
> you maimed my mamby-pamby
> Wagnered my Nietzsche
> and gotcha'd my sweatshop
>
> there ain't room in heaven for us (51)

If the language is oddball, the overall structure is quite simple: you [bleeped] me! This structure suggests a feeling of grievance or woundedness, but the poet machineguns so many allusions at us—from commercials to board games to political acronyms to philosophy—that we are suspended in its comic-furious catalogue. The first line, "you tongued my battleship" both references the commercial for the game "Battleship"—in which the boy says to his sister, "You sunk my battleship!"—and the bombing of the USS *Cole* off the coast of Yemen in 2001, summoning the strangeness of American subjectivity, where history is crosscut with advertising, and war itself is a commodity to be sold.

But the poem gains gravitas with its blues refrain and confuses any simplistic reading of who is the "us" and who is the "them." Is the "us" of the refrain, who have no room in heaven, the terrorists or the Americans who appear to be speaking the main stanzas? The poem ends:

> you prayed on my carpet
> you bombed my parade
>
> and there ain't room in heaven
> no there ain't room in heaven
> no there ain't room in heaven for us (52)

The voices get confused in ways that suggest that the "us" is the wider human race, since "you prayed on my carpet" could be the typical complaint of bin Laden about American military presence in Saudi Arabia, and "you bombed my parade" could refer either to the U.S. economic parade ending or the U.S. bombings of wedding parties in Afghanistan or Iraq. The grievances get melded together in ways that suggest that competing grievances become a vicious circle, a self-perpetuating psychology which collapses the distance between us and the terrorists. Magee thus uses and feels the strength of grievance even as the poem shows a deep distrust of that energy, and an awareness of the violence of acting out of grievance. Though the peace movement recognizes the fatality of a politics based principally on grievance, it has occasionally succumbed to its own rhetorics of blame—blaming the government system or blaming the peace movement. And poets have, at times, contributed to both polarities of blame. Mike Magee's poem dramatizes—and thus inoculates us from—demonization itself, which can only end with everyone sharing hell together.

Envoi

The debates between those who call for mobilizing poetry for war resistance and those who see poetry in and of itself as a mode of resistance recur because of a deep investment in the power and irreducibility of poetry; yet the latter view poetry as the end, while the former view poetry as a means to other ends. That poets have themselves disagreed so vociferously about the fundamental laws of war resistance poetry suggests the health of the movement and the care that poets accord both their craft and the work of resistance. The latest flap about Kent Johnson's *Lyric Poetry after Auschwitz* suggests that the questions about resistance poetry will not be resolved, but rather lived through by poetic and activist means. The ongoing work of national organizations like Poets against the War and localized nodes in networks of publication (O Books, Curbstone, Interlink, Dischord, to name a few) suggests that resistance work does not require unanimity. Certainly, poetry thrives most particularly in the local. As W. D. Ehrhart mused:

> What was the point of my reading antiwar poetry to the members of the
> Brandywine Peace Community? These are folks who chain themselves to
> fences and hammer on missile warheads. But what they hear in my
> poems confirms them in their beliefs (which are not easy to hold and
> maintain in this culture . . . and renews their spirit and commitment; it

gives them a sense of connectedness, of not being entirely alone. That's worth doing, even if it is on such a small scale (there were maybe 25 people there that night). (interview)

War resistance poems thus ask for our redeployment in multiple sites, returning poetry to where it thrives—at the local and in local resistance—as graffiti, in pamphlets, as performances, in political meetings, as songs, and in the classroom. Yet poetry can also serve as a part of a shared national and even global culture of resistance. After all, social movements that begin in the local necessarily seek a wider audience to promote wider cultural and political change. Likewise, war resistance poets attempt to address both the converted and unconverted, to praise the committed and also to hail the uncommitted, inviting them to partake in this collective subjectivity of resistance. As Mark LeVine has argued, "localism is only one of several strategies [of resistance]" (241), and in order to expand the relevance of social movements into a national and global context, one must engage in "culture jamming"—which brings together different people and different cultures in dialogue to "grasp and work through the unprecedented complexity of globalization . . . and to perform and struggle together in close dialogue with the very public whose views and attitudes they have great power to shape" (16). LeVine's work bringing together artists from across the globe to talk and perform together enables a cross-cultural exchange—not only between the artists themselves but between the artists and their audiences (who are not only consumers but participants in and transmitters of the art they experience and transform).

To those of us who consider poetry a medium and a tradition of the imagination of conscience, who see in it a useable past and a vital resource for social change, our work is to liberate what has already been written in books and recirculate it in the social networks where poetry can both inspire and interrogate war resistance and peace activism. Such a call requires us to articulate our own history and our own tradition, to recover that which we did not know was part of us—and, finding it lacking, to create our own. In some sense, that may require rejecting the tradition of poems and poetry that I have laid forth in this book—since I recall, as a college student, demonstrating against what would become the Persian Gulf War, the desire to reject the hippie "kumbaya" culture of Vietnam-era peace activism in favor of Fugazi's punk anthem "KYEO" (Keep Your Eyes Open). It also asks of us to enter into already existing local nodes and social networks of war resistance and to participate as citizen-poets in the mundane acts of community building such as weekly potlucks, flyering, sign making, and petitioning. Poets have a unique role to play in the peace movement, because we can bring our obsessive and nuanced attention to language, its rhetorical possibilities, and its formal limits.

As we extend our poetics into the peace movement, we will be writing the potential archive, writing the future—not just of war resistance poetry, but of our collective histories. In the tradition of the visionary anthologies of Jerome Rothenberg and Pierre Joris, where poetry is not gathered and contained but rather set loose in a larger structure toward symbolic action, our poems and acts will have the occasion to articulate themselves into possible futures. In Rothenberg's words: "the anthology [is] a kind of long poem. . . . In working as a poet, finding a space for different voices is probably at the center of what I think I'm doing in poetry. So translations are an arena of voicings, anthologies are an arena of voicings, found poetry and collage are an arena of voicings" ("Chanting" 53). Every demonstration—in the broadest sense of the term—is in some sense also an arena of voicings, and the work of war resistance poets is to allow that arena to reverberate beyond the space-time event, to echo in the eyes and ears of participants and passersby alike.

Poets can extend the mimeograph revolution of the twentieth century (and the ongoing independence of small literary presses, who have the ability to control the means of producing language-events) to electronic and other new media—including college radio, Internet sites, Weblogs, downloadable podcasts, You Tube—thus reframing Billy Bragg's ironic "Revolution is just a tee shirt away!" into a potentially empowering act of self-commodification. Whole Web sites devoted to linking poetry and political action, such as Brian Kim Stefans's 2003 project, "Circulars: Poets, Artists, and Critics Respond to U.S. Global Policy," suggest the ways in which this work is already engaged, if not always sustained. Other activists have taken to "freeway blogging"—writing pithy messages on bed sheets or cardboard and hanging them on highway overpasses (see www.freewayblogger.com). Further, poets and poetry can play a role in the use of digital filmography to document acts of repression and resistance. The recent *Investigation of a Flame* (2001) and its attendant Web site revisit the Catonsville Nine action, including original footage and other documentary materials not previously accessed by the public, thus enabling a new generation insight into the radical nonviolent resistance during the Vietnam War.

As we articulate poetry to the poetics of war resistance, we will keep it vital by finding and writing the broadest possible range of voicings: not only lyric poems, not only language-based poems, but poems as scripts for symbolic actions; poems that can be marched to, poems that are parodies of well-known songs or poems that others could easily perform, poems that enable something beyond comprehension to collective and bodily participation; not just solemn or angry poems, but poems that are funny; not just Apollonian poems of reason, but Dionysian poems that offend public morals and political correctness; in short, poems that use every means necessary—the lyric tradition's self-dialectic, the African American performance tradition's use of chant and audience dialectic, the experimental tradition's explosive play with language. In light of the Iraq War, such a range of voicings could include American war resistance poems such as the meditative and rationalist "Against Shock and Awe" by Bob Perelman, next to the stately jeremiad "Dithyramb and Lamentation" by David Wojahn, next to the Flarf-constructed "Chicks Dig War" by Drew Gardner, next to a fragment of the visionary multivocal *This Connection of Everyone with Lungs* by Juliana Spahr, next to the diatribe "Somebody Blew Up America" by Amiri Baraka, next to the fractured collage of "I Note in a Notebook" by Lawrence Joseph, next to the first-person witness "Here, Bullet" by Iraq War veteran Brian Turner. Following LeVine's notion of culture jamming and Edward Said's notion of contrapuntal reading, such U.S. war resistance poems could be read alongside the poetry of "enemy" nations; from the classic to the folk to the contemporary traditions, the enemy's poetic culture becomes a possible site of resistance, insofar as it demonstrates the humanity of the other. John Balaban's translations of Vietnamese folk poetry during the Vietnam War, Robert Auletta's retranslation of *The Persians* during the Persian Gulf War, Stephen Mitchell's version of *Gilagamesh* released during the Iraq War, the anthology *Iraqi Poetry Today*, and Dunya Mikhail's *The War Works Hard*—all create other ways for Americans to listen to and imagine the other. Nor ought the arena of global voicings be limited to poetry, since now we have voices audible from the sites of conflict, such as Salaam Pax's revolutionary day-by-day representation of a civilian voice on the Iraqi "front," or Riverbend's subsequent notes under occupation.

Poets bringing their keen attention to language ought to try not only poems— and thus repeat the embarrassment of the poet-activist in *I Heart Huckabees* (2004) dragging his poems to every demonstration—but also placard writing, media press releases, writing to government officials, and songwriting. In New York City, poet and environmentalist E. J. McAdams—who spearheaded the effort to return red-tailed hawk Pale Male's nest to its roost on a city building in 2005—wrote his daily statements to the press as if they needed to be as memorable as small poems. In terms of songwriting, perhaps only Neil Young—who penned the famous post–Kent State-shooting dirge "Ohio"— could so effectively suture the distance between the Vietnam War and the Iraq War with his recent *Living with War* (2006). Yet on almost every song of this album—gesturing toward the collectivity for whom he wishes to speak—Young's voice is accompanied by a chorus of 100 singers. And now there are dozens of singer-songwriters like protest singer David Rovics, who offers all his music for download free; nearly 500,000 downloadings of his songs had occurred as of this writing. Hip hop, as well, has contributed dozens of songs against war just since 2003; Chuck D, Dead Prez, KRS-One, Michael Franti, Nas, Paris, Talib Kweli, Wyclef Jean, and others have spoken out against the Iraq War. Songs can be the glue of movements, insofar as they crystallize in a pithy phrase and tune some undeniably shared utterance.

As we contribute to the poetics of the peace movement, we must actively become archivists of the movement itself. Save everything you write and make. Document how the texts came into being, when and how they were employed, and how they might be used in the future. Since many books have almost no information about the ephemeral conditions of a poem's making, they create the impression that war resistance poetry comes out of an ahistorical pacifism that lacks pragmatism and melts at the first sign of manufactured imminent threats. If possible, create website archives so that others may benefit from and use your work. Bequeath your archive to the Swarthmore College Peace Collection to allow future scholars access into the dynamic poetics of resistance.

In this making, in this composing, in this movement building, we know that our actions will not necessarily lead to immediate change and may never end war; yet, we ought to remember that when we resist war, we are participating in something that many people throughout history have struggled for, even given their lives for. Since war will not soon be sloughed off as a vestigial organ or an archaism in light of Pure War, war resistance will survive and persist—even thrive—because poets continue to articulate, question, motivate, and sustain it—in the symbolic action of their utterances and in the prose of their daily involvement making resistance. A visionary aspect of the peace movement, war resistance poems valorize the struggle inherent in resistance and argue against the mythologies of prowar discourse so that, when the next wars come, people will resist the manufacture of public consent. As Denise Levertov writes, "if we restructured the sentence our lives are making," we might find "an energy field more intense than war" where "each act of living [is] / one of its words, each word / a vibration of light" (MP 58). This is a fight worth writing for, and the lines made and broken are part of "millions of intricate moves" (Stafford WII 81), whose sentence might end with the word *peace.*

Notes

INTRODUCTION

1. We hear Thersites's voice echoing down to General Smedley Butler's 1933 speech, which called war "a racket . . . conducted for the benefit of the very few at the expense of the masses" (http://www.fas.org/man/ smedley.htm).

2. Crucial resources of war resistance literature from the ancient world would also necessarily include, among others: *Gilgamesh* (third millennium BCE) (cf. Stephen Mitchell's recent translation and introduction, which draws explicit links to the Iraq War); Hebrew and Christian scriptures; *The Persians* by Aeschylus (cf. Robert Auletta's Gulf War–inflected version); *Lysistrata* by Aristophanes, in which Greek women deny their warrior-husbands sex until they end their wars; and the poems of Simonides and Archilochus.

3. *The Iliad* presents a depiction of war that corroborates the *Encyclopedia of Poetry and Poetics*'s definition of patriotic war poetry as one that simultaneously "ennobles" and "debases" the enemy warriors, to show the slaughter to be "morally admirable" (777). The enemy Trojan warriors appear as human as the Greek warriors; in fact, Jonathan Shay has shown how the warriors actually talk to the enemy, and consistently demonstrate that the "enemy is worthy of respect, even honor" (103). Shay's excellent *Achilles in Vietnam: Combat Trauma and the Undoing of Character*, corroborates this reading, noting that "Homer minimized to the point of falsification these four universal realities of war: casualties from 'friendly fire,' 'fragging,' the suffering of the wounded, and the suffering of civilians, particularly women" (121).

4. I have used the compound "homefront" rather than "home front" in an attempt to parallel the militarized form "battlefront."

5. James Tatum argues that the narrative structure not only serves an aesthetic purpose—sustaining the dramatic tension of the epic from its emotional crisis to its resolution—but also represents, in its turbulence and chaos, the traumatic realism that a "true war story" requires. Yet Miriam Cooke has argued that the war story's archetypal narrative too frequently "gives order to wars that are generally experienced as confusion" (15) and ultimately "reinforces mythic wartime [gender] roles" (15).

6. Claims to the poem's universality underwrite a reading of human nature as essentially violent, thereby justifying post–Cold War American militarism. Bernard Knox's introduction follows the humanist dicta to the letter, arguing that *The Iliad* is universal precisely because it embraces human nature—i.e., the inherent violence of human beings, and by extension, the inevitability of war. The

poem "accepts violence as a permanent factor in human life and accepts it without sentimentality. . . . Three thousand years have not changed the human condition in this respect; we are still lovers and victims of the will to violence" (29). Since war is inevitable, even natural to human life, the argument follows that great civilizations only last as long as they maintain greater military might. Peace (and culture) comes, as the military saying goes, only through superior firepower. For Knox, the moral of the epic poem is that "no civilization, no matter how rich, no matter how refined, can long survive once it loses the power to meet force with equal or superior force" (37). Thus *The Iliad*, an ancient text about warring Greek city-states, becomes an apology for maintaining U.S. hegemony at the end of the Cold War. There is no telling, the implicit argument goes, when another fascist power could enslave us all. That Knox evokes the Second World War as a parallel to the poem's action—that historical moment when the United States achieved unchallenged world power—suggests not only how *The Iliad* speaks to the present but also how it underwrites American empire.

7. War poetry anthologies since the Second World War demonstrate that the war poetry canon continues to be dominated by Anglo-American male soldiers, except during the height of the Vietnam War. Further, their argument that war is inevitable even though modern war poetry is fundamentally "antiwar" obscures more than the anthologies' editors reveal. In *War and the Poet: An Anthology of Poetry Expressing Man's Attitudes to War from Ancient Times to the Present* (1945), Richard Eberhart suggests that the proper attitude of the poet is to hate war—"Note should be taken of Friederich Adolf Axel Detlev von Liliencron (1844–1909). He is the only poet in the book who boasts of loving war" (vi–vii). The message could not be any clearer: the only poet who "boasts" of loving war is a German named Adolf. Though shifts in critical consciousness altered the claim that war poetry is essentially antiwar, the war poetry canon has continued to marginalize pacifism. *Where Steel Winds Blow* (1968) also privileges antiwar poetry, but editor Robert Cromie distances himself from pacifist ideology. While in *The Faber Book of War Poetry* (1996), Kenneth Baker gestures toward it; but his "substantial section on the debate over pacifism" (xxv) consists of seventeen pages in this almost 600-page anthology. In this section, three of the poems are explicitly antipacifist (almost half of the entire section). The primary "debate" structured by Baker is one between Alex Comfort, whose "Letter to an American Visitor" is pure doggerel, and George Orwell's antipacifist retort, "As One Non-Combatant to Another." An exception to the rule, the balanced *Poets of World War II* (2003), edited by Harvey Shapiro, includes civilian poets because they often "wrote about war-related issues not covered by the war poets themselves. Segregation [in the U.S. military and at home], for instance" (xxxi). The recent *American War Poetry* (2006), edited by Lorrie Goldensohn, also offers a more inclusive selection, but by its very process of selection necessarily foregrounds soldier-poets.

8. In particular, the work on resistance literature by Barbara Harlow and Mary DeShazer and partisan poetics by Michael True, Walter Kaladjian, Cary Nel-

son, and Mark Van Wienen enable this investigation, shifting the critical discussion to poetry's cultural work. Resistance poetry, for Harlow, has been especially effective in mobilizing collective response, creating solidarity, acting as a source for cultural memory and popular consciousness, documenting the repressiveness of colonial and postcolonial regimes, imagining alternative political and social orders, and praising heroes of resistance. While Harlow's resistance literature primarily focuses on the writing of national liberation movements, Van Wienen's theorization of First World War "partisan poetry" contributes to my sense of how war resistance poetry hails its audience and relates dialogically with the peace movement.

9. William Stafford recounts an argument he had with a war resister who refused to believe the fantasy of his own efficacy to stop war: "Well, I can't stop war. Jesus couldn't stop war. Eisenhower couldn't stop war. Why should I blame myself for not stopping war? What I can do is do the things that are within my power. I can decide there's one person who won't be in it" (EWHTL 127–128). His interlocutor refused Stafford's position; Stafford went on to say, "That leads you to terrorist acts that don't really do any good, but they relieve your conscience. I don't want to relieve my conscience. I want to do good" (128).

10. See Bill Weinberg's "The Question of A.N.S.W.E.R." for insight into the political battles for peace movement coalition building between A.N.S.W.E.R. (run by the communist Workers World Party) and UFPJ (United for Peace and Justice) during the Iraq War. In many ways, this latest struggle over the means and aims of the peace movement is the latest manifestation of the negotiation between hardcore radicals and moderates, and between authoritarian and democratic methods of organizing movements and social institutions. See also Ward Churchill for an anarchist critique of the peace movement's reliance on nonviolent actions and symbolic (rather than armed) resistance; unfortunately, Churchill's argument unfairly psychologizes pacifism as pathological in ways that replicate the dominant narrative.

11. William James broached this argument in 1910: "[I]t may even be reasonably said that the intensely sharp competitive *preparation* for war by the nations is *the real war*" (italics his 66).

12. In his farewell address, President Eisenhower warned of the "total influence [of the military-industrial complex] — economic, political, even spiritual. . . . We recognized the imperative need for this development. Yet we must not fail to comprehend its grave implications." (http://mcadams.posc.mu.edu/ike.htm). Muriel Rukeyser phrased it this way: "[the empire of business includes in its] basic premise the concept of perpetual warfare. It is the history of the idea of war that is beneath our histories" (LP 61). In Thomas Pynchon's *Gravity's Rainbow*, Slothrop articulates that "[t]he real business of the War is buying and selling [and the actual combat] serves as spectacle, as diversion from the real movements of the War" (105). See also the Staff of the Defense Monitor's analysis of the militarization of American society, and the recent documentary *Why We Fight* (2005).

13. Looking through the Peace Action files during the Gulf War in the Swarthmore College Peace Collection, I found that the organization resembles the kind of work one associates with a think tank. Perhaps such institutionalized peace organizations have forgone the arts in order to appear more worthy of playing the game of "experts" and to enter the public discourse on the level of the mass media. Yet such national institutionalization of war resistance, while essential, may efface the crucial role played by the grassroots, suffused in the cultures of the local. The peace movement, as such, must emerge from the productive dialectic between local groups and national umbrella organizations.

14. See John Gery's *Ways of Nothingness: Nuclear Annihilation and Contemporary American Poetry* (1996) for a wide-ranging analysis of poems written in solidarity with the antinuclear movement, decrying the illogic of Mutually Assured Destruction and the low-intensity warfare of the nuclear arms race.

15. David Lindley isolates three qualities of the lyric: its first-person speaker, its present-tense immediacy, and its brevity. But Lindley's discomfort with overgeneralizing stems both from the lyric's protean qualities and from the dangers of genre study. The lyric is both notably elastic and infamously purist — its elasticity most visible in the modernist experiments with the form and its purist tendencies most visible in the legacy of Romanticism and Mallarmean pure poetry — yet criticism of the lyric mode spans from the aesthetic to the political. Critics aggrandizing the novel, from Bakhtin to Lukacs, have denigrated the lyric as monological and, in Lukacs's words, the "language of the absolutely lonely man" (45). W. R. Johnson has posited that the modern lyric defines the self as an inwardness that is "in opposition to the world outside" (178). Other critics focus on how the lyric poem — perhaps the form of the Romantic ideology par excellence — has tended to efface materiality, history, and often those others that trigger the poem in the first place. These criticisms expose the aesthetic and political limits of the lyric mode as a monological form.

16. Jed Rasula has suggested that the long poem might be a form that allows for the lyric impulse without being subsumed by it; for him, "lyricism as intermittent has a much greater chance of infiltrating the fabric of cultural life than does [the lyric's resurrection]" (332). W. R. Johnson and Antony Easthope have articulated the limits of the modern lyric insofar as it has abandoned the chorale and multivocal possibilities of poetry; indeed, modern poets themselves have since Pound engaged in their own attempts to stretch the lyric, even turn it inside out. The attempts to stretch the lyric have been variously described: as verse epics (cf. Michael Bernstein), as sequences (cf. M. L. Rosenthal), and as long poems (cf. Keller).

17. Other notable pacifist poets include Stanley Kunitz, who thought the war was just but refused to bear arms and was forced to go through basic training three times; Kenneth Rexroth, who worked in a mental hospital; and Robert Duncan and avant-garde poet Jackson Mac Low, both of whom received IV-F waivers. See Kunitz's essay "The Single Conscience" and *Passport to the War* (both reprinted in *The Poems of Stanley Kunitz*). Like the other CO poets, Ku-

nitz refused to write just out of a sense of political outrage, and instead articulated a poetic that privileges the encounter with the unconscious.

18. Covering KPFA radio station protests in 1999, Daily Show host Jon Stewart joked that KPFA was founded by conscientious objectors of the Second World War, who after the war split into three groups: "pussies, fairies, and hippies." In an uncanny way, these terms of derision echo the three condemned versions of masculinity seemingly proffered by the three poets—Lowell's castrated persona, Stafford's nonviolent man, and Everson's communitarian.

19. Though my focus is on CO poetry, war resistance poetry was not limited to the spaces of internment camps, nor was it always a rejection of the radical poetries of the 1930s. Sarah Cleghorn's *Poems of Peace and Freedom* (1945) and Kate Crane-Gartz's *Realistic Rhythms* (1941) continue the work of radical (and pacifist) politics through traditional forms and rhyme, like Elizabeth Jewett Easton and Daisy Marie Barteau had in *Mother Goose at War* (1931). Cleghorn's use of the ballad as a way of communicating the stories of struggle for peace and social justice, and her use of satirical blank verse in "The Poltroon"—in which a "patriotic" speaker expresses disgust with the nonviolence of Jesus Christ— and Kate Crane-Gartz's use of the couplet, suggest that formal subversion and agitprop were alive and well, and we ought to be careful about simply rejecting such poetry as propaganda. Further, these two women saw themselves as conscientious objectors (cf. Crane-Gartz's "Conscientious Objectors" in *Realistic Rhythms*) even though they were not interned because of their gender exemption from military conscription. Read alongside war resistance poetry by other homefront women during the Second World War (cf. Schweik's readings of Elizabeth Bishop's "Roosters," Gwendolyn Brooks's "Gay Chaps at the Bar," Marianne Moore's "In Distrust of Merits," and Muriel Rukeyser's "Letter to the Front" in particular), we can redraw our picture of the American homefront as a place of unreflective unanimity, and further explore the multiplicity of resistance poetry.

1. ROBERT LOWELL'S REFUSALS

1. That Hamilton and Peck misunderstood each other is further supported by Peck's *Underdogs vs Upperdogs*, in which the activist recalls how "next to Lepke's cell at one time there was a young CO from Iowa, Lowell Naeve. He tried to explain to Lepke what a CO was, but the gangster had trouble understanding. 'You mean they put you in here for not killing?' Lepke finally exclaimed—and he laughed and laughed" (23).

2. "Just War" theory, initiated by Saint Augustine of Hippo in the fifth century, began as a principle of inquiry to determine whether a war were just in the eyes of God. The theory marks the decisive break between the early Christian Church and the Constantinian Church, whose role as state religion required a reassessment of the apocalyptic and anti-worldly ethics of the early Church. In an interview twenty-five years after his refusal, Lowell states the connection

openly: "'I was a Roman Catholic at the time, and we had a very complicated idea of what was called 'the unjust war.' This policy of bombing German cities seemed to be clearly unjust'" (qtd. in Mariani 106).

3. First World War poet Siegfried Sassoon may have also influenced Lowell. Sassoon's letter to the *London Times* protesting the handling of the war reads like an Ur-text to Lowell's: "I believe that this war, upon which I entered as a war of defence and liberation, has now become a war of aggression and conquest. . . . I am not protesting against the war, but against the political errors and insincerities for which the fighting men are being sacrificed" (qtd. in Barker 3).

4. Jerome Mazzaro has argued, in his reading of Lowell's "early politics of apocalypse," that the poet may have been influenced by Christopher Dawson's critique of the decline of Western culture. Mazzaro intimates that Dawson and other Catholic writers often relied on the same critique of capitalism invoked by fascist and anti-Semitic discourse, and that inevitably Lowell's early politics and poetics are inflected by that discourse (325).

5. The *New York Times* unapologetically conflates Lowell's antiwar dissent with a Nazi Party member named Ernst Oscar Hopf by combining the stories of both Lowell's and Hopf's sentencing. Page thirteen of the October 14, 1943, edition announces Lowell's arraignment under the headline: "Nazi Draft Dodger Gets 3-Year Term." A second, smaller headline, reads "R.T.S. Lowell Jr. Also to Go to Prison for Defying Law." Lowell's letter to Roosevelt receives a three-line paraphrase, while the judge's admonition of the poet receives a direct three-line quotation.

6. In fact, Lowell's erasure of the Catholic phase does not occur only in "Memories of West Street." Even between *Land of Unlikeness* and *Lord Weary's Castle*, Lowell drops many of the antiwar poems; his revision may be due to the fact that the political poems were often marked by overtly religious address that Lowell dropped in favor of the psychoanalytic *Life Studies*.

7. Contrary to Meyers's assessment that the time "allowed the poets to become privileged beings: free to express rather than hide their illness and encouraged to use madness to exalt the authenticity of their work" (15), Lowell's other poems—such as "Home after Three Months Away"—characterize his manic self as infantile.

8. Though "Memories" implicates Lowell in Cold War containment discourse, Lowell's anti-Soviet stance dated at least from his "Declaration of Personal Responsibility" to President Roosevelt. In addition, it led him to confront publicly Soviet poets on the levels of personal freedoms provided under Soviet control. Typically, Hamilton's account of this confrontation, quoting heavily from Shostakovich's memoir about the incident, casts Lowell as naïve and disoriented. But Lowell's anti-Stalinism did not preclude critiquing U.S. foreign policy; his position against Stalinism also led, in his words, "to my being against our suppression of the Vietnamese" (qtd. in Axelrod 179).

9. Approximately 250 Jews performed alternative service or went to prison for pacifist beliefs. The case of Moshe Kallner, an Orthodox Jew who immigrated

from Nazi Germany in the 1930s and served for a year and a half in a Civilian Public Service camp before enlisting, suggests the complexity of maintaining pacifism in the face of fascism. Kallner "would continue to support the efforts of the peace movement" (Young 156), which had called for opening immigration to Jews from Germany and boycotting German goods in the 1930s. Lowell's pairing of Abramowitz with Bioff and Browne also dramatizes the split between nonpolitical religious objectors (particularly Black Israelites or Jehovah's Witnesses) and Social Actionists, who were by far the minority. Jehovah's Witnesses comprised 75 percent of all imprisoned war refusers.

10. Lowell's "Memories" demonstrates that poems cannot be read as transparent containers of information. W. R. Johnson, in *The Idea of Lyric*, argues similarly that, at its best, poetry is not an expression of identity but rather an offering of "paradigms of identity" (31) that might enable reflective action in the world. Confessionalism, as poetic mode, passes down a complex legacy. It provides an important way to theorize how lyric poetry functions as a performance to the Other. However, all too often, it has underwritten deceptive and oversimplified notions of the relation between autobiography and poetry, notions that have privileged the Oedipal (personal and familial) narrative over political—even global—narratives of subjectivity.

2. WILLIAM STAFFORD'S LOST LANDMARKS

1. For the exhaustive account of conscientious objection during the Second World War, see Mulford Q. Sibley and Philip E. Jacob's *Conscription of Conscience: The American State and the Conscientious Objector, 1940–1947*. Other important accounts include Gordon Zahn's *Another Part of the War: The Camp Simon Story* and William Stafford's *Down in My Heart*. See also *A Few Small Candles* (1999) for memoirs of war resisters, the documentary, *The Good War and Those Who Refused to Fight It* (2000), and *Prison Etiquette: A Convict's Compendium of Useful Information* (republished in 2001).

2. In *The Ethics of Psychoanalysis*, Lacan asks, "[I]s there anyone who doesn't evoke Antigone whenever there is a question of a law that causes conflict in us even though it is acknowledged by the community to be a just law?" (243). Though Lacan never broaches the question of conscientious objection, the "conflict in us" over laws that the community agrees are just is fundamental to discussions of conscience.

3. Stafford's involvement with the Fellowship of Reconciliation during his college years in the 1930s shaped his vision of nonviolent social change; see Stitt (170).

4. Stafford notes in the preface to an interview that "being a pacifist forces you into a strange kind of aggression sometimes . . . I found myself disagreeing—in a slant way—with some standard teaching practices," by "choosing to be a participant, not an evaluator of student writing" (*YMRL* 73). The notion of bringing structural violence to the surface was central to the methods of Mohandas Gandhi and Martin Luther King.

5. David Dellinger notes that "[women] had a less spectacular, more difficult path to journey without being adequately recognized as the brave and often lonely pioneers of a better future" (qtd. in *Against the Tide: Pacifist Resistance in the Second World War: An Oral History* unpaginated). See also Rachel Waltner Goossen's *Women against the Good War: Conscientious Objection and Gender on the American Homefront, 1941–1947* for a history of pacifist women in the Second World War, in which "approximately two thousand women, and perhaps half as many children, lived in and near Civilian Public Service camps" (2).

6. Stafford's privileging of the process of writing suggests his affinity with Jackson Mac Low and John Cage, poets whose aleatory methods are linked to their political pacifism. Mac Low and Cage saw in chance operations the possibility of suspending the egoic tendencies of lyric poetry, deconstructing their own will to literary mastery.

7. To be fair, Perelman's reading of "Traveling through the Dark" reads very little of the poem—which is much more tentative and ambiguous about its own power than Perelman allows—and is more concerned, in the end, with a critique of the contemporary lyric.

3. WILLIAM EVERSON AND THE FINE ARTS CAMP

1. After Everson sent a second poem, he felt what biographer Lee Bartlett calls "a pang of conscience" and wrote a confessional indictment of *Poetry*: "I sent the second in meanness, deliberately debased myself, deliberately joined the host of panderers and double-jointed pimps that make the age what it is. . . . Condemnation of me in no way absolves you. . . . As editor of the one journal upon which American poets heavily lean, at a time when poetic expression needs the most rigorous preservation of its ideals, to let yourself be swayed by the extraneous political mess speaks eloquently for itself" (26).

2. The anthology, while still unpublished, "only survives in a pile of submissions in the Brethren Historical Archives" (Wallach 25).

3. That Steve Clay and Rodney Phillips begin their study of postwar independent poetry presses, *A Secret Location on the Lower East Side*, with the Waldport work of Untide Press in 1943, suggests the symbolic importance of CO poetry to the independent experimental poetries that would proliferate from the 1950s.

4. BRINGING IT ALL BACK HOME

1. The ease with which these songs became artifacts of culture, commodities exchanged for jeans or sport, indicates the ongoing problem of employing mass cultural art forms as dissent. On the one hand, popular music and film played a central role in the New Left and countercultural experience; the folk rock music of the period is arguably a form of poetry, mediated by music. What account of 1960s war resistance could leave out Pete Seeger, Bob Dylan, Joan Baez, Phil Ochs, Country Joe and the Fish, or Creedence Clearwater Revival?

David Wojahn has recently argued that Bob Dylan's "Maggie's Farm" actually became a prototype for a new political poetry, a "surrealist-tinged condemnation of injustice," that "failed to fulfill its early promise" ("MFNM" unpaginated). On the other hand, that the message of the songs could so easily be excised in favor of the rousing feeling suggests at least one limitation of pop music as a means of dissent.

2. Jim Neilson, Lorrie Smith, Renny Christopher, Susan Jeffords, James William Gibson, and Jerry Lembcke have argued how Vietnam War literature may perpetuate, rather than complicate, revisionist thinking of the war as a military defeat at the hands of politicians, media, and protesters. For Neilson, the academy has contributed to this revision "by promoting a literature that favors individual lives over social relations, universal truths over historical contingency, and textured sophistication over social analysis" (6). If Neilson's generalizations gloss over the contribution of American veteran writers to an increasingly sophisticated and vexed Vietnam War literature, he does suggest that American veterans, too, had to struggle against their own first-person experience of Vietnam, since they too were subject to the war in a highly controlled and highly mediated way—that their own perspectives were often as profoundly limited and circumscribed as the civilian's, only in different ways.

3. For a fuller consideration of GI antiwar poetry in anthologies and journals, cf. Bibby, *Hearts and Minds*. Jan Barry notes how the anthology succeeded in becoming a script: "poems from that collection were reprinted into the NY Times and other newspapers across the country. A staged version that my wife created was featured in the NY Daily News. We read poems on radio programs. The book was reviewed in major publications and in a Pentagon publication, which urged its readers to take a serious look at what these dissident vets had to say about the war" (Barry interview). The tradition of asking people to copy poems and pass poems has a long history. In the Swarthmore College Peace Collection, I discovered a poem, "Men Wanted," which contained these instructions: "In the name of Peace, make at least five copies of this Peace Poem, send one or more to those who you believe are interested in preventing another world war. In ninety days, ten million people will have read it. Give it to your local newspapers, your radio stations, use it in every way possible."

4. See Oskar Castro's "Selling the American Nightmare: Recruiting Latinos," for an analysis of recent military recruitment of Latinos (both U.S. citizens and non-U.S. citizens) through the use of Spanish-language advertising. See also "Jose Vasquez: From Soldier to Objector," in which Jose Vasquez tells the story of his becoming a conscientious objector to the Iraq War in 2005. He is now a member of the Iraq Veterans against the War.

5. See Barrett Watten's "The Turn to Language and the 1960s" for another reading of Ginsberg's speech as the impossible politics of liberation of the 1960s.

6. For Ehrhart, poetry was the ideal mode because "it was a struggle to concentrate on painful details for more than a few hours" (qtd. in Nicosia 6). See also Ehrhart's version of the poetry event in his memoir *Passing Time* (247–248).

7. Despite the battle lines in poetry between traditionalists and experimentalists, poets from all schools and persuasions came together to protest the war; these aesthetic alliances broke down the boundaries between formerly bitter poetry enemies. Rothenberg recalls his participation in the Three-Penny Reading, in which organizers "managed to bring together, to make a united front of so-called academics and so-called experimentalists" (qtd. in Rothenberg "Chanting" 55).

8. Though some poets embraced the reading as a public act of resistance against the war—and some have argued, mistakenly, that these poets exploited the war for their own personal gain—others most certainly did not, and maybe to avoid personal or professional consequences. David Ray recalls giving a reading from the Old State Capital steps in Iowa City in which academic poets who had promised to read decided against stepping up to the microphone, possibly because of violence erupting in the audience: "They must have done a hasty cost-benefit analysis of truth telling and decided they didn't want their names and photographs to appear in the Des Moines *Register*, on television, or in the files of the F.B.I. . . . Later, incidentally, it was revealed that the photographers and journalists were getting paid to share their work with the F.B.I., doubling their salaries" (David Ray interview).

9. William Stafford wrote about a discomfort with public display as a mode of argument: "why does demonstration, assertiveness, parading, etc., disquiet me?. . . If public action creates turmoil, intimidation, distortion of the frequency and distribution of more quietly held views, then individual thought is damaged both in its occurrence and in its expression" (EWHTL 37).

10. Mac Low's range of techniques—from "simultaneities & other group forms, music & language intersections, phonemic sound poems, collage & assemblage, intermedia, high-tech computer work, concrete & visual poetry, acrostics & syllabics" (Rothenberg vi)—made him, in Jerome Rothenberg's words, "the principal experimental poet of his time" (v). Mac Low's earliest work shows the inextricability of his political pacifism and his experimental poetry. "HUNGER StrikE," written in 1938 at the age of 16, anticipates Mac Low's twinning interest in anarchopacifism and experimental poetics.

11. In a letter to Robert Duncan, Denise Levertov notes that she had written "a 'street ballad' in rhymed couplets (a 'come all ye') about the Fort Hood 3—not a good poem but something the Greenwich Village Peace Center may be able to use as a leaflet I hope" (Bertholf and Gelpi 555). Levertov and others saw the possibilities of agit-poetry that might not aspire to be "good" poetry, but still might be useful to the movement.

12. The Weather Underground, incidentally, also saw poetry as essential cultural work, publishing a book of women's poetry "as cultural workers, striving to create poems which are accessible to the people and responsible to the struggle" (Women of the Weather Underground Organization unpaginated).

13. For analyses of the Levertov-Duncan correspondence, see in particular Perloff, *Poetry on & off the Page*, and Davidson, "A Cold War Correspondence."

14. In choosing folk poems—which appear in *After Our War* and *Ca Dao Viet Nam: A Bilingual Anthology of Vietnamese Folk Poetry* (1980) and in more recent editions—rather than just contemporary or antiwar poems, Balaban avoids the emphasis on the Vietnam War in favor of a larger vision of Vietnamese culture and history. However, his vision is not simply the sanctioned vision provided by official national culture; rather, he focuses on an oral culture that is woven through the fabric of peasant life. Balaban's gamble is the humanist's gamble.

5. DENISE LEVERTOV'S DISTANT WITNESS

1. Jose Muñoz's "disidentification" is the strategic performance of hegemonic identities by oppressed groups in order to survive and subvert their influence; he looks at the performance artist Vaginal Davis, whose costumes (soldier, bureaucrat, etc.) threaten the ideological power of these roles. To avoid any confusion for those familiar with Muñoz's terminology, I will be using the term "disidentification" to mean Muñoz's "counteridentification." War resistance culture from the Vietnam period spanned from the notion of "authentic" naked subjectivity to bawdy theatricality. However, theatricality and performativity became strategies of an increasingly media-conscious Left. Abbie Hoffman, Jerry Rubin, the Fugs, and the Yippies capitalized on the subversive mimicry in the way that Vaginal Davis does. Despite the fact that many war resistance poets have written about the problem of counteridentification and the need to avoid "absolute" positions of resistance, Vietnam war resistance poetry—like war resistance activism—often transgressed that boundary.

2. On the one hand, then, the danger of identification is that it "aids and abets" identity, in which the other simply functions as a point in the circuit of identification that leads to the self. On the other hand, identification also "immediately calls that identity into question . . . keeps identity at a distance . . . a detour through the other that defines the self" (Fuss 2). The question then becomes, for Fuss, "[H]ow can the other be brought into the domain of the knowable without annihilating the other *as other*—as precisely that which cannot be known?" (italics hers 4).

3. Levertov's lines echo the Chorus in Sophocles's *Antigone*:

Many are the wonders, none
is more wonderful than man. . . .
The tribe of lighthearted birds he snares
and takes prisoner the races of savage beasts
and the brood of the fish of the sea,
with the close-spun web of nets. (174)

Thus Levertov begins her war resistance poetry as Sophocles and ends as Antigone.

4. Postcolonial scholars such as Edward Said, Ranajit Guha, and Gayatri Spivak have practiced a "reading against the grain" of Western literary and historical texts in order to deconstruct the fantasies, ambivalences, and exclusions implicit in the workings of colonialism. Spivak's "Can the Subaltern Speak?" calls upon postcolonial historians to enact a dialectic between a project of information retrieval and a consideration of what is irretrievable. The postcolonial historian must be, then, witness to a trauma that he cannot possess. Spivak forces the historian — and likewise, any narrator — to confront the limitations in discourses that speak for or about, rather than speak to. Similarly, the poet attempting to write about the experience of the other places herself in a perilous position; on the one hand, refusing to represent the subaltern — the one who "cannot speak" — is to risk being complicit in the actions taken against the subaltern. On the other hand, representing the subaltern runs the very same risk.

5. Cary Nelson lambasted these poems in *Our Last First Poets*, yet included both "Life at War" and "What Were They Like?" in his *Anthology of Modern American Poetry* (2000). Nelson's critical reversal marks his movement from canonizer to cultural archivist.

6. Ironically, the poems "The Pulse" and "Living," which frame the section titled "Life at War," articulate a Staffordian mode of resisting war. Both poems demonstrate a keen attentiveness to the fragility and evanescence of existence, in ways that, given the title of the section and the context, propose a provisional pastoral of war resistance through nonviolent affirmation. For Levertov, this pastoral approach proves insufficient over the course of the war.

7. Levertov's adoption of resistance poetry points to the limits of the Romantic oppositional mode articulated by Terrence Des Pres. Des Pres sets up politics and poetry in Manichean terms, calling politics "the play of impersonal force disrupting personal life; and politics, therefore, as a primary ground of misfortune" (xvi). Des Pres's formulation delimits politics (political process, political action, and political desire), partly because it derives its energy from a bourgeois false binary between public and personal lives. Further, poetry's role is reduced to one of refusing politics; the poet can only be "an outside observer distressed by the march of events but not — not yet — an inside participant overwhelmed and mute in the face of events themselves. . . . Poetry — anything more than raw cursing, is always language at a crucial remove" (23).

8. Paul Lacey notes, in "The Poetry of Political Anguish," how Levertov in the 1980s continued to expand the limits of the poetry collection by including speeches which she calls "not properly classifiable as a poem but not prose either" (151).

9. According to Martin Lee and Norman Solomon, in *Unreliable Sources: A Guide to Detecting Bias in News Media*, the media were so solidly behind the war that "only 1.5 percent of news sources were identified as American antiwar protestors, about the same percentage of people who were asked to comment on how the war affected their travel plans. Only one leader of a peace organization was quoted in news broadcasts, out of 878 sources cited" (xvii).

1. Robyn Wiegman's analysis deftly points out how the movie narrates the triumph of transnational capitalism; that is, despite racial segregation, the Vietnam War, and AIDS, Americans like Gump can traverse the globe and get rich in the process. That Gump wears Nike shoes—the corporation whose factories in Vietnam have exploited its workers—suggests that the U.S. may have lost a battle but ultimately won the war.

2. Numerous analyses of mass media coverage have shown the degree to which media acted as an extension of the military effort. In *Second Front: Censorship and Propaganda in the Gulf War*, John R. MacArthur details how Pentagon front man Pete Williams cajoled, coddled and ultimately convinced the major media industry into agreeing to press restrictions, in the form of "press pools"— thus assuring that all journalists would compete against each other for the same stories, distant from the scene of war and always mediated and censored by military escorts. In particular, the omnipresence of PAOs (military public affairs officers) compromised journalists' ability to have even a free interview with a soldier. According to NBC correspondent Gary Matsumoto, "Whenever I began interviewing a soldier, this PAO would stand right behind me, stare right into the eyes of the [soldier], stretch out a hand holding a cassette recorder, and click it on in the soldier's face. This was patent intimidation . . . which was clear from the soldiers' reactions. After virtually every interview, the soldier would let out a deep breath, turn to the PAO, and ask [something like], 'Can I keep my job?'" (qtd. in MacArthur 171). The Pentagon, even after delaying "unilateral access" to the front lines, delayed further coverage with news blackouts during the initial phases of the ground invasion. Unfortunately, "most of [reporters'] dispatches and film took so long to get back to Dhahran [the media base in Saudi Arabia] that they were too dated to use. The Pentagon's real Phase III was censorship by delay" (189). Media complicity in the military effort during the 2003 war was far more mutually satisfying (but no less problematic) due to the practice of "embedding" reporters with various divisions; this innovation granted reporters more "access" but paradoxically rendered them even more vulnerable to reporting the war from a partisan, indebted point of view.

3. Postmodernism's nebulous contours force us to ask the question—*whose* postmodernism, or, more important, *"in whose interests is it, exactly?"* (italics his Ross UA xiv). Kwame Anthony Appiah and Linda Hutcheon have critiqued various descriptions of postmodernism as inherently flawed, even imperial in their outlook. Appiah, Hutcheon, and Andrew Ross have all leveled critiques at Lyotard's "metanarrative of the end of metanarratives" (Appiah 423–424) as one that plays into U.S. hegemony.

4. Perhaps because of this cinematic quality of the media coverage, there will be less need to make movies about it. According to Sturken, "the Persian Gulf War will not need to be rescripted like the Vietnam War; it was expressly manufactured for the screen and a global audience, complete with a premiere date

(January 15th, 1991) and a cast of familiar characters (the evil, dark tyrant; the fearless newsman; the infallible weaponry)" (123). The Hollywood movies about the Gulf War—*Courage under Fire*, *Wag the Dog*, and *Three Kings*—bypassed the traditional war story in favor of exploring postwar trauma, war crimes, and government manipulation of mass media.

5. For Michael Rogin, the Gulf War was an imperial spectacle, built upon four unspoken American myths: (1) "racial domination," (2) "redemption through violence," (3) "belief in individual agency," and (4) "identification with the state" (508). Rogin, building on the work of Guy Debord and Richard Slotkin, provides a disturbing picture of the American spectacle, originating in the white supremacy of the KKK (*Birth of a Nation*) and the Western.

6. Baudrillard's first article on the Gulf War appeared just days before the war, arguing that the war "would not take place." Two succeeding articles round out his meditation on the eventlike quality of the Gulf War. A fuller treatment of this debate would enumerate the ways in which both critics demonstrate their theoretical blind spots. Oddly enough, Baudrillard shows himself at times to be an anti-image moralist. Norris, by contrast, willfully misreads Baudrillard and postmodern theory more generally.

7. See also Kent Johnson's "The Debate That Died."

8. In chapter 7, I examine how June Jordan's war resistance poetry marries the Chomskyan impulse of documentary evidence with the performative poetics of the Black Arts.

9. In chapter 8, I consider how Barrett Watten's *Bad History*, a book-length poem that addresses the Gulf War within the context of postmodernism, mediates between this Baudrillian approach and the Chomskyan approach of Norris.

10. Michael Parenti provides this example of unbalanced coverage during the height of the Gulf War; on January 26, 1991, despite a gathering of perhaps as many as 250,000, "CNN reports . . . noted that 'organizers were hoping for 50,000 but they appear well short of that goal.' . . . Various media conduits gave a few hundred counterdemonstrators . . . only slightly less, the same, or sometimes more exposure than the vastly larger antiwar protest" (107–109). The irony is that antiwar activism during the Persian Gulf War ramped up quickly, and according to Max Elbaum, was "more politically sophisticated than its 1960s predecessor" (143). (Cf. also Michael Klare's darker assessment of the peace movement during the Gulf War.)

11. In contrast to Harrison's finely honed attacks on the war, Calvin Trillin's columns of verse appearing in the *Nation*, reprinted in *Deadline Poet*, were more like linguistic mortars. "Thursday Night War" attacks the misinformation provided by "brave correspondents standing at the scene" and the dangers of the instant transfer of information by satellite broadcast—truth, he asserts, "usually takes a longer point of view." While he does not condemn the "costly toys" of technology, he asks us to "keep in mind: They [correspondents] ain't Thucydides" (66). Another satirical poem, "Suggested Cheers . . . " which ap-

peared on April 1, 1991, casts aspersions on the U.S. generals' corpulence ("Yeaaaaa, Norm! Big as a dorm!") or boring personalities ("Yeaaaa, Cheney! Rarely zany!") (67–68). By mocking the trumped-up joy over the victory of Allied forces over Iraq, the poem expresses the bitter cynicism of those who opposed the conflict. Moreover, it could have provided the scripts to chanted slogans. Recent poems, such as Gulf War veteran Kevin Honold's "Desert," published in 2006, suggests that it may be too early to make final judgments about the poetry of the Gulf War. See also Theodore Pelton's brilliant Steinien "Friendly Fire" from *Endorsed by Jack Chapeau* (2000) and David Ray's *The Death of Sardanapalus and Other Poems of the Iraq Wars* (2004).

12. Amateur collections *A Poetic Calm after the Desert Storm* (1991) and *A Diary for Heroes* (1992) offer examples of jingoistic poetry written for the cause of war. These collections point to a continued belief that poetic expression is a means to political ends, though they replicate the official rhetorical strategies to "support the troops," the catchphrase for conflating the antiwar movement with the mythic protestors who spat on troops coming home from Vietnam. Mattie Shavers Johnson's *Wings of Fire* (1993) critiques the war on pacifist grounds.

13. *Mother of Battles* fails to move beyond its own Orientalist vision of Iraq, where the gods of ancient Mesopotamia garner more interest than its present human inhabitants. Likewise *Desert Storm: A History* and *Persian Gulf Poems*, which fail to slip the generic constraints the poets place upon themselves; the former's haiku and the latter's Yeatsian lyric are so rigidly conceived they never move beyond the politics of description inherent in each form. Moore's haiku occasionally touch upon deeply politicized and mediated events but denude the images of context. One haiku records the conscientious objection of one GI to fight in the Gulf War by narrowing its gaze on the handcuffs: "the rainwet GI / who refused to go to the Gulf— / his handcuffs glisten" (3). A haiku inspired by the Kenneth Jarecke photograph has neither the shock of the picture nor the sardonic humor of Harrison's poem: "shimmering heat waves— / behind the truck's steering wheel / a charred corpse" (20). Another haiku on the infamous troop burial explored in Levertov's "News Report," completely erases the agent and the narrative of the atrocity: "bulldozers pushing / corpses into the deep hole / another dawn" (*ET* 53).

7. JUNE JORDAN'S RIGHTEOUS CERTAINTY

1. Jordan's advocacy on behalf of the Palestinians, which caused firestorms of controversy and death threats, led David Barsamian to call Palestine "the moral litmus of [Jordan's] life."

2. See Davidson, *Guys Like Us*, for a reading of the masculinism of Black Arts poetry and African American women poets' response to it.

8. BARRETT WATTEN'S BAD HISTORY

1. Watten's poetic project seems to have found its ideal mediating subject in the Persian Gulf War. His use of poetry as mode of theoretical inquiry, his obsession with the problem of the frame, and his "attempt to articulate a productive negativity" (Friedlander 124) all come to maximum use in "writing through" the Gulf War.

2. Relatedly, Charles Bernstein's verse essay, "The Artifice of Absorption," argues for a poetry that is antiabsorptive—one that is marked by "impermeability, imperviousness, ejection / repellence" (*Poetics* 20)—as a strategy to resist commodification and address postmodern conditions. In his words, "In contrast to—or is it an extension of?—Adorno's famous remarks about the impossibility of (lyric?) poetry after Auschwitz, I would say poetry is a necessary way to register the irrepresentable loss of the Second War" (*Poetics* 217). In "The New Sentence and the Commodity Form: Recent American Writing," Andrew Ross argues that language poetry's strategies of resisting commodification include a fourth proposal: in a time when "rhetoric no longer acts as agent provocateur" (377), the language poets challenge through form itself.

3. Watten asserts his poetic use of these discourses: "quite a lot of the impetus for *Bad History* came from my writing in that [art criticism] medium. For one thing, I was going against journalistic practice by writing long sentences, with tons of hypotaxis, and not breaking them up in small paragraph units" (email November 22, 1999).

4. Watten, a draft resister during the Vietnam War, wrote that his poetics attempts to articulate his traumatic experience of the Vietnam War, which was, in his words, "both totally threatening and a non-event . . . experienced . . . through resistance, negation" (email November 22, 1999). *Bad History* thus provides a revision of the Vietnam War even as it revises the Gulf War.

5. Though Watten's strategy is to pursue a Zukofskyan "thinking with things as they exist," the dates cannot represent only the time of writing, since in the section footed by the date January 16, Watten references how "only later did we find out that the success rate for Patriot missiles was only 6 percent" (9). Watten's use of the dates may represent an impossible desire for a writing that aims for full awareness of its subjective historical moment or a method of anchoring a meditation against a specific historical moment.

PROLIFERATIONS

1. If the mass media discussion of empire only glancingly addressed the implications of empire and the administration's adoption of the term—as early as November 2000, when Richard Haas called for an "informal" American empire (see Ferguson 4)—a profusion of political and cultural analyses of Empire (both pro and con) has emerged since September 11. Just a small sample would include *American Empire: The Realities and Consequences of U.S. Diplomacy*

(2002); *After the Empire: The Breakdown of the American Order* (2002); *The Imperial Tense: Prospects and Problems of American Empire* (2003); *Incoherent Empire* (2003); *The New Imperialism* (2003); *The Sorrows of Empire: Militarism, Secrecy, and the End of the Republic* (2004); and *Colossus: The Rise and Fall of the American Empire* (2005).

2. Other solid recent anthologies with a focus on war resistance include: *A Chorus for Peace: A Global Anthology of Poetry by Women* (2002), *Present/Tense: Poets in the World* (2004), *Voices in Wartime Anthology: A Collection of Narratives and Poems* (2005), and *Imagine a World: Poetry for Peacemakers* (2005).

3. Johnson is no stranger to provocation, like William Everson before him, who donned the mask of a more politically correct poet and thus executed one of the great contemporary literary hoaxes—that of the Hiroshima poet, Araki Yasusada, whose poems received wide acclaim and were published in esteemed poetry journals in the mid-1990s until it became clear that Yasusada was a fiction. Johnson was widely lambasted, and the poetry world did not entirely face its own complicity in holding old doxa about authenticity and authorship.

Works Cited

Adorno, Theodor. "On Lyric Poetry and Society." *Notes to Literature Vol. 1.* Ed. Rolf Tiedeman. Trans. Shierry Weber Nicholson. New York: Columbia UP, 1991. 37–54.

Aeschylus. *The Persians: A Modern Version by Robert Auletta.* Los Angeles: Sun & Moon, 1993.

Altieri, Charles. "Denise Levertov and the Limits of the Aesthetics of Presence." *Denise Levertov: Selected Criticism.* Ed. Paul A. Lacey. Ann Arbor: U Michigan P, 1993. 126–150.

Andrews, Bruce. *Ex Why Zee.* New York: Roof, 1995.

Andrews, Tom, ed. *On William Stafford: The Worth of Local Things.* Ann Arbor: U Michigan P, 1993.

Antin, David. *What It Means to Be Avant-Garde.* New York: New Directions, 1993.

Apocalypse Now. Dir. Francis Ford Coppola. Writ. John Milius and Francis Ford Coppola. http://film.tierranet.com/films/a.now/an_tscript.html accessed January 4, 2000.

Appiah, Kwame Anthony. "Is the 'Post' in 'Postcolonial' the 'Post' in 'Postmodern'?" *Dangerous Liaisons: Gender, Nation, and Postcolonial Perspectives.* Ed. Anne McClintock, Aamir Mufti, and Ella Shohat. Minneapolis: U Minnesota P, 1997. 420–444.

Axelrod, Steven Gould. *Robert Lowell: Life and Art.* Princeton, NJ: Princeton UP, 1978.

Bacevich, Andrew J. *American Empire: The Realities and Consequences of U.S. Diplomacy.* Cambridge, MA: Harvard UP, 2002.

———, ed. *The Imperial Tense: Prospects and Problems of American Empire.* Chicago: Ivan R. Dee, 2003.

Baker, Kenneth, ed. *The Faber Book of War Poetry.* London: Faber and Faber, 1996.

Bakhtin, M. M. and P. N. Medvedev. *The Formal Method in Literary Scholarship: A Critical Introduction to Sociological Poetics.* Trans. Albert J. Wehrle. Baltimore, MD: Johns Hopkins UP, 1978.

Balaban, John. *After Our War.* Pittsburgh, PA: U Pittsburgh P, 1974.

———. *Ca Dao Viet Nam: A Bilingual Anthology of Vietnamese Folk Poetry.* Trans. John Balaban. Greensboro, NC: Unicorn P, 1980.

———. *Locusts at the Edge of Summer: New and Selected Poems.* Port Townsend, WA: Copper Canyon, 1997.

———. *Remembering Heaven's Face: A Moral Witness in Vietnam.* New York: Poseidon P, 1991.

———. *Vietnam Poems*. Oxford, England: Carcanet P, 1970.

Baraka, Amiri. "Somebody Blew Up America." http://www.amiribaraka.com/blew.html accessed August 31, 2006.

Baritz, Loren. *Backfire: A History of How American Culture Led Us into Vietnam and Made Us Fight the Way We Did.* New York: William Morrow, 1985.

Barker, Pat. *Regeneration.* New York: A Plume Book, 1993.

Barks, Coleman. "Becoming Milton." *Rooster Crows at Light from the Bombing: Echoes from the Gulf War.* Ed. Anthony Signorelli and Paul MacAdam. Minneapolis, MN: Inroads, 1992. 60–61.

Barry, Jan. Interview with author. July 10, 2005.

———, ed. *Peace Is Our Profession: Poems and Passages of War Protest.* Montclair, NJ: East River Anthology, 1981.

Barry, Jan, Basil Paquet, and Larry Rottman. *Winning Hearts and Minds: War Poems by Vietnam Veterans.* New York: McGraw Hill, 1972.

Barsamian, David. "June Jordan: Childhood Memories, Poetry & Palestine" (2000) http://www.alternative radio.org/Jordan02.html accessed December 5, 2003.

Bartlett, Lee. *William Everson: The Life of Brother Antoninus.* New York: New Directions, 1988.

Bates, Scott, ed. *Poems of War Resistance from 2300 B.C. to the Present.* New York: Grossman, 1969.

Baudrillard, Jean. *The Gulf War Did Not Take Place.* Trans. Paul Patton. Bloomington: Indiana UP, 1995.

Bawer, Bruce. "A Plague of Poets." *Hudson Review.* LVI: 4 (Winter 2004). http://www.hudsonreview.com/BawerWi04.pdf accessed August 31, 2006.

"The Beat Friar." *Time* LXXIII: 21 (May 25, 1959). http://jcgi.pathfinder.com/time/magazine/article/0,9171,865912,00.html accessed August 30, 2006.

Beidler, Philip. *American Literature and the Experience of Vietnam.* Athens, GA: Georgia P, 1982.

Bennis, Phyllis and Michel Moushabeck, ed. *Beyond the Storm: A Gulf Crisis Reader.* Brooklyn, NY: Olive Branch P, 1991.

Benveniste, Emile. *Problems in General Linguistics.* Trans. Mary Elizabeth Meek. Coral Gables, FL: Miami P, 1971.

Berkeley in the Sixties. Dir. Mark Kitchell. 1989.

Bernstein, Charles. *A Poetics.* Cambridge, MA: Harvard UP, 1992.

———. "War Stories." http://epc.buffalo.edu/authors/bernstein/poems/war_stories.html.

Bernstein, Michael Andre. *The Tale of the Tribe: Ezra Pound and the Modern Verse Epic.* Princeton, NJ: Princeton UP, 1980.

Berrigan, Daniel. "A Meditation." *The Catonsville Nine: An Act of Conscience* (pamphlet). Ed. Daniel Berrigan et al. The Catonsville Nine Defense Committee, 1968.

———. *The Trial of the Catonsville Nine.* Boston: Beacon, 1970.

Bertholf, Robert J. "From Robert Duncan's Notebooks: On Denise Levertov." http://www.jacketmagazine.com/28/dunc-bert-notebooks.html accessed August 31, 2006.

———— and Albert Gelpi. *The Letters of Robert Duncan and Denise Levertov.* Stanford, CA: Stanford UP, 2004.

Bey, Hakim. "Involution." *The Vernalist.* Spring 1998. 21–27.

Bibby, Michael. *Hearts and Minds: Bodies, Poetry and Resistance in the Vietnam Era.* New Brunswick, NJ: Rutgers UP, 1996.

Birth of a Nation. Dir. D. W. Griffith. 1915.

Bly, Robert. "For these States." *Rooster Crows at Light from the Bombing: Echoes from the Gulf War.* Ed. Anthony Signorelli and Paul MacAdam. Minneapolis, MN: Inroads, 1992. 25.

————. Introduction. *The Darkness Around Us Is Deep: Selected Poems of William Stafford.* William Stafford. New York: HarperPerennial, 1993. vii–xxii.

————. "Leaping Up into Political Poetry." *Poetry and Politics: An Anthology of Essays.* Ed. Richard Jones. New York: William Morrow, 1985. 129–137.

————. *The Teeth Mother Naked at Last.* San Francisco: City Lights, 1970.

————. Interview with author. November 11, 2002.

———— and David Ray, ed. *A Poetry Reading Against the Vietnam War.* Madison, MN: American Writers Against the Vietnam War; distr. Sixties P, 1966.

Bowen, Kevin, Nguyen Ba Chung, and Bruce Weigl, ed. *Mountain River: Vietnamese Poetry from the Wars, 1948–1993.* Amherst: U Massachusetts P, 1998.

Bowen, Kevin and Bruce Weigl, ed. *Writing Between the Lines: An Anthology of War and Its Social Consequences.* U Massachusetts P, 1997.

Breslin, Paul. *The Psycho-Political Muse: American Poetry since the Fifties.* Chicago: U Chicago P, 1987.

Burke, Kenneth. *Language as Symbolic Action: Essays on Life, Literature, and Method.* Berkeley: U California P, 1966.

Butler, Smedley. Excerpt from a speech delivered in 1933. http://www.fas.org/man/smedley.htm accessed June 26, 2006.

Cargas, Harry. *Daniel Berrigan and Contemporary Protest Poetry.* New Haven, CT: College and University P, 1972.

Castro, Oskar. "Selling the American Nightmare: Recruiting Latinos." *The Nonviolent Activist.* March–April 2006. http://www.warresisters.org/nva0306-2.htm accessed May 25, 2006.

Chomsky, Noam. "On Resistance" (1967). *Against the Current: Readings for Writers.* Ed. Pamela J. Annas and Robert C. Rosen. Upper Saddle River, NJ: Prentice, 1998. 672–684.

Christopher, Renny. *The Viet Nam War, the American War: Images and Representations in Euro-American and Vietnamese Exile Narratives.* Amherst: U Massachusetts P, 1995.

Churchill, Ward, with Mike Ryan. *Pacifism as Pathology: Reflections on the Role of Armed Struggle in North America.* Winnipeg: Arbeiter, 1998.

Clark, Ramsey. *The Fire This Time: U.S. War Crimes in the Gulf.* New York: Thunder's Mouth P, 1992.

———— et al. *War Crimes: A Report on United States War Crimes against Iraq.* Washington, DC: Maisonneuve P, 1992.

Clausen, Jan. *A Movement of Poets: Thoughts on Poetry and Feminism*. Brooklyn, NY: Long Haul, 1982.

Clay, Steve and Rodney Phillips. *A Secret Location on the Lower East Side: Adventures in Writing, 1960–1980*. New York: New York Public Library and Granary Books, 1998.

Cleghorn, Sarah. *Poems of Peace and Freedom*. The New York State Branch of the Women's International League for Peace and Freedom, 1945.

Coffield, Glen. *The Horned Moon*. Waldport, OR: Untide P, 1944.

Coleman, Wanda. "Notes of a Cultural Terrorist." *War after War*. Ed. Nancy J. Peters. *City Lights Review* Number Five. San Francisco: City Lights, 1992. 111–112.

Cooke, Miriam. *Women and the War Story*. Berkeley: U California P, 1996.

Cooney, Robert and Helen Michalowski, ed. *The Power of the People: Active Nonviolence in the United States*. Philadelphia, PA: New Society, 1987.

Cortez, Jayne. "Global Inequalities." *After the Storm: Poems on the Persian Gulf War*. Ed. Jay Meek and Frank Reeve. Washington, DC: Maisonneuve P, 1992. 22–23.

Courage Under Fire. Dir. Edward Zwick. 1996.

Crane-Gartz, Kate. *Realistic Rhythms*. Altadena, CA: self-published, 1941.

Cromie, Robert, ed. *Where Steel Winds Blow*. New York: David McKay, 1968.

D, Davey. "Give the Hip Hop Credit for Anti-War Songs." http://po76.ezboard.com/fpoliticalpalacefrm73.showMessage?topicID = 57.topic accessed September 3, 2006.

Dacey, Philip. "The Neighbors." *After the Storm: Poems on the Persian Gulf War*. Ed. Jay Meek and Frank Reeve. Washington, DC: Maisonneuve P, 1992. 24–25.

Davidson, Michael. "A Cold War Correspondence: The Letters of Robert Duncan and Denise Levertov." *Contemporary Literature* XLV: 3 (2004). 538–556.

———. *Ghostlier Demarcations: Modern Poetry and the Material Word*. Berkeley: U California P, 1997.

———. *Guys Like Us: Citing Masculinity in Cold War Poetics*. Chicago: U Chicago P, 2004.

———. *San Francisco Renaissance: Poetics and Community at Mid-Century*. Cambridge, England and New York: Cambridge UP, 1989.

Des Pres, Terrence. *Praises and Dispraises: Poetry and Politics, the 20th Century*. New York: Viking, 1988.

DeShazer, Mary K. *A Poetics of Resistance: Women Writing in South Africa, El Salvador, and the United States*. Ann Arbor: U Michigan P, 1994.

Driestadt, Anne Magruder, ed. *A Diary for Heroes: A Collection of Poems Covering the Persian Gulf War*. New York: Vantage, 1992.

Duncan, Robert. "From Robert Duncan's Notebooks: On Denise Levertov." *Jacket* 28. October 2005. http://jacketmagazine.com/28/dunc-bert-notebooks.html accessed August 31, 2006.

Easthope, Antony. *Poetry as Discourse*. New York: Methuen, 1983.

Easton, Elizabeth Jewett and Daisy Marie Barteau. *Mother Goose and War*. Minneapolis: Art Service P, 1931.

Eberhart, Richard and Selden Rodman, ed. *War and the Poet: An Anthology of Poetry Expressing Man's Attitudes to War from Ancient Times to the Present*. New York: Devin Adair, 1945.

Ehrhart, W. D. *Passing Time: Memoir of a Vietnam Veteran against the War*. Amherst: U Massachusetts P, 1995.

———. Interview with author. July 10, 2005.

Ehrhart, W. D., ed. *Carrying the Darkness: American Indochina: The Poetry of the Vietnam War*. New York: Avon, 1985.

Eisenhower, Dwight D. "Farewell Address to the Nation." January 17, 1961. http://mcadams.posc.mu.edu/ike.htm accessed August 31, 2006.

Elbaum, Max. "The Storm at Home." *Beyond the Storm: A Gulf Crisis Reader*. Ed. Phyllis Bennis and Michel Moushabeck. Brooklyn, NY: Olive Branch P, 1991.

Eller, Cynthia. *Conscientious Objectors and the Second World War: Moral and Religious Arguments in Support of Pacifism*. New York: Praeger, 1991.

Ellul, Jacques. *Propaganda: The Formation of Men's Attitudes*. Trans. Konrad Kellen and Jean Lerner. New York: Knopf, 1968.

Engelhardt, Tom. *The End of Victory Culture: Cold War America and the Disillusioning of a Generation*. New York: Basic Books, 1995.

Eshelman, William R. "Everson and the Fine Arts at Waldport." *Perspectives on William Everson*. Ed. James B. Hall, Bill Hotchkiss, and Judith Shears. Grants Pass, OR: Castle Peak Editions, 1992. 9–21.

———, ed. *Take Hold upon the Future: Letters on Writers and Writing: 1938–1946 (William Everson and Lawrence Clark Powell)*. Metuchen, NJ: Scarecrow P, 1994.

Everson, William. *Chronicle of Division*. Reprinted in *The Residual Years: Poems 1934–1948*. William Everson. Santa Rosa, CA: Black Sparrow, 1997. 149–190.

———. "The Fine Arts at Waldport." *Compass* (Fall 1944). 20–27.

———. *Waldport Poems*. Illus. Clayton James. Waldport, OR: Untide Press, 1944.

———. *X War Elegies*. Illus. Kemper Nomland. Waldport, OR: Untide P, 1944.

——— et al., ed. "An Indelicate Commission." Broadside (unpaginated). Waldport, OR. May 6, 1944.

Everts, Philip P. "Where the Peace Movement Goes When It Disappears." *The Bulletin of Atomic Scientists*. November 1989. 26–30.

Farrow, Kenyon. "Not Showing Up: Blacks, Military Recruitment and Antiwar Movement." *The Nonviolent Activist*. March–April 2006. http://www.warresisters .org/nva0306-1.htm accessed May 25, 2006.

Fenn, J. W. *Levitating the Pentagon: Evolutions in the American Theatre of the Vietnam War Era*. Newark, NJ: Delaware P, 1992.

Ferguson, Niall. *Colossus: The Rise and Fall of American Empire*. New York: Penguin, 2004.

The Fine Arts at Waldport Writers' Group. *An Importunate Proposition* (broadside). 1944 (?).

Finley, Karen. "The War at Home." *War after War*. Ed. Nancy J. Peters. *City Lights Review* Number Five. San Francisco: City Lights, 1992. 85–89.

Flanzbaum, Hilene. "Surviving the Marketplace: Robert Lowell in the Sixties." *New England Quarterly* LXVIII:1 (March 1995). 44–57.

Forché, Carolyn. *The Country between Us*. New York: Harper and Row, 1981.

———, ed. *Against Forgetting: Twentieth-Century Poetry of Witness*. New York: W. W. Norton, 1993.

Forrest Gump. Dir. Robert Zemeckis. 1994.

Fowler, Alastair. *Kinds of Literature: An Introduction to the Theory of Genres and Modes*. Cambridge, MA: Harvard UP, 1982.

Freeway Blogger. http://www.freewayblogger.com accessed September 3, 2006.

Friedlander, Benjamin. "A Short History of Language Poetry/According to Hecuba Whimsy." *Qui Parle* 12.2 (2001). 107–142.

Frontline. "The Gulf War." http://www.pbs.org/wgbh/pages/frontline/gulf/ accessed July 7, 2006.

Fugazi. "KYEO." *Steady Diet of Nothing*. France: Dischord, 1991.

Fuss, Diana. *Identification Papers*. New York: Routledge, 1995.

Fussell, Paul. *The Great War and Modern Memory*. New York: Oxford, 1975.

Gara, Larry and Lenna Mae Gara. *A Few Small Candles: War Resisters of World War II Tell Their Stories*. Kent, OH: Kent State UP, 1999.

Gardner, Drew. "Chicks Dig War." http://lists.ibiblio.org/pipermail/lucipo/2006 -January/006974.html accessed July 7, 2006.

Garfinkle, Gwynne. "Beyond Vietnam." *Journal of the Gulf War: Poetry from Home*. Ed. Michael Logue et al. Fullerton, CA: Poets Reading, 1991. 15.

Gery, John. *Ways of Nothingness: Nuclear Annihilation and Contemporary American Poetry*. Gainesville: Florida UP, 1996.

Gibbons, Reginald. "Poetry after the Recent War." *After the Storm: Poems on the Persian Gulf War*. Ed. Jay Meek and Frank Reeve. Washington, DC: Maisonneuve P, 1992. 33–34.

Gibbs, Nancy. "If You Want to Humble an Empire." *Time*. September 14, 2001. (Special Issue.) Unpaginated.

Gibson, James William. "American Paramilitary Culture and the Reconstitution of the Vietnam War." *Vietnam Images: War and Representation*. Ed. Jeffrey Walsh and James Aulich. New York: St. Martin's, 1989. 10–42.

———. *The Perfect War: Technowar in Vietnam*. Boston: Atlantic Monthly P, 1986.

Gilbert, Roger. "Textured Information: Politics, Pleasure, and Poetry in the Eighties." *Contemporary Literature* 33:2 (Summer 1992). 243–274.

Ginsberg, Allen. *Collected Poems 1947–1980*. New York: HarperPerennial, 1984.

———. "Hūm Bom." *Journal of the Gulf War: Poetry from Home*. Ed. Michael Logue et al. Fullerton, CA: Poets Reading, 1991. 52–55.

Giovanni, Nikki. "The Great Pax Whitie." *Vietnam and Black America: An Anthology of Protest and Resistance*. Ed. Clyde Taylor. Garden City, NY: Anchor Books, 1973. 4–6.

Gitlin, Todd. *The Sixties: Years of Hope, Days of Rage* (1987). New York: Bantam, 1993.

————. *The Whole World Is Watching: Mass Media in the Making and Unmaking of the New Left.* Berkeley: U California P, 1980.

————, ed. *Campfires of the Resistance: Poetry from the Movement.* Indianapolis: Bobbs-Merrill, 1971.

Goldensohn, Lorrie, ed. *American War Poetry: An Anthology.* New York: Columbia UP, 2006.

Goldman, Judith and Leslie Scalapino, ed. *War and Peace 2.* Oakland, CA: O Books, 2005.

Gonzalez, Ray. "Going to the Mailbox: An Interview with Robert Bly." *Bloomsbury Review* (September/October 2002). 3, 21, 22.

The Good War and Those Who Refused to Fight It. Dir. Judith Ehrlich and Rick Tejada-Flores. 2000.

Goodman, Mitchell, ed. *The Movement toward a New America: The Beginnings of a Long Revolution; A Collage; A What?* New York: Knopf, 1970.

Goodman, Paul. Preface. *A Field of Broken Stones.* Lowell Naeve, with David Wieck. Glen Gardner, NJ: Libertarian P, 1951.

Goossen, Rachel Waltner. *Women against the Good War: Conscientious Objection and Gender on the American Homefront, 1941–1947.* Chapel Hill: U North Carolina P, 1997.

Greiner, Donald J., ed. *American Poets since World War II.* Vol 2. 2 vols. Detroit: Gale Research, 1980.

Gundy, Jeff. "Without Heroes, without Villains: Identity and Community in *Down in My Heart.*" *On William Stafford: The Worth of Local Things.* Ed. Tom Andrews. Ann Arbor: U Michigan P, 1993. 95–103.

Gwiazda, Piotr. "The Aesthetics of Politics/The Politics of Aesthetics: Amiri Baraka's 'Somebody Blew Up America.'" *Contemporary Literature* 45:3 (2004). 460–485.

Hadas, Moses. *A History of Greek Literature.* New York: Columbia UP, 1950.

Hall, Donald. "The Coalition." *After the Storm: Poems on the Persian Gulf War.* Ed. Jay Meek and Frank Reeve. Washington, DC: Maisonneuve P, 1992. 15.

Hallin, Daniel. *The Uncensored War: The Media and Vietnam.* New York: Oxford UP, 1986.

Hamill, Sam, ed. *Poets against the War.* New York: Nation Books, 2003.

Hamilton, Ian. *Robert Lowell: A Biography.* London: Faber and Faber, 1982.

Hampl, Patricia. "A Witness of Our Time." *Denise Levertov: Selected Criticism.* Ed. Paul A. Lacey. Ann Arbor: U Michigan P, 1993. 167–172.

Hanley, Lynne. *Writing War: Fiction, Gender, and Memory.* Amherst: U Massachusetts P, 1991.

Hansen, Ron Rockwell, ed. *A Poetic Calm after the Desert Storm.* Monterey, CA: Monterey Poetry Society, 1991.

Hardt, Michael and Antonio Negri. *Empire.* Cambridge, MA: Harvard UP, 2000.

Harlow, Barbara. *Resistance Literature.* New York: Methuen, 1987.

Harper, Phillip Brian. "Nationalism and Social Division in Black Arts Poetry of the 1960s." *Critical Inquiry* 19 (Winter 1993). 235–255.

Harrison, Tony. *A Cold Coming*. Newcastle upon Tyne, England: Bloodaxe Books, 1991.

Harvey, David. *The New Imperialism*. New York: Oxford UP, 2003.

Heaney, Seamus. *The Government of the Tongue: Selected Prose, 1978–1987*. New York: Farrar, Straus and Giroux, 1990.

Heyen, William. *Ribbons: The Gulf War*. St. Louis: Time Being Books, 1991.

Himes, Andrew, with Jan Bultmann and others, ed. *Voices in Wartime Anthology: A Collection of Narratives and Poems*. Seattle: Whit, 2005.

Holden, Jonathan. "Gulf: January 17, 1991." *After the Storm: Poems on the Persian Gulf War*. Ed. Jay Meek and Frank Reeve. Washington, DC: Maisonneuve P, 1992. 47–48.

Hollis, J. T. *Persian Gulf Poems*. New Castle, DE: American Poetry & Literature P, 1992.

Homer. *The Iliad* (1990). Trans. Robert Fagles. Intro. Bernard Knox. New York: Viking, 1996.

Honold, Kevin. "Desert." *Pleiades* 26:1 (2006). 37–45.

Hoover, Paul, Ed. *Postmodern American Poetry: A Norton Anthology*. New York: W. W. Norton, 1994. xxv–xxxix.

Howlett, Charles F. and Glen Zeitzer. "The History of the American Peace Movement." *Making War/Making Peace: The Social Foundations of Violent Conflict*. Ed. Francesca M. Cancian and James William Gibson. Belmont, CA: Wadsworth, 1990. 225–238.

Hulse, Michael. *Mother of Battles*. Todmorden, England: Littlewood Arc, 1991.

Hurwitz, Deena and Craig Simpson, ed. *Against the Tide: Pacifist Resistance in the Second World War, an Oral History*. New York: War Resisters League, 1984.

Hutcheon, Linda. "The Post Always Rings Twice: the Postmodern and the Postcolonial." *Textual Practice* 8:2 (1994). 205–238.

I Heart Huckabees. Dir. David O. Russell. 2004.

I Was a Communist for the FBI. Dir. Gordon Douglas. 1951.

Ingram, Mira. "POWs." *Journal of the Gulf War: Poetry from Home*. Ed. Michael Logue et al. Fullerton, CA: Poets Reading, 1991. 21.

Investigation of a Flame. Dir. Lynne Sachs. 2001.

Isaacson, Bruce. "January 15, 1991." *Journal of the Gulf War: Poetry from Home*. Ed. Michael Logue et al. Fullerton, CA: Poets Reading, 1991. 29–31.

James, William. "The Moral Equivalent of War" (1910). *Approaches to Peace: A Reader in Peace Studies*. Ed. David P. Barash. New York: Oxford UP, 2000. 65–69.

Jameson, Fredric. *Postmodernism: Or, the Cultural Logic of Late Capitalism*. Durham, NC: Duke UP, 1991.

Jeffers, Robinson. *Selected Poems of Robinson Jeffers*. New York: Random, 1938.

Jeffords, Susan. *The Remasculinization of America: Gender and the Vietnam War*. Bloomington: Indiana UP, 1986.

——— and Lauren Rabinovitz, ed. *Seeing through the Media: the Persian Gulf War*. New Brunswick, NJ: Rutgers UP, 1994.

Johnson, Chalmers. *The Sorrows of Empire: Militarism, Secrecy, and the End of the Republic*. New York: Metropolitan/Henry Holt, 2004.

Johnson, Kent. "The Debate That Died." http://flashpointmag.com/ debate.htm accessed June 1, 2006.

———. *Lyric Poetry after Auschwitz: Eleven Submissions to the War*. Austin, TX: effing press, 2005.

Johnson, Mattie Shavers. *Wings of Fire*. Nashville, TN: Post Oak Productions, 1993.

Johnson, W. R. *The Idea of Lyric: Lyric Modes in Ancient and Modern Poetry*. Berkeley: U California P, 1982.

Jordan, June. *Affirmative Acts: Political Essays*. New York: Anchor/Doubleday, 1998.

———. *Civil Wars*. Boston: Beacon, 1981.

———. *Directed by Desire: The Collected Poems of June Jordan*. Port Townsend, WA: Copper Canyon, 2005.

———. "From the Persian Gulf to the Invasion—Poet, Activist, Essayist and Teacher June Jordan Speaks About the U.S. and Iraq in 1991." http://www.pacifica.org/ programs/dn/031119.html accessed August 31, 2006.

———. *Kissing God Goodbye: Poems 1991–1997*. New York: Anchor Books, 1997.

———. *On Call*. Cambridge, MA: South End, 1985.

———. *Passion*. Boston: Beacon, 1980.

Joseph, Lawrence. "I Note in a Notebook." *Into It*. Lawrence Joseph. New York: Farrar, Straus and Giroux, 2005. 10–11.

Kaladjian, Walter. *Languages of Liberation: The Social Text in Contemporary American Poetry*. New York: Columbia UP, 1989.

Keller, Lynn. *Forms of Expansion: Recent Long Poems by Women*. Chicago: U Chicago P, 1997.

King, Martin Luther Jr. "Beyond Vietnam." *Vietnam and Black America: An Anthology of Protest and Resistance*. Ed. Clyde Taylor. Garden City, NJ: Anchor Books, 1973. 79–98.

Kitchen, Judith. *Understanding William Stafford*. Columbia: U South Carolina P, 1989.

Klare, Michael. "The Peace Movement's Next Steps." *Nation*. 252.7 (March 25, 1991). 361–363.

Kroker, Arthur and Marilouise Kroker, eds. *The Body Invaders: Panic Sex in America*. New York: St. Martin's, 1987.

Kunitz, Stanley. *A Kind of Order, a Kind of Folly: Essays and Conversations*. Boston: Little, Brown, and Company, 1975.

———. *The Poems of Stanley Kunitz: 1928–1978*. Boston: Little, Brown, and Company, 1979.

Lacan, Jacques. *The Ethics of Psychoanalysis, 1959–1962*. Trans. Dennis Porter. New York: W. W. Norton, 1992.

Lacey, Paul A. *The Inner War: Forms and Themes in Recent American Poetry*. Philadelphia: Fortress P, 1972.

———. "The Poetry of Political Anguish." *Denise Levertov: Selected Criticism*. Ed. Paul A. Lacey. Ann Arbor: U Michigan P, 1993. 151–161.

Larsen, Wendy Sue and Tran Thi Nga. *Shallow Graves: Two Women and Vietnam.* New York: Perennial Library, 1986.

Lee, Martin and Norman Solomon. *Unreliable Sources: A Guide to Detecting Bias in News Media.* New York: Carol Publishing Group, 1991.

Lembcke, Jerry. *The Spitting Image: Myth, Memory, and the Legacy of Vietnam.* New York: New York UP, 1998.

Levertov, Denise. *Evening Train.* New York: New Directions, 1992.

———. *The Freeing of the Dust.* New York: New Directions, 1975.

———. *Making Peace.* Ed. Peggy Rosenthal. New York: New Directions, 2006.

———. *New and Selected Essays.* New York: New Directions, 1992.

———. "On the Edge of Darkness: What Is Political Poetry?" *Poetry and Politics: An Anthology of Essays.* Ed. Richard Jones. New York: William Morrow, 1985. 162–174.

———. *Poems 1960–1967.* New York: New Directions, 1983.

———. *Poems 1968–1972.* New York: New Directions, 1987.

———. *The Poet in the World.* New York: New Directions, 1967.

LeVine, Mark. *Why They Don't Hate Us: Lifting the Veil on the Axis of Evil.* Oxford, England: OneWorld, 2005.

Lindley, David. *Lyric.* London and New York: Methuen, 1985.

Logue, Michael et al., ed. *Journal of the Gulf War: Poetry from Home.* Fullerton, CA: Poets Reading, 1991.

London, Rick and Leslie Scalapino, ed. *enough.* Oakland, CA: O Books, 2003.

Lorde, Audre. "Power." *What Is Found There: Notebooks on Poetry and Politics.* Adrienne Rich. New York: W. W. Norton, 1993. 68–69.

Lowell, Robert. *Collected Poems.* New York: Farrar, Straus and Giroux, 2003.

———. *Collected Prose.* Ed. Robert Giroux. New York: Farrar, Straus and Giroux, 1987.

———. *Land of Unlikeness.* Cummington, MA: Cummington P, 1944.

———. *Life Studies* (1956). New York: Farrar, Straus and Cudahy, 1960.

———. *Lord Weary's Castle* (1946) and *The Mills of the Kavanaughs* (1951). New York: Meridian Books, 1966.

———. "Memories" drafts. Houghton Archives. Cambridge, MA: Harvard University.

———. *Notebook 1967–1968.* New York: Farrar, Straus and Giroux, 1969.

———. *Selected Letters.* Ed. Saskia Hamilton. New York: Farrar, Straus and Giroux, 2005.

———. *Selected Poems.* New York: Farrar, Straus and Giroux, 1976.

Lowenfels, Walter. *Where Is Vietnam? American Poets Respond.* Garden City, NY: Anchor, 1967.

Lukacs, Gyorgy. *The Theory of the Novel: A Historico-Philosophical Essay on the Forms of Great Epic Literature.* Trans. Anna Bostock. Cambridge, MA: MIT P, 1970.

Lyotard, Jean-François. *The Postmodern Condition: A Report on Knowledge.* Trans. Geoff Bennington and Brian Massumi. Minneapolis: U Minnesota P, 1984.

MacArthur, John R. *Second Front: Censorship and Propaganda in the Gulf War.* Berkeley: U California P, 1993.

Mac Low, Jackson. *Representative Works: 1938–1985.* New York: Roof, 1986.

Magee, Michael. *MS.* New York: Spuyten Duyvil, 2003.

Mahoney, Phillip, ed. *From Both Sides Now: The Poetry of the Vietnam War and Its Aftermath.* New York: Scribner, 1998.

Mailer, Norman. *The Armies of the Night: History as a Novel; the Novel as History.* New York: New American Library, 1968.

The Man in the Gray Flannel Suit. Dir. Nunally Johnson. 1956.

Mann, Michael. *Incoherent Empire.* New York: Verso, 2003.

Marable, Manning. *Race, Reform and Rebellion.* Jackson: UP Mississippi, 1991.

Mariani, Paul. *Lost Puritan: A Life of Robert Lowell.* New York: W. W. Norton, 1994.

Mariscal, George, ed. *Aztlán and Viet Nam: Chicano and Chicana Experiences of Viet Nam.* Berkeley: U California P, 1999.

Masland, Tom. "Beyond the Caricatures of Hussein and His Society." *Philadelphia Inquirer.* September 1, 1991. 2F.

Mazzaro, Jerome. "Robert Lowell's Early Politics of Apocalypse." *Modern American Poetry: Essays in Criticism.* Ed. Jerome Mazzaro. New York: David McKay, 1970. 321–350.

McGann, Jerome. "Contemporary Poetry, Alternate Routes." http://www.writing .upenn.edu/~afilreis/88/megann.html, accessed September 1, 2006.

———. "The Third World of Criticism." *Rethinking Historicism: Critical Readings in Romantic History.* Ed. Marjorie Levinson, Marilyn Butler, Jerome McGann, and Paul Hamilton. New York: Basil Blackwell, 1989. 85–107.

McNamara, Robert S., with Brian VanDeMark. *In Retrospect: The Tragedy and Lessons of Vietnam.* New York: Times Books, 1995.

Meek, Jay. Personal correspondence. December 3, 1999.

Meek, Jay and Frank Reeve, ed. *After the Storm: Poems on the Persian Gulf War.* Washington, DC: Maisonneuve P, 1992.

Mersmann, James. *Out of the Vietnam Vortex: A Study of Poets and Poetry against the War.* Lawrence: Kansas UP, 1974.

Metres, Philip. "Chanting in the House of Nabokov: An Interview with Jerome (and Diane) Rothenberg." *Combo* 13 (Winter/Spring 2004). 47–56.

———. *Prison Etiquette: A Convict's Compendium of Useful Information* (1950). Carbondale: Southern Illinois UP, 2001.

Meyers, Jeffrey. *Manic Power: Robert Lowell and His Circle.* New York: Arbor House, 1987.

Mitchell, Stephen. *Gilgamesh: A New English Version.* New York: Free P, 2004.

Monroe, Jonathan. *A Poverty of Objects: The Prose Poem and the Politics of Genre.* Ithaca, NY: Cornell UP, 1987.

Montefiore, Jan. *Feminism and Poetry: Language, Experience, and Identity in Women's Writing.* San Francisco: Pandora, 1994.

Moore, Lenard D. *Desert Storm: A Brief History.* San Diego: Los Hombres, 1993.

Muller, Lauren and the Poetry for the People Collective, ed. *June Jordan's Poetry for the People: A Revolutionary Blueprint*. New York: Routledge, 1995.

Muñoz, Jose. " 'The White to Be Angry': Vaginal Davis's Terrorist Drag." *Social Text* Fall/Winter 1997. 52–53.

Muske, Carol. "To the Muse." *After the Storm: Poems on the Persian Gulf War*. Ed. Jay Meek and Frank Reeve. Washington, DC: Maisonneuve P, 1992. 82–83.

Nadel, Alan. *Containment Culture: American Narratives, Postmodernism, and the Atomic Age*. Durham, NC: Duke UP, 1995.

Naeve, Lowell, with David Wieck. *A Field of Broken Stones*. Glen Gardner, NJ: Libertarian P, 1951.

"Nazi Draft Dodger Gets 3-Year Term." *New York Times* October 14, 1943. A13.

Neal, Larry. "The Cultural Front" (1965). *The Liberator*. http://www.umich.edu/~eng499/documents/neal1.html accessed December 5, 2003.

Neilson, Jim. *Warring Fictions: American Literary Culture and the Vietnam War Narrative*. Jackson: UP Mississippi, 1998.

Nelson, Cary. *Our Last First Poets: Vision and History in Contemporary American Poetry*. Urbana: U Illinois P, 1981.

———. *Repression and Recovery: Modern American Poetry and the Politics of Cultural Memory, 1910–1945*. Madison: U Wisconsin P, 1989.

———, ed. *Anthology of Modern American Poetry*. New York: Oxford UP, 2000.

Newton, Huey P. "Letter to the National Liberation Front of South Vietnam (with reply)." *Vietnam and Black America: An Anthology of Protest and Resistance*. Ed. Clyde Taylor. Garden City, NY: Anchor Books, 1973. 290–295.

Nicosia, Gerald. *Home to War: A History of the Vietnam Veterans' Movement*. New York: Crown, 2001.

———. "A Poem for the Human Voice." *Journal of the Gulf War: Poetry from Home*. Ed. Michael Logue et al. Fullerton, CA: Poets Reading, 1991. 34–35.

Norris, Christopher. *Uncritical Theory: Postmodernism, Intellectuals, and the Gulf War*. London: Lawrence & Wishart, 1992.

Norris, Margot. "Military Censorship and the Body Count in the Persian Gulf War." *Cultural Critique* (Fall 1991). 223–245.

Olds, Sharon. "May 1968." *American War Poetry: An Anthology*. Ed. Lorrie Goldensohn. New York: Columbia UP, 2006. 304–305.

Orwell, George. "Politics and the English Language" (1946). *Essays in Context*. Ed. Sandra Fehl Tropp and Ann Pierson-D'Angelo. New York: Oxford UP, 2001. 186–199.

Parenti, Michael. *Inventing Reality: The Politics of the News Media*. New York: St. Martin's, 1993.

Parkinson, Thomas. "William Everson: A Poet, Anarchist and Printer Emerges From Waldport." *Perspectives on William Everson*. Ed. James B. Hall, Bill Hotchkiss, and Judith Shears. Grants Pass, OR: Castle Peak Editions, 1992. 28–32.

Patchen, Kenneth. *An Astonished Eye Looks Out of the Air*. Waldport, OR: Untide P, 1945.

Pawlak, Mark, ed. *Present/Tense: Poets in the World*. Brooklyn, NY: Hanging Loose, 2004.

Pease, Donald. "Hiroshima, the Vietnam Veterans War Memorial, and the Gulf War: Postnational Spectacles." *Cultures of United States Imperialism*. Ed. Amy Kaplan and Donald Pease. Durham, NC: Duke UP, 1993. 557–580.

Peck, James. *Underdogs vs Upperdogs*. Canterbury, NH: Greenleaf Books, 1969.

Pelton, Theodore. "Friendly Fire." *Endorsed by Jack Chapeau*. Buffalo, NY: Starcherone, 2000. 9–33.

Perelman, Bob. "Against Shock and Awe." Online version. http://www.arras.net/circulars/archives/cat_poems.html accessed August 31, 2006.

———. *The Marginalization of Poetry: Language Writing and Literary History*. Princeton, NJ: Princeton UP, 1996.

Perloff, Marjorie. *Poetry on & off the Page: Essays for Emergent Occasions*. Evanston, IL: Northwestern UP, 1998.

———. "Postmodernism and the Impasse of Lyric." *Formations* 1:2 (Fall 1984). 43–63.

Peters, Nancy J., ed. *War after War*. *City Lights Review* Number Five. San Francisco: City Lights, 1992.

Peterson, Michael. Catalogue Essay for Art Against War Exhibit, March 3–7, 1991. Unpaginated. Eau Claire, WI: Poets and Artists Against War, 1991.

Preminger, Alex, ed. *Encyclopedia of Poetry and Poetics*. Princeton, NJ: Princeton UP, 1965.

Prevallet, Kristin. "The Exquisite Extremes of Poetry (Watten and Baraka on the Brink)." *Jacket* (12): July 2000. http://jacketmagazine.com/12/prevallet-orono.html accessed August 31, 2006.

Pynchon, Thomas. *Gravity's Rainbow* (1973). New York: Penguin, 1995.

Rasula, Jed. *The American Poetry Wax Museum: Reality Effects, 1940–1990*. Urbana, IL: NCTE, 1996.

Ray, David. *The Death of Sardanapalus and Other Poems of the Iraq Wars*. Berthoud, CO: Howling Dog, 2004.

———. Email interviews with author. 2002.

Rich, Adrienne. *An Atlas of the Difficult World: Poems 1988–1991*. New York: W. W. Norton, 1991.

———. *What Is Found There: Notebooks on Poetry and Politics*. New York: W. W. Norton, 1993.

———. *The Will to Change: Poems 1968–1970*. New York: W. W. Norton, 1971.

Rizzo, Fred. "Brother Antoninus: of Radical Catholicism." *Perspectives on William Everson*. Ed. James B. Hall, Bill Hotchkiss, and Judith Shears. Grants Pass, OR: Castle Peak, 1992. 152–165.

Rogin, Michael. "Make My Day!: Spectacle as Amnesia in Imperial Politics." *Cultures of United States Imperialism*. Ed. Amy Kaplan and Donald Pease. Durham, NC: Duke UP, 1993. 499–534.

Rosenthal, M. L., ed. (1959) *The New Poets: American and British Poetry since World War II*. New York: Oxford UP, 1967.

Rosenthal, Peggy, ed. *Imagine a World: Poetry for Peacemakers*. Erie, PA: Pax Christi USA, 2005.

Ross, Andrew. "The New Sentence and the Commodity Form: Recent American Writing." *Marxism and the Interpretation of Culture*. Ed. Cary Nelson and Lawrence Grossberg. Urbana: U Illinois P, 1988. 361–380.

———, ed. *Universal Abandon? The Politics of Postmodernism*. Minneapolis: U Minnesota P, 1988.

Rothenberg, Jerome. Introduction. *Representative Works: 1938–1985*. Jackson Mac Low. New York: Roof, 1986. v–x.

Rottman, Larry. *Voices from the Ho Chi Minh Trail: Poetry of America and Vietnam, 1965–1993*. Desert Hot Springs, CA: Event Horizon P, 1993.

Rovics, David. http://www.soundclick.com/pro/view/01/default.cfm?bandid=111310 &content=main&songid=0 accessed July 7, 2006.

Rukeyser, Muriel. *Collected Poems*. New York: McGraw Hill, 1978.

———. *The Life of Poetry*. Williamsburg, MA: Paris P, 1996.

Said, Edward. *Culture and Imperialism*. New York: Vintage, 1993.

Sanchez, Sonia. "The Final Solution/The Leaders Speak." *Vietnam and Black America: An Anthology of Protest and Resistance*. Ed. Clyde Taylor. Garden City, NY: Anchor Books, 1973. 169–170.

Scalapino, Leslie. *The Front Matter, Dead Souls*. Wesleyan, CT: Wesleyan UP, 1996.

———, ed. *War and Peace*. Oakland, CA: O Books, 2004.

Schulte-Sasse, Jochen and Linda Schulte-Sasse. "War, Otherness, and Illusionary Identifications with the State." *Cultural Critique* 19 (Fall 1991). 67–95.

Schumacher, Michael. *Dharma Lion: A Biography of Allen Ginsberg*. New York: St. Martin's, 1992.

Schweik, Susan. *A Gulf So Deeply Cut: American Women Poets and the Second World War*. Madison: U Wisconsin P, 1991.

Scott, Peter Dale. *Coming to Jakarta: A Poem about Terror*. New York: New Directions, 1989.

Scully, James. *Line Break: Poetry as Social Practice*. Seattle: Bay P, 1988.

Shapiro, Harvey, ed. *Poets of World War II*. New York: Library of America, 2003.

Shapiro, Karl. *Trial of a Poet and Other Poems*. New York: Reynal & Hitchcock, 1947.

Sharp, Gene. *The Politics of Nonviolent Action*. 3 vols. Boston: Porter Sargent, 1973.

Shaw, Robert B. "The Poetry of Protest." *American Poetry since 1960: Some Critical Perspectives*. Ed. Robert B. Shaw. Cheadle, England: Carcanet P, 1973. 45–54.

Shay, Jonathan. *Achilles in Vietnam: Combat Trauma and the Undoing of Character* (1994). New York: Touchstone, 1995.

Sheldon, Sayre P., ed. *Her War Story: Twentieth-Century Women Write about War*. Carbondale: Southern Illinois UP, 1999.

Shown, Leslie. "What I Mean." *June Jordan's Poetry for the People: A Revolutionary Blueprint*. Ed. Lauren Muller and the Poetry for the People Collective. New York: Routledge, 1995. 200.

Sibley, Mulford Q. and Philip E. Jacob. *Conscription of Conscience: The American State and the Conscientious Objector, 1940–1947.* Ithaca, NY: Cornell UP, 1952.

Sifry, Micah L. and Christopher Cerf, ed. *The Gulf War Reader: History, Documents, Opinions.* New York: Times Books, 1991.

Signorelli, Anthony. "New York Honors Troops." *Rooster Crows at Light from the Bombing: Echoes from the Gulf War.* Ed. Anthony Signorelli and Paul MacAdam. Minneapolis, MN: Inroads, 1992. 28–29.

Signorelli, Anthony and Paul MacAdam, ed. *Rooster Crows at Light from the Bombing: Echoes from the Gulf War.* Minneapolis, MN: Inroads, 1992.

"Signs of Dissent." *Nation* 252, 9 (March 11, 1991). 292.

Silliman, Ron, Carla Harryman, Lyn Hejinian, Steve Benson, and Barrett Watten. "Aesthetic Tendency and the Politics of Poetry: A Manifesto." *Social Text* (Fall 1988). 19–20, 261–275.

Silverman, Kaja. *Male Subjectivity at the Margins.* New York: Routledge, 1992.

Simawe, Saadi, Daniel Weissbort, and Norma Rinsler, ed. *Iraqi Poetry Today.* London: King's College, 2003.

Sloan, Jacob. *The Generation of Journey.* Waldport, OR: Untide P, 1945.

Sloterdijk, Peter. *A Critique of Cynical Reason.* Trans. Michael Eldred. Minneapolis: U Minnesota P, 1987.

Smith, Lorrie. "Songs of Experience: Denise Levertov's Political Poetry." *Denise Levertov: Selected Criticism.* Ed. Paul A. Lacey. Ann Arbor: U Michigan P, 1993. 177–197.

Sophocles. *Antigone. Sophocles I.* Ed. David Grene and Richard Lattimore. Chicago: U Chicago P, 1991. 159–212.

Spahr, Juliana. *This Connection of Everyone with Lungs.* Berkeley: U California P, 2005.

Spivak, Gayatri Chakravorty. "Can the Subaltern Speak?" *Marxism and the Interpretation of Culture.* Ed. Cary Nelson and Lawrence Grossberg. Urbana: U Illinois P, 1988. 271–313.

Staff of the Defense Monitor. "Militarism in America" (1986). *A Peace Reader: Essential Readings on War, Justice, Non-violence and World Order.* Ed. Joseph J. Fahey and Richard Armstrong. New York: Paulist P, 1992. 61–75.

Stafford, Kim, ed. *Every War Has Two Losers: William Stafford on Peace and War.* Minneapolis, MN: Milkweed, 2003.

Stafford, William. *The Darkness around Us Is Deep: Selected Poems of William Stafford.* New York: HarperPerennial, 1993.

———. *Down in My Heart* (1947). Swarthmore, PA: Bench P, 1985.

———. Introduction. *The Achievement of Brother Antoninus.* William Everson. Glenview, IL: Scott Foresman, 1967. 1–18.

———. *The Way It Is: New and Selected Poems.* St. Paul, MN: Graywolf, 1998.

———. *Writing the Australian Crawl: Views on the Writer's Vocation.* Ann Arbor: U Michigan P, 1978.

———. *You Must Revise Your Life.* Ann Arbor: U Michigan P, 1986.

Stallworthy, Jon, ed. *The Oxford Book of War Poetry.* New York: Oxford UP, 1984.

Stitt, Peter. "William Stafford's Wilderness Quest." *On William Stafford: The Worth of Local Things.* Ed. Tom Andrews. Ann Arbor: U Michigan P, 1993. 165–202.

Sturken, Marita. *Tangled Memories: The Vietnam War, the AIDS Epidemic, and the Politics of Remembering.* Berkeley: U California P, 1997.

Sullivan, James. "Investing the Cultural Capital of Robert Lowell." *Twentieth-Century Literature* 38:2 (Summer 1992). 194–213.

———. *On the Walls and in the Streets: American Poetry Broadsides from the 1960s.* Urbana: U Illinois P, 1997.

Swift, Todd, ed. *100 Poets Against the War.* Cambridge, England: Salt, 2003.

Tatarunis, Paula. "Guernica Pantoum." *Poets Against the War.* Ed. Sam Hamill. New York: Nation Books, 2003. 225–226.

Tatum, James. *The Mourner's Song: War and Remembrance from* The Iliad *to Vietnam.* Chicago: U Chicago P, 2003.

Taylor, Clyde, ed. *Vietnam and Black America: An Anthology of Protest and Resistance.* Garden City, NY: Anchor Books, 1973.

Three Kings. Dir. David O. Russell. 1999.

Tillinghast, Richard. *Robert Lowell's Life and Work: Damaged Grandeur.* Ann Arbor: U Michigan P, 1995.

Todd, Emmanuel. *After the Empire: The Breakdown of the American Order.* Trans. C. Jon Delogu. New York: Columbia UP, 2003.

Tracy, James. *Direct Action: Radical Pacifism from the Union Eight to the Chicago Seven.* Chicago: U Chicago P, 1996.

Trillin, Calvin. *Deadline Poet: Or, My Life as a Doggerelist.* New York: Warner Books, 1994.

Tritle, Lawrence A. *From Melos to My Lai: War and Survival.* New York: Routledge, 2000.

True, Michael. *An Energy Field More Intense than War: The Nonviolent Tradition and American Literature.* Syracuse, NY: Syracuse UP, 1995.

Turner, Brian. *Here, Bullet.* Farmington, ME: Alice James Books, 2005.

VanDevanter, Linda and Joan A. Furey, ed. *Visions of War, Dreams of Peace: Writings of Women in the Vietnam War.* New York: Warner Books, 1991.

Van Wienen, Mark. *Partisan and Poets: The Political Work of American Poetry in the Great War.* Cambridge, England and New York: Cambridge UP, 1997.

Vasquez, Jose. "Jose Vasquez: From Soldier to Objector." Interview by Francesca Fiorentini and Steve Theberg. *The Nonviolent Activist* (March–April 2006). http://www.warresisters.org/nva0306-5.htm accessed May 25, 2006.

Vendler, Helen. *The Given and the Made: Strategies of Poetic Redefinition.* Cambridge, MA: Harvard UP, 1995.

Vincent, Stephen and Ellen Zweig, ed. *The Poetry Reading: A Contemporary Compendium on Language and Performance.* San Francisco, CA: Momo's P, 1981.

Virilio, Paul, with Sylvere Lotringer. *Pure War.* New York: Semiotext(e), 1997.

Von Eschen, Penny M. *Race against Empire: Black Americans and Anticolonialism, 1937–1957.* Ithaca, NY: Cornell UP, 1997.

Von Hallberg, Robert. *American Poetry and Culture, 1945–1980*. Cambridge, MA: Harvard UP, 1985.

Wag the Dog. Dir. Barry Levinson. 1997.

Walker, Margaret. "The Ballad of the Free." *Vietnam and Black America: An Anthology of Protest and Resistance*. Ed. Clyde Taylor. Garden City, NY: Anchor Books, 1973. 310–311.

Wallach, Glenn. "The C.O. Link: Conscientious Objection to World War II and the San Francisco Renaissance." *Brethren Life and Thought* 27 (Winter 1982). 15–34.

Walsh, Jeffrey. "'After Our War': John Balaban's Poetic Images of Vietnam." *Vietnam Images: War and Representation*. Ed. Jeffrey Walsh and James Aulich. New York: St. Martin's, 1989. 141–152.

Watten, Barrett. *Bad History*. Berkeley, CA: Atelos, 1998.

———. *Frame: 1971–1990*. Los Angeles: Sun & Moon, 1997.

———. "Intention and Identity." *Artweek* (April 4, 1991). 18–19.

———. "Michal Rovner." *Artweek* (February 20, 1992). 14.

———. "No More War! 'An Unwanted Animal at the Garden Party of Democracy' at Southern Exposure Gallery." *Artweek* (February 7, 1991). 1, 22–23.

———. "The Turn to Language and the 1960s." *Critical Inquiry* 29 (Autumn 2002). 139–183.

———. Email correspondence with the author. November 22, 1999.

Weil, Simone. "The Iliad, Poem of Might." *Simone Weil Reader*. Ed. George Panichas. Mt. Kisco, NY: Moyer Bell Limited, 1977. 153–183.

Weinberg, Bill. "The Question of A.N.S.W.E.R." *The Nonviolent Activist* (Nov.–Dec. 2005). http://www.warresisters.org/nva1105-1.htm accessed May 25, 2006.

Whitehead, Kim. *The Feminist Poetry Movement*. Jackson: UP Mississippi, 1996.

Why We Fight. Dir. Eugene Jarecki. 2005.

Wiegman, Robyn. "Whiteness Studies and the Paradox of Particularity." *Boundary 2* 26:3 (1999). 115–150.

Wilbur, Richard. "Advice to a Prophet." *The Oxford Book of War Poetry*. Ed. Jon Stallworthy. New York: Oxford UP, 1984. 336–337.

Williams, Juan. *Eyes on the Prize: America's Civil Rights Years, 1954–1965*. New York: Penguin, 1987.

Williamson, Alan. *Pity the Monsters: The Political Vision of Robert Lowell*. New Haven, CT: Yale UP, 1974.

Wittner, Lawrence. *Rebels against War: The American Peace Movement, 1933–1983*. Philadelphia, PA: Temple UP, 1984.

Wojahn, David. *Interrogation Palace: New and Selected Poems 1982–2004*. Pittsburgh, PA: U Pittsburgh P, 2006.

———. "Maggie's Farm No More: The Fate of Political Poetry." Unpublished manuscript.

Women of the Weather Underground Organization. *Sing a Battle Song: Poems*. U.S.: Inkworks, 1975.

Woolf, Virginia. *The Virginia Woolf Reader*. Ed. Mitchell A. Leaska. New York: Harcourt Brace Jovanovich, 1984.

Wordsworth, William. Preface [to *Lyrical Ballads* (1802)]. *Lyrical Ballads and Related Writings*. Ed. William Richey and Daniel Robinson. New York: Houghton Mifflin, 2002.

Yeats, William Butler. "Easter 1916." *Norton Anthology of Poetry*. Fourth Edition. New York: W. W. Norton, 1996. 1089–1090.

———. "Per Amica Silentia Lunae" (1917). *Mythologies* (1959). New York: Touchstone, 1998. 319–368.

Young, David. "'1940': Shivers of Summer Wind." On William Stafford: *The Worth of Local Things*. Ed. Tom Andrews. Ann Arbor: U Michigan P, 1993. 260–267.

Young, Michael. "Facing a Test of Faith: Jewish Pacifists during the Second World War." *The Challenge of Shalom: The Jewish Tradition of Peace and Justice*. Ed. Murray Polner and Naomi Goodwin. Philadelphia, PA: New Society, 1994. 156–167.

Young, Neil. *Living with War*. Reprise. 2006.

Zahn, Gordon. *Another Part of the War: The Camp Simon Story*. Amherst: U Massachusetts P, 1979.

Zinn, Howard. *A People's History of the United States*. New York: Harper and Row, 1980.

Zizek, Slavoj. *Enjoy Your Symptom!: Jacques Lacan in Hollywood and Out*. New York: Routledge, 1992.

———. *The Indivisible Remainder: An Essay on Schelling and Other Related Matters*. New York: Verso, 1996.

———. *The Sublime Object of Ideology*. New York: Verso, 1989.

Index

Gara, Larry, 17
Gardner, Drew: "Chicks Dig War," 235
Garfinkle, Gwynne: "Beyond
    Vietnam," 167
Gaye, Marvin: "What's Goin' On," 212
Gelpi, Albert, 102, 103, 106, 107, 127, 133
gender, 83, 114, 182
GI samizdat poetry, 101
Gibbons, Reginald: "Poetry after the
    Recent War," 173
Gibbs, Nancy: "If You Want to Humble
    an Empire," 220
Gibson, James William, 245n2; and
    Technowar, 98
Gilbert, Roger, 14
Ginsberg, Allen, 20, 21, 96, 107, 108, 116,
    117, 169, 205; "America," 36; "hare om
    namo shiva" chant, 104; "Howl," 108;
    "Hūm Bom," 167; "Kaddish," 108;
    "Pentagon Exorcism," 109; "Wichita
    Vortex Sutra," 110, 116
Giovanni, Nikki: "The Great Pax
    Whitie," 100
Gitlin, Todd, 6, 111, 115, 128, 138, 139;
    Sixties, 106, 129; The Whole World Is
    Watching, 21
Goldman, Judith, 226
González, Juan Carlos, 101
Goodman, Paul, 41
Grahn, Judy, 182–183
Greiner, Donald J., 49
Griffin, Susan, 182
Gulf War. See Persian Gulf War
Gulf War Syndrome, 159, 160
Gundy, Jeff, 52
Gwiazda, Piotr, 221

Hadas, Moses, 3
Hall, Donald, 169; "The Coalition," 170
Hallin, Daniel, 98
Hamill, Sam, 225; Poets against the War,
    222, 223
Hamilton, Ian, 27, 30, 33, 42, 241n1,
    242n8
Hamilton, Saskia, 30, 31
Hanley, Lynne, 4
Hardt, Michael, 10, 11, 100

Harlow, Barbara, 9, 99, 238n8;
    "resistance literature," 138
Harper, Phillip Brian, 7, 182, 192
Harrison, Tony, 165, 250n11; "A Cold
    Coming," 164; "Initial Illumination,"
    164
Heaney, Seamus, 4
Herber, William. See Everson, William
Heyen, William: "The Reich," 175; "The
    Truth," 176; Ribbons, 23, 174, 175–177;
    September 11, 2001, 220; The Swastika
    Poems, 175–176
Hobbes, Thomas, 212
Holden, Jonathan, 172
Hollis, J. T.: Persian Gulf Poems, 174
homefront, 3, 5, 10, 21, 93, 97, 110, 111,
    113, 114, 131, 175, 179, 199, 207, 241n19
Homer, 1, 2, 23, 237n3
Hoover, Paul, 160
Howlett, Charles F.: "The History of the
    American Peace Movement," 7
Hulse, Michael: Mother of Battles,
    174, 251n13
Hutcheon, Linda, 249n3

I Heart Huckabees, 235
I Was a Communist for the FBI, 34
identification, 127–129, 131–135, 137, 139,
    140, 142–147, 186, 230
imagined community, 7, 9, 51, 81
imperialism, 10, 20, 49, 76, 99, 121, 122,
    136, 157, 160, 173, 181, 183, 190, 192,
    220, 230
Ingram, Mira: "POWs," 166
internment, 19, 40, 53, 60, 70, 78, 79, 84,
    86, 241n19
Investigations of a Flame, 234
Iraq, 159, 166, 214, 216, 232, 251n13
Iraq War, 9, 16, 24, 222, 224, 226, 230, 235,
    236, 237n2, 245n4
Iraqis, 22, 23, 129, 147–149, 164, 189, 190,
    192, 194, 198, 199, 206, 210, 228, 235,
    245n4
Isaacson, Bruce, 167

Jacob, Philip P., 16, 53, 55, 62;
    Conscription of Conscience, 243n1

Prins, Gwyn, 8
propaganda, 52, 75, 76, 161, 230, 241n19
psychoanalysis, 34, 36, 48, 55–56, 86
Public Enemy, 180
Pure War, 7, 9–11, 22, 24, 60, 66, 147, 197, 207, 212, 215, 220, 236

Ra, Sun, 17
Rasula, Jed, 156, 240n16; subjectivity racket, 161
Ray, David, 98, 134, 246n8; *A Poetry Reading against the War*, 5, 6, 97; *The Death of Sardanapalus and Other Poems of the Iraq Wars*, 251n11
Reeve, Frank: *After the Storm*, 169, 170
representation, 15, 28, 29, 62, 111, 133, 138, 144, 147, 166, 169, 183, 198, 202, 211, 213, 219, 226
resistance communities, 7, 20, 160
Rexroth, Kenneth, 52, 90, 240n17
Reyes, Ben; "Juan Carlos Gonzalez," 101; *Aztlán and Viet Nam*, 100–101
Rich, Adrienne, 13, 14, 21, 114, 182; "An Atlas of the Difficult World," 160; *An Atlas of the Difficult World*, 12, 155; "Newsreel," 114; "Shooting Script," 93; *What Is Found There*, 13, 184; *The Will to Change*, 114
Riverbend, 235
Rogin, Michael, 250n5
Romanticism, 65, 116, 139, 183, 200, 201, 206, 211, 240n15
Rosenthal, M. L., 34, 240n16; "Poetry as Confession," 31
Rothenberg, Jerome: "Chanting," 105, 234; Three-Penny Reading against the War in Vietnam, 104, 105, 234, 246n10
Rottman, Larry: 1st Casualty Press, 98
Rovics, David, 236
Rovner, Michal, 199; "Decoy#1," 198
Rukeyser, Muriel, 90, 142, 239n12; "Book of the Dead," 138; "Letter to the Front," 241n19; *The Life of Poetry*, 144, 230
Rustin, Bayard, 17, 52, 179

Said, Edward, 235, 248n4
San Francisco Renaissance, 19, 74, 75, 90
Sanchez, Sonia, 99, 180
Sanders, Ed: "Levitating the Pentagon," 96
Sassoon, Siegfried, 4, 242n3
Savio, Mario, 106
Scalapino, Leslie, 14, 225, 229; *enough*, 222; *The Front Matter, Dead Souls*, 226
Schulte-Sasse, Jochen and Linda, 10
Schumacher, Michael, 108
Scott, Paul Dale: *Coming to Jakarta*, 12
Second World War, 3, 4, 6, 9, 15, 16, 19, 20, 22, 23, 25, 28–32, 34, 40, 41, 45, 48, 51, 52, 54, 63, 67, 70, 74, 76, 84, 89, 91, 107, 120, 127, 131, 157, 158, 179, 186, 207, 214, 227, 230, 243n1, 244n5
Seeger, Pete, 244n1
Seeing through the Media, 214
September 11th, 9, 24, 219, 220, 222, 225, 231
Shapiro, Harvey: *Poets of World War II*, 238n7
Shapiro, Karl, 4, 17; "The Conscientious Objector," 26
Sharp, Gene: *The Politics of Nonviolent Action*, 9
Shaw, Robert B.: "The Poetry of Protest," 5
Shay, Jonathan: *Achilles in Vietnam*, 237n3
Sheldon, Sayre P., 4
Shown, Leslie, 190; "What I Mean," 189
Signorelli, Anthony: "New York Honors Troops," 168
Silliman, Ron, 199, 201, 229
Silverman, Kaja, 36, 48, 129
Simonides, 237n2
Simpson, Louis, 4
simulacra, 157, 159, 163
Sloan, Jacob, 79; "From New Hampshire," 78; *The Generation of Journey*, 77
Sloterdijk, Peter, 166
Smith, Lorrie, 245n2

soldier-poet, 4, 5, 112
Spahr, Juliana: *This Connection of
Everyone with Lungs*, 235
Spearhead, 180
Spellman, A. B., 99
Spicer, Jack, 90
Spivak, Gayatri Chakravorty, 148; "Can
the Subaltern Speak?" 22, 248n4
Stafford, Kim, 63
Stafford, William, 5, 17, 18, 51–71, 74,
169, 191, 226, 236, 239n9, 243n3, 243n4,
244n6, 246n9; *The Achievement of
Brother Antoninus*, 91, 92; *The
Darkness around Us Is Deep*, 63;
Down in My Heart, 18, 51–60, 62, 63,
70, 92; "Entering History," 66, 69, 70;
Every War Has Two Losers, 63, 239n9;
"History Display," 66; "How It Is," 62;
"The Jet Planes Dive," 80; "Not in the
Headlines," 66; "Peace Walk," 68, 69;
"Poetry," 70; "Something to Declare,"
71; "Traveling through the Dark,"
66n; "Watching the Jet Planes Dive,"
66, 68, 69; *The Way It Is*, 62–63,
67–71, 236; *Writing the Australian
Crawl*, 66; *You Must Revise Your Life*,
62–64, 243n4
Starr, Edwin: "War," 95
Stefans, Brian Kim: "Circulars: Poets,
Artists, and Critics Respond to U.S.
Global Policy," 234
Stitt, Peter, 64, 243n3
Student Non-Violent Coordinating
Committee, 99
Students for a Democratic Society
(SDS), 21, 128
Sullivan, James, 15, 46, 101, 102
Swarthmore College Peace Collection,
236, 240n13; "Men Wanted," 245n3
Swift, Todd: *100 Poets against the
War*, 222
symbolic action, 15, 18, 20, 21, 102, 104,
106, 109, 111, 201, 229, 234, 236

Tatarunis, Paula: "Guernica Pantoum,"
224, 225

Taylor, Clyde: *Vietnam and Black
America*, 99
Technowar, 118
Thersites, 1–3
Thoreau, Henry David, 67, 106;
"Resistance to Civil Government," 70
Three Kings, 250n4
Tillinghast, Richard, 46
Todorov, Tsvetan, 201
Tomorrow, Tom: "This Modern
World," 153
Toscano, Rodrigo, 226
Touré, Askia Muhammed, 99
Tracy, James: *Direct Action*, 17
translations, 125–126
Trillin, Calvin: "Thursday Night War,"
250–251n11
Tritle, Lawrence A., 2
Turner, Brian, 4; "Here, Bullet," 235

Valdez, Luis: *Pensamiento Serpento*, 101
Van Wienen, Mark, 4, 160, 239n8
Vargas, Adrian: "Blessed Amerika," 101
Vasquez, Jose: "Jose Vasquez: From
Soldier to Objector," 245n4
Vendler, Helen, 33
Vietnam Veterans against the War, 7,
107, 110
Vietnam War, 2, 4, 5, 9, 15–18, 20–22, 45,
46, 61, 93–151, 156, 160, 161, 163, 166,
168, 172, 173, 176, 180, 186, 199, 201, 203,
206–208, 224, 225, 230, 234, 235, 249n14
Vincent, Stephen, 108
Virilio, Paul, 9–11, 22, 60, 197, 205, 207
visionaries, 21, 112, 113, 115, 126
Voices in Wartime, 225
Von Eschen, Penny, 180; *Race against
Empire*, 179
Von Hallberg, Robert, 13, 49; *American
Poetry and Culture, 1945–1980*, 5
Vosnesensky, Andrei: Three-Penny
Reading against the War in
Vietnam, 105

Wag the Dog, 158, 250n4
Waldman, Anne, 226

Contemporary North American Poetry Series

Industrial Poetics: Demo Tracks for a Mobile Culture
BY JOE AMATO

Jorie Graham: Essays on the Poetry
EDITED BY THOMAS GARDNER
UNIVERSITY OF WISCONSIN PRESS, 2005

Gary Snyder and the Pacific Rim: Creating Countercultural Community
BY TIMOTHY GRAY

History, Memory, and the Literary Left: Modern American Poetry, 1935–1968
BY JOHN LOWNEY

Paracritical Hinge: Essays, Talks, Notes, Interviews
BY NATHANIEL MACKEY
UNIVERSITY OF WISCONSIN PRESS, 2004

Behind the Lines: War Resistance Poetry on the American Homefront
BY PHILIP METRES

Frank O'Hara: The Poetics of Coterie
BY LYTLE SHAW